Applying Cultural Historical Activity Theory in Educational Settings

Applying Cultural Historical Activity Theory in Educational Settings harnesses research and development for educational improvement, bridging the gap between research and practice. Exploring how collaborations between researchers and practitioners can be used to co-construct solutions to real-world problems, this book considers key concepts in cultural historical activity theory (CHAT), including models as resources that can be used to build and facilitate collaboration between researchers and practitioners.

The chapters of the book draw on research findings from the practices of learning communities in diverse educational settings: teacher education, the education of school leaders, early childhood education and driving teacher education.

Applying Cultural Historical Activity Theory in Educational Settings is an excellent resource for researchers and practitioners seeking to construct new knowledge and develop practice, or wishing to expand their knowledge of CHAT.

May Britt Postholm is Professor in pedagogy and qualitative methodology in the Department of Teacher Education at the Norwegian University of Science and Technology, Norway.

Kirsten Foshaug Vennebo is Associate Professor in the Department of Education at the University of Tromsø, Norway.

Routledge Research in Education

This series aims to present the latest research from right across the field of education. It is not confined to any particular area or school of thought and seeks to provide coverage of a broad range of topics, theories and issues from around the world.

Recent titles in the series include:

Issues in Teaching and Learning of Education for Sustainability
Theory into Practice
Edited by Chew-Hung Chang, Gillian Kidman and Andy Wi

Young People's Transitions into Creative Work
Navigating Challenges and Opportunities
Julian Sefton-Green, S. Craig Watkins and Ben Kirschner

The Complex Web of Inequality in North American Schools
Investigating Educational Policies for Social Justice
Edited by Gilberto Q. Conchas, Briana M. Hinga, Miguel N. Abad, and Kris D. Gutiérrez

Fear and Schooling
Understanding the Troubled History of Progressive Education
Ronald W. Evans

Applying Cultural Historical Activity Theory in Educational Settings
Edited by May Britt Postholm and Kirsten Foshaug Vennebo

Sonic Studies in Educational Foundations
Echoes, Reverberations, Silences, Noise
Edited by Walter S. Gershon and Peter Appelbaum

Designing for Situated Knowledge Transformation
Edited by Nina Bonderup Dohn, Stig Børsen Hansen and Jens Jørgen Hansen

Challenging Perceptions of Africa in Schools
Critical Approaches to Global Justice Education
Edited by Barbara O'Toole, David Nyaluke and Ebun Joseph

For a complete list of titles in this series, please visit www.routledge.com/Routledge-Research-in-Education/book-series/SE0393

Applying Cultural Historical Activity Theory in Educational Settings

Learning, Development and Research

Edited by
May Britt Postholm and
Kirsten Foshaug Vennebo

LONDON AND NEW YORK

First published 2020
by Routledge
2 Park Square, Milton Park, Abingdon, Oxon OX14 4RN

and by Routledge
52 Vanderbilt Avenue, New York, NY 10017

Routledge is an imprint of the Taylor & Francis Group, an informa business

© 2020 selection and editorial matter, May Britt Postholm and Kirsten Foshaug Vennebo; individual chapters, the contributors

The right of May Britt Postholm and Kirsten Foshaug Vennebo to be identified as the authors of the editorial material, and of the authors for their individual chapters, has been asserted in accordance with sections 77 and 78 of the Copyright, Designs and Patents Act 1988.

All rights reserved. No part of this book may be reprinted or reproduced or utilised in any form or by any electronic, mechanical, or other means, now known or hereafter invented, including photocopying and recording, or in any information storage or retrieval system, without permission in writing from the publishers.

Trademark notice: Product or corporate names may be trademarks or registered trademarks, and are used only for identification and explanation without intent to infringe.

British Library Cataloguing-in-Publication Data
A catalogue record for this book is available from the British Library

Library of Congress Cataloging-in-Publication Data
Names: Postholm, May Britt, editor. | Vennebo, Kirsten Foshaug
Title: Applying cultural historical activity theory in educational
settings : learning, development, and research / edited by May Britt
Postholm and Kirsten Foshaug Vennebo.
Description: Abingdon, Oxon ; New York, NY : Routledge, 2020. |
Series: Routledge research in education | Includes bibliographical references and index.
Identifiers: LCCN 2019033076 (print) | LCCN 2019033077 (ebook) |
ISBN 9780367321314 (hardback) | ISBN 9780429316838 (ebook)
Subjects: LCSH: Action research in education. | Culturally
relevant pedagogy.
Classification: LCC LB1028.24 .A628 2020 (print) | LCC LB1028.24
(ebook) | DDC 370.21--dc23
LC record available at https://lccn.loc.gov/2019033076
LC ebook record available at https://lccn.loc.gov/2019033077

ISBN: 978-0-367-32131-4 (hbk)
ISBN: 978-0-429-31683-8 (ebk)

Typeset in Galliard
by Taylor & Francis Books

Contents

List of illustrations   vii
List of contributors   viii
Preface   x

1   The texts in context   1
    MAY BRITT POSTHOLM AND KIRSTEN FOSHAUG VENNEBO

2   Schools conducting research in collaboration with researchers   12
    MAY BRITT POSTHOLM

3   Young refugees meeting another road safety culture: Development work in bridging a road safety gap   26
    EVA BRUSTAD DALLAND

4   Inspired by the concept of boundary objects in arts education   42
    NINA SCOTT FRISCH

5   Cultural-historical activity theory as the basis for mentoring student teachers in triads   58
    JANNE MADSEN

6   Encouraging working and communicating like mathematicians: An illustrative case on dialogic teaching   73
    VIVI NILSSEN AND TORUNN KLEMP

7   Realizing data-driven changes and teacher agency in upper secondary schools through formative interventions   91
    LISE VIKAN SANDVIK AND ANNE BERIT EMSTAD

8   A study of case-based problem-solving work in groups of principals participating in a school leadership programme   108
    KIRSTEN FOSHAUG VENNEBO

9 Cultural-historical activity theory framing and guiding professional
  learning in school-based development   126
  NINA A. VASSELJEN

Index   145

Illustrations

Figures

1.1 Vygotsky's (1978) triangle showing the intermediary step between stimulus and response through the auxiliary stimulus, representing the first generation of CHAT — 3
1.2 The activity system representing the second generation of CHAT — 4
1.3 A network of activity systems representing the third generation of CHAT — 4
1.4 The expansive learning cycle — 6
1.5 The R&D model — 8
2.1 The activity system — 15
2.2 The expansive learning cycle — 18
3.1 Tensions in an activity system emphasizing road safety — 28
3.2 Two activity systems in collaboration in a DWR project — 30
3.3 Sequences of epistemic actions in an expansive learning cycle — 31
4.1 Photos of installations from the toddler festival 'Playing with Light' — 50
6.1 Polygon figures to be sorted — 79
6.2 Sheet for naming, pasting and explaining a group of polygons — 80
6.3 Rogers and Naomi's work on the task presented in Figure 6.2 — 84
6.4 The mini-pitch — 86
7.1 DWR model for PD and literacy assessment — 94
9.1 Co-learning and co-leadership in school-based development — 140

Table

7.1 The DWR seen through the lens of the expansive learning cycle — 99

Contributors

Eva Brustad Dalland, Traffic section, Nord University, is associate professor in pedagogy. Her teaching and practical experiences are inside the education of driving teachers and – examiners. Her research and publishing deal with the driving test, formative assessment, cultural differences as road users, and about horse-users in road traffic.

Anne Berit Emstad, Innovation manager, Department of Teacher Education, Norwegian University of Science and Technology. Her responsibility is to realize more of the innovation potential in research and research collaboration. Her research interests are school management and leadership, school evaluation, newly educated teachers and teacher education.

Nina Scott Frisch, Department of Art Education, Queen Maud University College of Early Childhood Education, is associate professor in art education. Frisch has published articles focusing on children`s drawing processes seen from a socio-cultural perspective in national and international journals and she is section editor for the international journal *FORMacademic*.

Torunn Klemp is associated professor in pedagogy at the Norwegian University of Science and Technology, Department of Teacher Education. She has participated in a multidisciplinary intervention project established around collaboration between researchers and practitioners. National and international publications from these projects focus on language and learning and early mathematics.

Janne Madsen, University of South-Eastern Norway, is professor in educational science. Madsen is working in the intersection between the fields of education and practice. She mentors student teachers, teachers and school leaders and is researching with cultural-historical activity theory as a frame and action research as the preferred strategy.

Vivi Nilssen is professor in pedagogy at the Norwegian University of Science and Technology, Department of Teacher Education. Nilssen has been the leader of multidisciplinary intervention projects established around collaboration between researchers and practitioners. She has national and international publications focusing on both collaboration and on mathematics in early years.

List of contributors ix

May Britt Postholm, Department of Teacher Education, Norwegian University of Science and Technology, is professor in pedagogy and qualitative methodology. Postholm has published articles focusing on classroom research and school development in both national and international journals. Postholm is the coordinator for the Nordic and Baltic countries in the ISCAR-organization.

Lise Vikan Sandvik, Associate Professor, Department of Teacher Education, Norwegian University of Science and Technology. Her professional field of interest revolves around educational assessment, teacher professionalism and school development. Sandvik currently leads a developmental work research project aiming to develop assessment literacy in upper secondary schools in Norway.

Nina A. Vasseljen, Department of Teacher Education, Norwegian University of Science and Technology, is assistant professor in pedagogy. Vasseljen is a PhD candidate. In her thesis she is focusing on Lesson Study and school-based development using cultural-historical activity theory as the theoretical framework.

Kirsten Foshaug Vennebo, Associate Professor, Department of Education, University of Tromsø The Arctic University of Norway. Vennebo's research interests are leadership and innovation in schools and professional development for school leaders. In an innovative way, she has developed and applied cultural-historical activity theory for understanding leadership in innovative work processes.

Preface

The authors of this book's chapters are members of an activity theory group established in the early 1990s. Sigrun Gudmundsdottir (1948–2003), a professor of pedagogy at the Norwegian University of Science and Technology (NTNU) in Trondheim, introduced the tradition of holding special seminars with her master's degree students. Some of those students – Vivi Nilssen, Janne Madsen and May Britt Postholm – also completed their doctoral theses under Sigrun's supervision and are now the group's elder members. May Britt Postholm leads the group and, with Kirsten Foshaug Vennebo, is the editor of this book.

We meet twice a year. At some of these gatherings, we meet for one day to discuss articles that we have read beforehand (either our own forthcoming texts or articles published by other researchers). The gatherings conclude with an informal dinner at one of the members' homes. The other type of gathering is a three-day seminar at which we write texts and provide feedback to one another.

The eight members of the group, including Eva Brustad Dalland, Anne Berit Emstad, Nina Scott Frisch and Lise Vikan Sandvik in addition to those mentioned above, come from five universities and university colleges in various regions of Norway. We are experienced researchers, publishing articles in national and international journals. Our research focuses on education in various settings: teacher education, the education of school leaders, early childhood education and driving teacher education. This book presents the latest findings related to the themes that the group's members are studying. Torunn Klemp has been invited as a co-author and Nina A. Vasseljen as a guest author.

We hope that you will find our texts interesting and instructive!

Trondheim and Oslo, 1 June 2019
May Britt Postholm and Kirsten Foshaug Vennebo

1 The texts in context

May Britt Postholm and Kirsten Foshaug Vennebo

The intention of this introductory chapter is, as the title indicates, to position the chapters within their theoretical perspective, which is cultural-historical activity theory (CHAT). We present key concepts in CHAT that the researchers use in their chapters to make a running red line within and across the chapters in the book. Before we deal with CHAT and its concepts and models, we place our research in the political discussion of today.

Currently, there are strong expectations placed on national governments to meet European and international challenges of achieving high educational quality. For example, governments are increasingly striving to develop collaborative universal models that bring practitioners and researchers together and engage them in this important work. By 'universal', the meaning is that a model should be applicable to different educational settings whilst being flexible at the same time to meet local needs. Nowadays, it is not unusual that governments provide funding for practice development, which has the requirements of researcher involvement and collaboration between academia and educational institutions, such as schools. Our research findings are culled from practices of learning communities in different educational settings. They will give future researchers and practitioners who are seeking to co-construct new knowledge and develop practice with an idea of the complexity of the processes for handling challenges. Likewise, the findings are expected to encourage them to take advantage of the possibilities in such collaborative environments that are locally established.

CHAT is developed on the basis of Lev Vygotsky's thoughts and ideas. In the western part of the world, in Europe and in the US, perhaps the most common label for CHAT is socio-cultural theory (Wertsch, 1991; Wertsch, Rio, & Alvarez, 1995). The roots of this theory are usually associated with Russian scholars Alexi Leont´ev and Alexander Luria, in addition to Vygotsky. However, it is Leont´ev's theoretical work that has had the influence on the consolidation and integration of the ideas of Vygotsky into what is known as theory of activity (Wertsch, 1981). In the following, we will use the label CHAT that Cole (1996) has given to name the theory.

CHAT has several features that correspond to Vygotsky's fundamental thoughts. Leont´ev claimed that *activity* breaks down the distinction between the external world and the world of internal phenomena (Wertsch, 1981). In CHAT, activity has a prominent place and is analysed on three different levels. The constructs *activity*, *action* and *operation*, developed by Leont´ev, indicate that activities are distinguished on the basis of their motive and the object toward which they are oriented, actions on the basis of their goals and operations on the basis of the conditions under which they are carried out (Wertsch, 1981). In Chapter 6, Vivi Nilssen and Torunn Klemp use these three levels to identify goal-directed actions, their conditions and how the goal-directed actions move a teacher's practice towards the object.

These three levels of analyses are the first features of CHAT. The second major feature of the theory is that it involves the notion of goal and goal-directed action, and these actions are concerned with conscious goals that are conducted to move the practice towards the object. The third main feature is that activity is mediated (Wertsch, 1981). Vygotsky (1978) extended the notion of mediation by tools to mediation by signs and thus also the use of language. Words likewise became a central mediating artefact in CHAT (Cole, 1996). The fourth main feature of CHAT is its emphasis on development or genetic explanation, and both culture and history are considered in the understanding of development. The fourth main feature is closely related to the fact that development approaches are important. This feature implies that human activity and the artefacts, tools and signs that mediate it have emerged through social interaction. The sixth and final feature is internalisation (Wertsch, 1981). This feature refers to Vygotsky's (1978) general genetic law of cultural development. Vygotsky explained the relationship between internal and external processes as follows:

> An interpersonal process is transformed into an intrapersonal one. Every function in the child's cultural development appears twice: first, on the social level, and later, on the individual level; first, between people (inter-psychological), and then inside the child (intrapsychological).
>
> (p. 57)

Although Vygotsky (1981) and his colleges saw social reality as having a primary role in determining the nature of the mental processes, the individual was not looked upon as a passive part of this process. According to Vygotsky, the consciousness is not a product of society; rather, it is produced in the interactions between individuals and society. The Vygotskian approach rejects the assumptions that the structures of external and internal activities are identical and that they are unrelated. External and internal activities have a developmental relationship – external processes are transformed to create internal processes. Vygotsky (1981) said that 'It goes without saying that internalization transforms the process itself and changes its structure and function' (p. 163). Thus, the individual is active with both transforming the process and also changing its structure. In CHAT, the externalisation process is likewise central (Leont´ev, 1981; Engeström, 1999). The two processes, internalisation and externalisation, continuously operate at every level in human activity. Internalisation is related to the reproduction of the culture in question. Externalisation refers to the processes that create new artefacts or new ways to use them, thus enabling development and creative processes (Engeström, 1999). We will come back to the relationship between internalisation and externalisation when we present the expansive learning cycle, which represents the actions conducted to move practice towards the object of an activity (Engeström, 1987, 2001). We have now mentioned the word 'object' several times. Before we describe the three generations of CHAT, we first reflect on this concept.

Leont´ev (1978) wrote

> The object of the activity is twofold: first, in its independent existence as subordinating to itself and transforming the activity of the subject, second; as an image of the object, as [a] product of its property of psychological reflection that is realized as an activity of the subject.
>
> (p. 52)

The object may therefore be material or ideal. The object could, for instance, be a lump of clay and its properties (its independent existence) that one is attempting to shape into a nice vase (as an image of the object), or it could be classroom management, which schools are required to work on, as mandated by national authorities (its independent existence); however, both teachers and leaders in schools can focus their effort on, for instance, developing communication between themselves (as an image of the object) to enhance pupils' learning (outcome). As we have already written as a part of CHAT's first feature, activities are distinguished on the basis of their motive and the object towards which they are oriented. Leont´ev (1981) pointed out that 'the object is the true motive' (p. 59) for people's actions. This means that people in educational settings aiming to develop their practice towards an object at least need to know about or, even better, share a collective motive to act on the object. In this way, the object becomes 'invested with meaning and motivating power' (Sannino, Engeström, & Lemos, 2016, p. 602). In school, teachers' motivation should thus be built into the object because it is their practice and needs that serve as the starting point of loading them 'with initiative and commitment' (Sannino & Engeström, 2017, p. 81). In Chapter 2, May Britt Postholm describes the start-up phase in a research and development work project and how time is needed to develop a shared object amongst teachers.

The first generation of CHAT is represented by Vygotsky's (1978) triangle. The intermediate link between stimulus (S) and response (R) is not just an improvement of this operation, but it is a qualitatively new process. This is visualised in Figure 1.1 below:

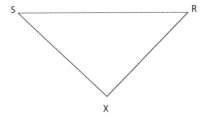

Figure 1.1 Vygotsky's (1978) triangle showing the intermediary step between stimulus and response through the auxiliary stimulus, representing the first generation of CHAT

The limitation of the first generation of CHAT is that individuals are the unit of analysis. This was overcome by the second generation of CHAT developed by Leont´ev. In his example of the collective hunt (Leont´ev, 1981), he introduced division of labour and thus described collective activity. Every person conducts goal-directed actions that together can satisfy their needs, as in the example of hunting directed to the object of obtaining food. One person is chasing, another is preparing for the ambush and another should fire the rifle. Engeström (1987, 2001) developed this second generation of CHAT into the activity system. The upper triangle in the activity system (see Figure 1.2 below) is the same as Vygotsky's fundamental triangle, but it is turned upside down, with the mediating artefacts at the top.

The activity system as a unit of analysis is presented and used in several chapters of the book (Chapters 2, 3, and 9), and the nodes constituting it are thoroughly described in Chapters 2 and 3. The third generation of CHAT was developed by Engeström (1987, 2015). This generation focuses on collaboration between two or more activity systems and thus forms networks of interacting systems. The basic model of CHAT, the activity system, is therefore expanded to include, at the minimum, two systems in the graphical development of the third generation. In their networking, the subjects acting in various systems act on the object that is partially shared between the systems. The third generation of CHAT is visualised in Figure 1.3 below.

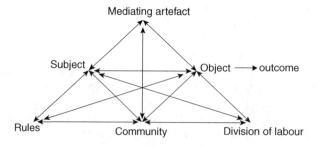

Figure 1.2 The activity system representing the second generation of CHAT

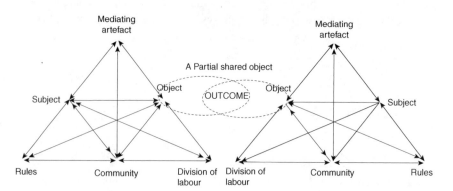

Figure 1.3 A network of activity systems representing the third generation of CHAT

In Chapter 3, Eva Dalland uses the third generation of CHAT to describe and analyse the collaboration between students, two researchers and two supervisors in one activity system and eight refugees, a centre leader, one employee and interpreters in another activity system. The primary objectives of this study are to find a way to communicate with newly arrived refugees about road safety and to identify some pedagogical tools and methods to do so. The intention of this research, therefore, is to create knowledge that can enhance the education of immigrants. In this chapter, learning is emphasised for all parties. Learning for both participants and the researcher is also the topic in Nina A. Vasseljen's chapter (Chapter 9). In Chapter 5, Janne Madsen focuses on learning in the triads of teacher education, student teachers and schools. A critique of some of our studies that focus on the collaboration between two arenas is that they do not adequately emphasise the learning potential for researchers' own activity system.

Boundary crossing is an important concept in CHAT. Akkerman and Bakker (2011) wrote a review article on the concepts of boundary, boundary crossing, boundary object, dialogicality and learning theory, and this article is frequently referred to in the book. According to Engeström, Engeström and Kärkkäinen (1995), boundary crossing is characterised as 'horizontal expertise where practitioners must move across boundaries to seek and give help, to find information and tools wherever they happen to be available' (p. 332). The concept of boundary crossing is useful when focusing on the collaboration between, for instance, teacher educators, leaders and teachers in school. The adoption of ideas from one another in a 'shared meeting ground' (Engeström & Toiviainen, 2011, p. 35) can lead to developmental transfer (Engeström & Sannino, 2010), for instance, from school to teacher education and vice versa. The findings in our studies, as already mentioned, focus mainly on learning in settings that are supported and researched on, not on horizontal learning that goes both ways. This situation can be a remnant of the traditional view of learning, in which someone teaches people who need to learn. Research questions grounded in the third generation of CHAT could or even should focus on the development transfer between networking activity systems in both ways. This perspective should be more present both in our future research and, in general, in studies of networking activity systems.

The researcher's role in studies framed by CHAT is defined by Engeström and Sannino (2010) as follows: 'In linear interventions the researcher aims at control of all the variables. In formative interventions, the researcher aims at provoking and sustaining an expansive transformation process led and owned by the practitioners' (p. 15). Formative interventions, conducted as developmental work research (DWR) (Engeström & Engeström, 1986), therefore mean that the researcher's role is to support practitioners in their development work and conduct research on these development processes. This definition also indicates, as we see it, that someone is going to learn (practitioners) and that others (researchers) will support this learning. In our opinion, the definition of the researcher's role underlines the one-way direction of learning, not learning in both parties' activity system. With this definition of the researchers' role, researchers can be considered as mediating artefacts that support practitioners by presenting the model (the activity system as an analysis unit), ideas and tools, as well as mirror data, and the researcher takes the role of an interventionist researcher (Engeström, 2001). This role of the researcher is prevalent in all chapters of the book, except Chapters 4, 5 and 8, which present studies in which the researchers collect data on their own teaching in higher education to understand students' perceptions of the teaching processes and thus help enhance their education. In Chapter 4, Nina Scott Frisch builds mainly on the first generation of CHAT and the concepts of boundary objects and artefacts to identify common grounds for music, drama, and arts and crafts in arts education in early childhood education. In Chapter 8, Kirsten Foshaug Vennebo focuses on case-based instruction that was used at a university in a national school leadership programme in Norway to challenge groups of principals to do problem-solving work based on a case narrative. In her chapter, CHAT provides the conceptual tools required to examine the situated work activities in depth. In Chapter 5, Madsen uses CHAT to analyse communication, collaboration and mutual learning in triads in teacher education. The context of the other studies in the book (Chapters 2, 3, 6, 7 and 9) is that the researchers collaborate with and support practitioners in their concrete practice to develop these processes, focusing on learning in both ways but in varying degrees. The findings of the studies presented in Chapters 4, 5 and 8 bring forward knowledge that can contribute to further development in these settings. The studies therefore map the situation and contribute with knowledge about the actual empirical setting, which constitutes one part of the second step in the expansive learning cycle (Engeström, 1987, 2001). In the studies presented in Chapters 2, 3, 7 and 9, the expansive learning cycle is used as a theoretical model to guide the action in development processes. The expansive learning cycle is presented in Figure 1.4 below.

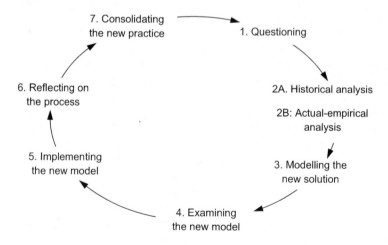

Figure 1.4 The expansive learning cycle
Source: Engeström, 1987, 2001

The steps constituting the processes guided by this cycle are presented and exemplified in detail in Chapter 2.

The two processes, internalisation and externalisation, continuously operate at every level in human activity. Internalisation is related to reproduction of the culture in question. Externalisation refers to the processes that create new artefacts or new ways to use them, thus enabling development and creative processes. The expansive cycle of an activity begins with an emphasis on internalisation. In this process, the novice members of a community are trained and socialised into the activity that is routinely executed. Externalisation as a creative action occurs in innovative, individual processes. When the activity becomes more demanding, self-reflection and externalisation increase. The process of externalisation reaches its peak when a new model has come into existence. Then, the process of internalisation again becomes conspicuous, as the inherent ways and means of the new model have to be learnt (Engeström, 1999).

Expansive learning is 'to learn something that is not yet there' (Engeström & Sannino, 2010, p. 2). According to Virkkunen (2006), transformative agency can be defined as 'breaking away from the given frame of action and taking the initiative to transform it' (p. 49). Engeström and Sannino (2016) stated that expansive learning requires and fosters transformative agency. Engeström (1987) wrote the following:

> The essence of [an expansive] learning activity is [the] production of objectively, societally new activity structures (including new objects, instruments, etc.) out of actions manifesting the inner contradictions of the preceding form of the activity in question. [Expansive] learning activity is mastery of expansion from actions to a new activity. While traditional schooling is essentially a subject-producing activity and traditional science is essentially an instrument-producing activity, [expansive] learning activity is an activity-producing activity.
>
> (p. 125)

The above quote means that a new collective activity is developed through expansive learning. In educational settings, it can take a long time before a new collective practice is consolidated (step 7 in the expansive learning cycle). The actions conducted can be perceived as potentially expansive, meaning that they can lead to expansive learning, or they can be miniature cycles and isolated events that do not lead to expansive learning. It is the latter case in which the overall cycle of organisational learning can be stagnant (Engeström & Sannino, 2010). The example project presented in Chapter 2 lasted over a period of two years, and the researcher collaborated regularly with the teacher and the leaders in the school. In the project, many cycles can be described as potentially expansive, but after two years of collaboration, there was no expansion from actions to a new activity. Various changes in the school's activity system can explain this stagnation; for instance, the school had a new leadership group that had not taken part in the development processes from the start-up phase of the project. The researcher collaborating with the teacher and leaders at the lower secondary school also developed a model modifying and building on the expansive learning cycle. The researcher had to develop a model that could help her determine which hat she was wearing – the development hat or the researcher's hat. This model, named the R&D model (Postholm & Moen, 2011), is presented in Figure 1.5 below.

This model that represents DWR (Engeström & Engeström, 1986) provides an analysis of the premises behind the activity in which the focus is on both content and work processes. This is also the basis for the three columns used by Coghlan and Brannick (2005), identified as *content, process* and *premise*, and shown as pillars in Engeström's modified expanding learning cycle at the bottom of the figure. The cycle is named the primary circle because it represents the core activity in practice and its development. These factors are represented in all the phases and levels of DWR, thus also in the circle placed centrally but above the modified expanding learning cycle, the primary circle. In the secondary circle, reflections occur on the specific development processes represented by the primary circle. Thus, the secondary circle represents meta-reflections on all activities conducted in the primary circle (illustrated by arrows in both ways between the primary circle and reflections on the meta-level).

The R&D model also includes a third level. On this level, the researcher brings all of the experiences and collected materials to a meta-meta-level, highlighting the

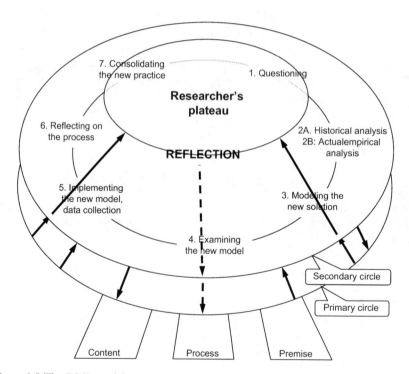

Figure 1.5 The R&D model

activities that prove to be essential in the development processes without connecting these directly to the defined phases of the work. This level is described as a transparent plateau in which the researchers view the DWR activities in their entirety (shown by arrows pointing to the third level in Figure 1.5). On this level, researchers are not in direct cooperation with participants, but from this transparent plateau, they can focus their research gaze telescopically and study the processes framed by focused research questions. As there is no direct cooperation between researchers and practitioners on this level, it is called the researcher's plateau. This model was used in the study presented in Chapter 9.

In the following, we briefly provide the content and some findings of the eight studies presented in the book. In Chapter 2, May Britt Postholm presents a study that shows how the activity system and the expansive learning cycle introduced by the researcher can be applied in researching schools. Furthermore, Postholm describes how CHAT and its models can be used by school leaders and teachers acting as leaders of research activities in their own school. In Chapter 3, Eva Brustad Dalland focuses on the challenges that arise when immigrants and refugees meet a foreign road safety culture when arriving in Norway. To bridge the gap on cultural differences related to road safety amongst refugees and immigrants, the findings in Dalland's study indicate a great need to include educational processes about road safety in programmes designed to help this group of individuals integrate into the community. In Chapter 4, Nina Scott Frisch presents a study focusing on the identification of common grounds for music, drama, and arts and crafts in arts education in early childhood education. The concept of a boundary object is used as a thinking tool to identify common grounds of art education at this level of education. The study shows that teachers can find specific common foci within the respective art disciplines and coordinate these to function as boundary objects when needed. In Chapter 5, Janne Madsen uses CHAT to uncover the communication, collaboration and mutual learning in triads (student teacher, teacher educators in the field of practice (practice mentors) and teacher educators who teach theory (subject teachers) in teacher education). The findings show that some triads are characterised by minimal communication, whereas some are open to communication but lack an arena for collaboration, and others collaborate but fail to achieve mutual learning. Vivi Nilssen and Torunn Klemp focus in Chapter 6 on how a primary teacher performs dialogic teaching by encouraging her pupils to work and communicate like mathematicians. They use the three levels of activity, action and operation developed by Leont'ev in their analyses. In Chapter 7, Lise Vikan Sandvik and Anne Berit Emstad focus on the collaboration between schools and a university in a school-based development of assessment for learning. They found that top-down processes may prevent commitment and that specialisation can lead to greater interaction between schools and universities. They argue that the concept of expansive learning is useful for investigating and developing inquiry-based teaching. In Chapter 8, Kirsten Foshaug Vennebo gives insight into how groups of principals participating in a national Norwegian school leadership program do problem solving work based on a case narrative. She found that case-based instruction is useful as a strategy for problem solving training in teams of principals. The principals managed to activate and make representations of the case relevant in their work and to identify, frame and examine the challenges at hand. However, they strived consecutively to include these findings in their problem-solving trajectory that resulted in that they arrived on an open-ended resolution and direction, meaning that the course of action was not kept in an acceptable frame. In Chapter 9, Nina A. Vasseljen focuses on lesson study and how this method for learning and development can contribute to teachers' learning and the development of professional learning communities that enhance school-based development. The purpose of the chapter is to show how CHAT can frame and guide these processes.

References

Akkerman, S. F., & Bakker, A. (2011). Boundary crossing and boundary objects. *Review of Education Research, 81*(2), 132–169. doi:10.3102/0034654311404435

Coghlan, D., & Brannick, T. (2005). *Doing Action Research in Your Own Organization.* London: Sage Publications.

Cole, M. (1996). *Cultural Psychology: A Once and Future Discipline.* Cambridge, MA: The Belknap Press of Harvard University Press.

Engeström, Y. (1987). *Learning by Expanding.* Helsinki: Orienta-Konsultit Oy.

Engeström, Y. (1999). Activity theory and individual and social transformation. In Y. Engeström, R., Miettinen, & R. Punamaki (Eds.), *Perspectives on Activity Theory* (pp. 19–38). Cambridge, MA: Cambridge University Press.

Engeström, Y. (2001). *Expansive Learning at Work. Toward an Activity-Theoretical Reconceptualization.* London: Institute of Education, University of London.

Engeström, Y. (2015). *Learning by Expanding. An Activity-Theoretical Approach to Development Research* (2nd edn). New York: Cambridge University Press.

Engeström, Y., & Engeström, R. (1986). Developmental work research. The approach and the application in cleaning work. *Nordisk Pedagogik, 6,* 2–15.

Engeström, Y., & Sannino, A. (2010). Studies of expansive learning: Foundations, findings and future challenges. *Educational Research Review, 5*(1), 1–24. doi:10.1016/j.edurev.2009.12.002

Engeström, Y., & Sannino, A. (2016). Expansive learning on the move: Insights from ongoing research. *Journal of the Study of Education and Development, 39*(3), 401–435. doi:10.1080/02103702.2016.1189119

Engeström, Y., & Sannino, A. (2017). Co-generation of societally impactful knowledge in change laboratories. *Management Learning, 48*(1), 80–96. doi:10.1177/1350507616671285

Engeström, Y., & Toiviainen, H. (2011). Co-configurational design of learning instrumentalities: An activity-theoretical perspective. In S. R. Ludvigsen, R. Säljö, I. Rasmussen, & A. Lund (Eds.), *Learning Across Sites: New Tools, Infrastructures and Practices* (pp. 33–52). Abingdon: Routledge.

Engeström, Y., Engeström, R., & Kärkkäinen, M. (1995). Polycontextuality and boundary crossing in expert cognition. Learning and problem solving in complex work activities. *Learning and Instruction, 5*(4), 319–335. doi:10.1016/0959-4752(95)00021-00026

Leont'ev, A. N. (1978). *Activity, Consciousness, and Personality*. Englewood Cliffs: Prentice-Hall.
Leont'ev, A. N. (1981). The Problem of Activity in Psychology. In J. V. Wertsch (Ed.), *The Concept of Activity in Soviet Psychology* (pp. 37–71). Armonk: M.E. Sharpe, Inc.
Postholm, M. B., & Moen, T. (2011). Communities of development: A new model for R&D work. *Journal of Educational Change*, 12(4), 385–401. doi:10.1007/s10833-10010-9150-x.
Sannino, A., Engeström, Y., & Lemos, M. (2016). Formative interventions for expansive learning and transformative agency. *Journal of the Learning Sciences*, 25(4), 599–633. doi:10.1080/10508406.2016.1204547.
Virkkunen, L. S. (2006). Dilemmas in building shared transformative agency. *Activités*, 3, 43–66. doi:10.4000/activites.1850
Vygotsky, L. S. (1978). *Mind in Society. The Development of Higher Psychological Processes*. Cambridge, MA: Harvard University Press.
VygotskyL. S. (1981). The genesis of higher mental functions. In J. V. Wertsch (Ed.), *The Concept of Activity in Soviet Psychology* (pp. 144–188). Armonk: M.E. Sharpe, Inc.
Wertsch, J. V. (1981). The concept of activity in Soviet psychology. An introduction. In J. V. Wertsch (Ed.), *The Concept of Activity in Soviet Psychology* (pp. 3–36). Armonk: M.E. Sharpe, Inc.
Wertsch, J. V. (1991). *Voices of the Mind. A Sociocultural Approach to Mediated Action*. Cambridge, MA: Harvard University Press.
Wertsch, J. V., Rio, D. P., & Alvarez, A. (1995). Sociocultural studies: History, action, and mediation. In J. V. Wertsch, D. R. Pablo, & A. Alvarez (Eds.), *Sociocultural Studies of Mind* (pp. 1–34). New York: Cambridge University Press.

2 Schools conducting research in collaboration with researchers

May Britt Postholm

Introduction

Norwegian schools and teachers are facing more and stronger requirements to focus on a form of systematic learning. To develop this teaching practice in an entire school, the teachers will need to interact in a shared professional environment (Ministry of Education and Research, 2009, 2010, 2013). Teachers can, of course, learn from their actions and what they do in the classroom during the learning activity with their pupils (Postholm & Jacobsen, 2011). But having insight into scientific methods and understanding and applying relevant research is what Lærerløftet (a strategy focusing on raising teachers' competence) highlights as typical of a school where teachers collaborate and reflect on their practice to improve the professional environment at the school (Ministry of Education and Research, 2014). Collective learning in a school may be improved if the teachers participate in shared observations of teaching practices and reflect on these observations with other teachers. Learning based on activities in the classroom is called action learning (Revans, 1982, 1984; Tiller, 2006). I will return to this approach below.

Research has shown that if schools are to learn, the focus must be on the teachers' learning. Bearing this in mind, it is not the school that learns, rather it is the individuals in the organization who learn, and their learning must be facilitated and supported by the school leaders (Postholm et al., 2013). According to Avalos (2011), the professional development of teachers refers to teachers' learning, how they learn to learn, and how they practically apply their knowledge to support the pupils' learning outcomes. Many research findings show that participation in collaborative communities impacts the practices of teachers and improves the learning outcomes of pupils (Robinson, 2011; Timperley, Wilson, Barrar, & Fung, 2007). Studies also show that teachers' observations of each other in class and their feedback to each other based on the observed practice lead to the most changes in the teaching practice (Given et al., 2010; Zwart, Wubbels, Bergen, & Bolhuis, 2009). But for this to happen, the improvement efforts must be based on collective research questions connected to the teaching practice. This must occur if collaborating teachers are to improve the learning outcomes of their pupils in a better way than individualistic schools (Little, 1990).

In this chapter, I refer to the schools' and teachers' research activities as development work, meaning that this work is systematic. If the learning and professional development are to include the entire school, the teachers and leaders must arrive at common object, and work systematically and collectively towards this object. Leont´ev (1981) stated that 'the object is the true motive', meaning that motivation is embedded in the overall goal of the work (p. 59). According to Virkkunen and Newnham (2013), action research contributes to the gradual development of a practice, while cultural-historical activity theory (CHAT) forms the basis for development towards a future collective object which is constructed according to historical and contemporary analyses of a practice. The purpose of this chapter is to show how CHAT can give direction to the work in researching schools. Thus, the content of this chapter guided by the following research question: *How can cultural-historical activity theory contribute to promoting researching schools?* When using CHAT as the theoretical framework, the activity of the entire organization is included. In specific studies, the focus may be on a small system within the greater organization. In this chapter, I will focus on the teacher team as the smallest unit for collective learning in schools.

First, this chapter presents the method for a study where the intention was to both develop and research the teaching practices at a lower secondary school. Thereafter CHAT is presented as a theory and method for researching schools. The chapter points out that this theory and its models can be used by researchers[1] collaborating with leaders and teachers, and also by leaders and teachers even if researchers do not take part in the research activity in the school. The chapter concludes with a discussion on premises and possibilities relating to researching schools. This discussion is conducted within the framework of relevant research studies.

A completed study used as an example

This chapter builds on research from a project carried out in a lower secondary school with twelve teachers. The project focused on systematics and hence was a research-based approach on the development of teaching practice. It can therefore be described as a development work research (DWR) project, an approach developed within CHAT (Engeström & Engeström, 1986). A qualitative case study (Creswell, 2013) was used as an approach to study the collaboration between the researcher and research participants where the intention was to improve teaching practices. The object of the DWR project, which lasted for two years, was to develop varied ways of working with a focus on learning strategies to improve the academic and social development of each pupil. I, the researcher, attended the school at least once every two weeks, either in meetings with teachers or leaders, or together with the teachers during their teaching.

CHAT constituted the framework and direction of DWR. The data material was collected through observations, interviews with leaders, teachers and pupils, through questionnaires given to pupils, and reflection conversations with teachers based on observations of actual teaching situations. The data material was transcribed on an on-going basis and analysed using the constant comparative analysis method developed by Strauss and Corbin (1998). This means that the researcher continuously asks questions of the teachers and compares the material collected to develop an understanding of the processes in practice. The transcriptions and the preliminary analyses of these were also applied to aid the development processes by being presented to teachers as mirror data (Cole & Engeström, 2007). This data material allowed the teachers to have their own practices and understanding mirrored to them by reading what was said and how this was understood by the researcher. The categories developed in the open coding phase (Strauss & Corbin, 1998) are the key topics of the discussion in the concluding section of this chapter. The following categories were developed: 'The launch phase as the basis of development', 'Reflection, the key to development' and 'The role of the school leader and lasting change'. This study is used to exemplify how CHAT can frame and give direction to researching schools.

Cultural-historical activity theory as a guide for researching schools

CHAT is a development of socio-cultural theory, where Vygotsky is the prominent theoretician. An important aspect of this theory is that learning occurs first on a social level (inter-psychological level) and is then internalized (intra-psychological level) (Vygotsky, 1978). Human beings are perceived as active in the learning process, and Vygotsky (2000) saw language as an important instrument in the learning process. His focus was on the learning child, but his ideas have also been applied in the context of teachers' learning (Postholm, 2012; Postholm & Wæge, 2015). In socio-cultural theory, learning is defined as a process where one masters the use of learning tools to enable thinking and acting (Wertsch, 1991; Säljö, 1999). It is thus the 'appropriation and mastering of communicative and specific tools that contributes to social practice' (Säljö, 1995, p. 91, my translation). This means that both language and specific tools, such as a teaching programme, may be actively used in the learning process, such as a team's shared observation and reflection process.

Vygotsky (1978) saw the actual development level, which represents what individuals know they can do and are able to carry out without assistance, and the zone of proximal development in connection with individual assessment and instruction. His definition of the zone of proximal development is the difference between the problem-solving skills of the learner and his/her ability to solve problems when given assistance by an adult or a more competent child. Based on Vygotsky's theory, Engeström (1987) has developed a definition of the zone of proximal development in a collectivist and social perspective. He writes: 'It is the distance between the present everyday actions of the individuals and the historically new form of the societal activity that can be collectively generated' (p. 174). This definition includes the activity both in a team and in the school as a whole and how this activity can be developed collectively into a new form of social activity.

The origin and content of the activity system

The activity system is a graphic development of the activity theory (Engeström, 1987, 2001). This system is shown in Figure 2.1 below.

The nodes included in the activity system are 'subject', 'mediating artefacts', 'object', 'outcome', 'rules', 'community', and 'division of labour'. This is a dynamic system where the nodes in the system have a mutual impact on each other. If a change occurs in one node, this will influence the other nodes in the system. As an acting subject, an individual utilizes cultural artefacts to move the practice towards the object. Above, I described a teachers' team as the smallest unit for collective learning in schools, and for this reason I place the teachers' team as an acting subject in the system. The 'mediating artefact' node comprises many physical artefacts, such as the blackboard, chalk, books, and computers, but also language, which therefore brings dialogue and reflection between the teachers into the picture. Teaching programmes in schools may also be defined as an aid or thinking tool which may support or inspire other teachers in the development of their teaching. The object in the example project was to develop varied ways of working with a focus on learning strategies to promote the academic and social development of each individual pupil. The 'outcome' factor expresses how the individual or the group of individuals has moved towards the object and the desired result of the activity. In this context, the 'outcome' factor also represents what the pupils have learnt when the attention has been on varied work methods and learning strategies. The uppermost triangle in the activity system, which is formed by the nodes 'subject', 'mediating artefacts' and, 'object', is called the action triangle (Postholm, 2010a).

The context of the actions is represented by the 'rules', 'community', and 'division of labour' nodes. These nodes form the three lowermost triangles of the activity system. The 'rules' node means guidelines, norms and conventions for actions. These may be white papers, regulations, the national curriculum in force, and local curricula. 'Community' refers to all the people in a community who share the same object. In schools, this means the teachers and leaders. This does not, however, mean that there needs to be complete agreement amongst the colleagues in terms of the object for the work, or how to move the practice in the direction of the object. 'Division of labour' means that the work or actions focusing on a goal have been distributed between the

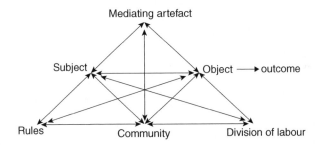

Figure 2.1 The activity system

people in the shared community. This represents the horizontal work division. Roles may also be distributed vertically, which may also reveal the power perspective in a team or between colleagues. These nodes on the bottom line of the activity system may determine the premises or possible limitations for actions to be carried out (Engeström, 1987). The activity system is used to describe and analyse the activities of people in an organization, such as the activity in a school. This is therefore a good tool for discovering areas in a school's activities that have development potential.

Tensions, conflicts, and ownership as the basis for development

In CHAT, tensions and contradictions are the point of departure for change and development. There may be contradictions within the nodes. When a teacher team is placed as the acting subject in the activity system, some members of the team might want changes, whilst others want stability. If the motivation for promoting development in the team differs, it may be necessary to focus on the learning culture and how the team functions as a practice community before the development of the teaching content commences. According to Timperley et al. (2007), a good point of departure is that everybody must be familiar with the purpose of the development work, and that it is not to be based on voluntary participation. The teachers in the example project designed the overarching goals and development questions for the DWR in the spring before we started the work in September. I found that it took approximately six months before the teachers really understood that they were the ones who 'owned' the project (Postholm, 2008a). In an interview at the start of November of the first year, the main team leader, who was the leader for all the teachers working in Years 8, 9, and 10, reminded me that they should be allowed to move at their own tempo. I would need to be sensitive and balance my actions between supporting and pushing the teachers. At the end of the same month it became clear, however, that they saw the project as their own, and that they wanted to develop the teaching based on common observations and reflections in their subject teams (Postholm, 2008b). It took a long time before the project was truly anchored in the teaching staff, but I found that this start-up phase, which continued for almost half a year, formed a firm foundation for the development work (Postholm, 2008a). When focusing on the 'division of labour' node in the analyses, a contradiction between working individually or collectively may be revealed in conversations, observations, and reflections. This may also be a challenge that should be addressed while also focusing on the content of the work.

There may also be contradictions between nodes in the activity system. An example may be that the teachers in the team, as the acting subject, do not quite agree on how to formulate the object for the activity. Another tension or conflict may be that the team does not find that they have sufficient artefacts to satisfy the object they have decided to work towards. They may have to call in extra resources to acquire new knowledge which can help them move towards the constructed object. There may also be a contradiction between new and leftover parts of the old practice in a school. Some teachers may find it difficult to discard teaching methods they have used for years and feel confident about, but it is when tensions and contradictions are resolved or dissolved that change and development occurs, according to Engeström and Miettinen (1999).

The activity system and the expansive learning cycle as tools in researching schools

The activity system may be a useful tool when a school activity is analysed to pinpoint tensions and contradictions when preparing to design and implement measures. A team can also, as a rule, decide which topics they want to work with after having experienced a contradiction between the current and the desired practice. The other nodes in the activity system are then analysed in relation to the object that was designed according to the chosen topic. Since the activity system is a dynamic system, a new object will impact the other nodes in the system. The teachers in the example project wanted to contribute further to the academic and social development of their pupils, but they felt that there was a contradiction between the object and the teaching practice. Bearing this in mind, they wanted to try to vary the teaching more and introduce learning strategies for the pupils. They also eventually found that they wanted to observe each other's practice and reflect on these observations later. Varied work methods, learning strategies, and observation and reflection are all cultural aids that they want to use to move the practice towards the desired object. The teachers also practised a division of their work when observing and reflecting; some taught and others observed before joining a reflection session.

To visualize mediated actions in development activities, Engeström (2001) has developed the expansive learning cycle. Expansive learning is 'to learn something that is not yet there' (Engeström & Sannino, 2010, p. 2). In the example project, the teachers developed a new structure for collaboration in teams. This meant that they would observe and reflect on the teaching of the others to enable the development of varied ways of working with a focus on learning strategies. In the reflection conversations, language was used as a tool (Vygotsky, 2000) to share and discuss the experiences connected to the object they wanted to strive for. The new collective practice helped the teachers to develop a culture where the common practice was perceived as a learning community. The main team leader stated the following after they had observed and reflected on the practices of the team members over half a year:

> We have found out that when we work together we become more visibly competent. We have received many tips and had epiphanies through observation and through reflections on our own practice. We have gained more insight into our colleagues and pupils. We trust each other more and support each other. Very useful. We are the ones, the teachers, who are supposed to learn from this, but our action learning will also help the pupils to learn more. Therefore, we will continue doing this next year too; we'll follow the same plan.
>
> (Postholm, 2010b)

18 M. B. Postholm

With these structural and cultural changes, they were able to develop their teaching. They learned in the shared community. The teachers and staff had moved within the zone of proximal development, defined within a collective and social perspective (Engeström, 1987). This meant, as mentioned above, that both the activity and culture of a team or school had been developed and changed. They had learned something new that was 'not yet there' (Engeström & Sannino, 2010, p. 2). The expansive learning cycle, representing expansive learning, is presented in Figure 2.2 below.

The object in the example project was to vary the teaching and apply learning strategies to promote the academic and social development of each pupil. The teachers' development question was: 'How can different ways of working with a focus on learning strategies contribute to the academic and social development of each individual pupil?' Preparing the development question and linking it to the object is the first step in the learning cycle (1). The next step in the expansive learning cycle is to carry out historic and actual-empirical analyses (2). To understand how their teaching was performed, the teachers may together and individually reflect on how their lessons went. To understand the present situation, the teachers in the example project observed their own teaching during the first six months and wrote observation notes. Additionally, I observed the teachers and gave them feedback based on the collected mirror data (Cole & Engeström, 2007). Over the subsequent six months, the teachers reflected on both their own teaching and that of the others. In their reflections, they analysed the teaching that had been observed together. The observations and reflections took place according to a plan which had been prepared at the start of the semester, a plan which I, in my capacity as the researcher, made based on the teachers' wishes for observation and reflection time. In addition to individual year teams and the main team, in which all the teachers in lower secondary school were together, they wanted to work in subject teams.

The teachers teaching the same subject observed each other and thereafter they reflected together on the observed activity. There was one teacher for each of the

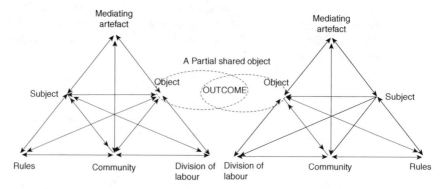

Figure 2.2 The expansive learning cycle
Source: Engeström, 1987, 2001

three years, meaning that there were three teachers in the subject teams. When the mathematics teacher in Year 8 taught the pupils, the mathematics teachers in Years 9 and 10 observed. Prior to the lesson, the teacher would send a lesson plan to the two teachers who would observe and to the researcher, who also participated in the observation and reflection. This document presented the topic for the lesson, questions to be used in the class with the topic as the framework, and what the teacher would like feedback on. The teachers who taught the same subject reflected together on the same day the observation was carried out. They were also able to reflect together in year team meetings about each observation, and in the main team when one third of the programme had been completed. Based on the plan during each semester, there was space for each teacher to teach once and reflect on this, and to observe twice and reflect on these observations with the specific practice and the desired focus as the point of departure.

When teachers feel that they are familiar with the current situation and its history, they can start developing a new model or solution to promote the collective practice in school so that the pupils develop both in their subject and socially. Developing a new model or solution means bringing new content into the nodes in the activity system. It took until the end of the first year before the teachers in the example project were familiar with and aware of what they themselves did and what the others did in their classes. They needed the first six months of the project to develop a sense of belonging to the activity. They spent the second half of the year getting to know each other in the observation and reflection processes and developing an understanding of how the subjects were taught in lower secondary school. They became more aware of what they themselves did and what others did in their teaching. This may be perceived as if they were on a joint actual development level (Vygotsky, 1978). It was after this first year that they were able to start planning development of the practice, which they now felt familiar with (Postholm, 2010b). Observation and reflection became important for getting to know one's own and each other's practice, but they also wanted to observe and reflect together to develop the practice further. Observation and reflection therefore became key tools in the development activity.

After new content had been introduced in the activity system (3), the new model (4) was analysed for possible outcomes. In the phase after the solution/model has been analysed and before it has been implemented, the teachers may undertake small tests of the practice based on specific issues with the development question as the framework. One of the questions in this testing phase within the scope of the development question in the example project was 'How do I give the pupils assignments that will activate them?' During the second year of the project, the teachers implemented programmes in single classes or sessions in classes with the development question as the framework. These classes represented small innovative learning circles. Together, these might constitute a new collective practice of varied ways of working with a focus on learning strategies which would eventually be implemented. Innovative circles may also be left as single events without becoming expansive, while other small innovative learning circles may present a new solution which thereafter will be implemented and put into practice (5) (Engeström & Sannino, 2010). In this phase, the teachers learn from the experiences they gain. They conduct research on their own practice. I call this research in the testing phase action learning (Revans, 1982, 1984) rather than action research because the teachers do not have to present their findings (Pedler & Burgoyne, 2009). Prior to this testing phase, the teachers had researched their own practice and had learnt how to prepare development questions, how to develop a sense of ownership of the projects, and how to work in a learning community. They had also gained some insight into how to observe and reflect together to enhance their own teaching and that of the others. They experienced becoming more confident and trusting in each other, while also learning from each other during the second six-month period of the project. The action learning was indeed intensified when both the learning culture and the structure for observation and reflection were in place when they started the second year of the project (Postholm, 2011). After the new solution/model has been implemented (6), the teachers reflect in teams, and then with the whole teaching staff, on how this solution/model works in practice (7). If they find that the solution/model works, the tests of individual teams will then be merged into a unified programme which over time will be consolidated in practice (7). The teams have developed a new collective practice (Engeström, 1987). After this, a new focus and new testing of the practice can be started with new development questions.

The lower secondary school teachers shared experiences in subject teams and in the main team, but there was no permanent structure for observations in the classroom. As the researcher, I was the facilitator in the project, and my role could probably have been less explicit so that the school leaders or a teacher could have taken more control of the development work. The school leaders were also replaced over the two years of the project. When I conducted a follow-up study two years after the project had ended, I found that one of the new leaders was unaware of the project. The leaders also told me that the teachers wanted time for observation, but that there were no resources that could be used to give them at that time. The teachers had wanted to continue in a learning community, but the school leaders were unable to satisfy this wish. The teachers stated that they still shared experiences and that the project was important for both their own planning and their actual teaching. They also stated that they found the project to be meaningful, but that it was difficult to continue with the formal collective practice when observation and reflection were no longer on the timetable (Postholm, 2011). The project therefore stopped at the point where the teachers tested the practice in their teaching, without their reflections being collected, implemented or consolidated (step 7 in the expansive learning cycle).

I have now presented CHAT with the activity system and the expansive learning cycle as tools for DWR in school. As the researcher, I used the theories and models in collaboration with the teachers and leaders in schools to analyse and develop teaching methods. According to Timperley et al. (2007), it may be necessary to invite external resources persons in research activities in school to co-construct new knowledge for development, but CHAT, and the models developed according to this theory, may also be good resources for school leaders and teachers to conduct research activities in their own school if they had learned about CHAT and its models.

Schools conducting research: premises and possibilities

In the following discussion, school leadership, reflection, ownership developed in the start-up phase and lasting change are the main themes.

Many research findings show that school leadership is important for facilitating and promoting teachers' learning in school (Little, 2012; Thoonen, Sleegers, Oort, & Peersma, 2014; Timperley et al., 2007). According to Robinson (2011), school leaders may also be indirectly important for pupils' learning outcomes through the teachers. If the teachers in a school are to be researchers, and thus are to be systematic in their teaching, they must have school leaders who both support and push them. Hargreaves and Fullan (2012) point out that leaders in research must be confident and humble, resolute and empathetic in their encounter with the teachers, and must also be able to understand when they need to back off a little if they have pushed too hard. This means that school leaders must be sensitive to situations that occur when the teachers are collaborating. Teachers in a researching school do not only need to be supported and pushed by someone leading the research activity, they also need a shared understanding of the object which should be the primary impetus for the systematic work. The example project shows that it may take a long time before the teachers experience it as *their* project. According to Timperley et al. (2007), it is essential that everybody understands the purpose of the work, which means that ample time must be given for the research activity's start-up phase so that it can form a firm foundation for further development. The teachers may then, as in the example project, be able to experience the research as autonomous and meaningful and not as something that has been ordered from above (Postholm, 2008a). Moreover, leaders of this type of work should function as buffers for the teachers against constant pressure from external sources to launch new projects, so the teachers can concentrate on their work (Elmore, 2000).

According to Hargreaves and Fullan (2012), collective collaboration must be a permanent feature of the teachers' work in the same way that teaching together with the pupils is. In the example project, we found that it was necessary to put observation and reflection on the timetable at the start of the semester for this activity to be realized (Postholm, 2008b). This is supported by Kennedy (2011), whose research shows that the timetable can impede collaboration between teachers and thus undermine collective research activity. One study has shown that documentation of the pupils' learning and teachers' teaching processes with a defined focus on dialogue and reflection led to changes in the teaching practice and strengthened the teachers' group processes. This work also improved the teachers' abilities to observe, note, analyse, represent, and respond to the teaching and learning that took place in their classrooms, which in turn led to a cultural change in the teachers' learning community (Given et al., 2010). Observation and reflection may thus lead to an improvement in the research activity in the school, and to the development of the teachers' learning culture. This was also clear in the example project. The main team leader stated, as mentioned above, that the teachers trusted each other and supported each other more than they did previously. They also experienced the work as meaningful (Postholm, 2011). Research findings show that collaboration between teachers in schools promotes a higher level of engagement as well as job satisfaction and well-being (Slavin, 2006, Postholm & Wæge, 2015; Soini, Pietarinen, & Pyhältö, 2016). Collaboration, as in a researching school, may thus help to prevent teachers from quitting the profession due to the stress they might experience at work (Skaalvik & Skaalvik, 2011). A collective systematic collaboration in schools may also help new teachers to join a community that appreciates learning and works systematically to develop everybody's teaching. Researching schools should therefore have strategies for how to include newly trained teachers and newly hired teachers in the school so that they also have the opportunity to develop a sense of belonging to the research activity that is taking place. In the example project, the school leaders were replaced in the middle of the project period. The ideal situation would have been continuity in the leadership team so that the same leaders could have continued to support and push the teachers in their development activities. However, ideal situations are rarely found in reality, and it would therefore be useful for researching schools to give teachers the opportunity to be support persons for school leaders in the development activity. Then development activities would not be so vulnerable to turnover in the schools' leadership, there would be more continuity in the systematic work, and a researching attitude among the teaching staff would more easily prevail. Researching schools also need collaborating researchers that are aware of these factors if possibilities for development is to be utilized.

In collaboration between teachers, leaders and researchers, new knowledge can be co-constructed, a knowledge that can be used underway in development processes, and thus contribute to boundary crossing (Engeström, Engeström, & Kärkkäinen, 1995) within schools. Researchers can also adopt ideas from collaboration with leaders and teachers and learn from the activity. Thus DWR in school supported by researchers can also lead to developmental transfer (Engeström & Sannino, 2010) and thus boundary crossing across institutions, from school to the teacher education institution. As a consequence, more knowledge-based teaching can take place in teacher education. Researchers can also publish findings from DWR projects in schools, meaning that the co-constructed knowledge can function as a thinking tool for other researchers, teachers and leaders aiming for development in DWR.

Note

1 Researchers in this chapter are considered to be teacher educators supporting development in school and at the same time conducting research on these processes.

References

Avalos, B. (2011). Teacher professional development in teaching and teacher education over ten years. *Teaching and Teacher Education*, 27(1), 10–20. doi:2010.08.007

Cole, M., & Engeström, Y. (2007). Cultural-historical approaches to designing for development. In J. Valsiner & A. Rosa (Eds.), *The Cambridge Handbook of Sociocultural Psychology* (pp. 484–507). New York: Cambridge University Press.

Creswell (2013). *Qualitative Inquiry & Research Design: Choosing among Five Approaches*, 3rd edn. Los Angeles: Sage.
Elmore, R. F. (2000). Building a new structure for school leadership. *American Educator*, 23(4), 1–9.
Engeström, Y. (1987). *Learning by Expanding*. Helsinki: Orienta-Konsultit Oy.
Engeström, Y. (2001). *Expansive Learning at Work. Toward an Activity-Theoretical Reconceptualization*. London: Institute of Education, University of London.
Engeström, Y., & Engeström, R. (1986). Developmental work research. The Approach and the application in cleaning work. *Nordisk Pedagogik*, 6, 2–15.
Engeström, Y., & Miettinen, R. (1999). Introduction. In Y. Engestrøm, R. Miettinen & R. Punamaki (Eds.), *Perspectives on Activity Theory* (pp. 1–16). Cambridge, MA: Cambridge University Press.
Engeström, Y., & Sannino, A. (2010). Studies of expansive learning: Foundations, findings and future challenges. *Educational Research Review*, 5(1), 1–24. doi:10.1016/j.edurev.2009.12.002
Engeström, Y., Engeström, R., & Kärkkäinen, M. (1995). Polycontextuality and boundary crossing in expert cognition. Learning and problem solving in complex work activities. *Learning and instruction*, 5(4), 319–335. doi:10.1016/0959-4752(95)00021-00026
Given, H., Kuh, L., LeeKeenan, D., Mardell, B., Redditt, S., & Twombly, S. (2010). Changing school culture: Using documentation to support collaborative inquiry. *Theory into Practice*, 49(1), 36–46. doi:10.1080/00405840903435733
Hargreaves, A., & Fullan, M. (2012). *Professional Capital. Transforming Teaching in every School*. New York: Teachers College Press.
Kennedy, A. (2011). Collaborative continuing professional development (CPD) for teachers in Scotland: Aspirations, opportunities and barriers. *European Journal of Teacher Education*, 34(1). 25–41. doi:10.1080/02619768.2010.534980
Leont'ev, A. (1981). The problem of activity in psychology. In J. Wertsch (Ed.), *The Concept of Activity in Soviet Psychology* (pp. 37–71). Armonk, NY: M.E. Sharpe.
Little, J. W. (1990). The persistence of privacy. Autonomy and initiative in teachers' professional relations. *Teachers College Record*, 91(4), 509–536.
Little, J. W. (2012). Professional community and professional development in the learning-centered school. In M. Kooy & K. van Veen (Eds.), *Teacher Learning that Matters: International Perspectives* (pp. 22–46). New York, NY: Routledge.
Ministry of Education and Research (2009). *Report to the Storting no. 11(2008–2009). Læreren, rollen og utdanningen* [The teacher, the role and the education]. Oslo: Ministry of Education and Research.
Ministry of Education and Research (2010). *Rundskriv [Circular] F-05–10*. Oslo: Ministry of Education and Research.
Ministry of Education and Research (2013). *Report to the Storting 18(2012–2013) Lange linjer – kunnskap gir muligheter* [Long lines – knowledge gives opportunities]. Oslo: Ministry of Education and Research.
Ministry of Education and Research (2014). *Lærerløftet. På lag for kunnskapsskolen* [Strategy to raise teachers' competence. Teaming up for the knowledge school]. Retrieved from www.regjeringen.no/globalassets/upload/kd/vedlegg/planer/kd_strategiskole_web.pdf (accessed 1 March 2016).
Pedler, M., & Burgoyne, J. (2009). Action learning. In P. Reason & H. Bradbury (Eds.), *The Sage Handbook of Action Research. Participative Inquiry and Practice* (pp. 319–332). London: SAGE Publications Ltd.

Postholm, M. B. (2008a). The start-up phase in a research and development work project: A foundation for development. *Teaching and Teacher Education*, 24(3), 575–584. doi:10.1016/j.tate.2007.08.001

Postholm, M. B. (2008b). Teachers developing practice: Reflection as key activity. *Teaching and Teacher Education*, 24(7), 1717–1728. doi:10.1016/j.tate.2008. 02. 024

Postholm, M. B. (2010a). *Kvalitativ metode. En innføring med fokus på fenomenologi, etnografi og kasusstudier* [Qualitative method. An introduction with the focus on phenomenology, ethnography and case studies]. Oslo: Universitetsforlaget.

Postholm, M. B. (2010b). Læring i reflekterende lærerteam: prosess og forutsetninger [Learning in reflecting teacher teams: Process and requirements]. In Andreassen, R.A., E. Irgens, & E. M.Skaalvik, (Eds.), *Kompetent skoleledelse* [Competent school leadership] (pp. 195–209). Trondheim: Tapir Akademisk Forlag.

Postholm, M. B. (2011). A completed research and development work project in school: The teachers' learning and possibilities, premises and challenges for further development. *Teaching and Teacher Education*, 27(3), 560–568. doi:10.1016/j.tate.2010. 10. 010

Postholm, M. B. (2012). Teachers' professional development: A theoretical review: *Educational Research*, 54(4), 405–429. doi:10.1080/00131881.2012.734725

Postholm, M. B., & Jacobsen, D. I. (2011). *Læreren med forskerblikk. En innføringsbok i vitenskapelig metode for lærerstudenter* [The teacher with the researcher's eye. An introduction into scientific methods for student teachers]. Kristiansand: Høyskoleforlaget.

Postholm, M. B., & Wæge, K. (2015). Teacher' learning in school-based development. *Educational Research*, 58(1), 24–38. doi:10.1080/00131881.2015.1117350

Postholm, M. B., Dahl, T., Engvik, G., Fjørtoft, H., Irgens, E. J., Sandvik, L., & Wæge, K. (2013). *En gavepakke til ungdomstrinnet? En undersøkelse av piloten for den nasjonale satsingen på skolebasert kompetanseutvikling* [A gift for lower secondary school? A study of the pilot programme for the national focus on school-based competence development]. Trondheim: Akademika forlag.

Revans, R. W. (1982). *The Origins and Growth of Action Learning*. Bromley: Chartwell-Bratt Ltd.

Revans, R. W. (1984). *The Sequence of Managerial Achievement*. Bradford: MCB University Press.

Robinson, V. (2011). *Student-Centered Leadership*. San Francisco, CA: Jossey-Bass.

Säljö, R. (1995). Mental and physical artefacts in cognitive practices. In P. Reimann & H. Spada (Eds.), *Learning in Humans and Machines. Towards an Interdisciplinary Learning Science* (p. 83–96). New York: Pergamon.

Säljö, R. (1999). Learning as the use of tools. A sociocultural perspective on the human-technology link. In K. Littleton & P. Light (Eds.), *Learning with Computers. Analysing Productive Interaction* (pp. 144–161). New York: Routledge.

Skaalvik, E., & Skaalvik, S. (2011). Teacher job satisfaction and motivation to leave the teaching profession: Relations with school context, feeling of belonging, and emotional exhaustion. *Teaching and Teacher Education*, 27(6). 1029–1038. doi:10.1016/j. tate.2011. 04. 001

Slavin, R. E. (2006). *Educational Psychology: Theory and Practice*. Boston: Pearson/Allyn & Bacon.

Soini, T., Pietarinen, J., & Pyhältö, K. (2016). What if teachers learn in the classroom? *Teacher Development. An International Journal of Teachers' Professional Development*, 20 (3), 380–397. doi:10.1080/13664530.2016.1149511

Strauss, A., & Corbin, J. (1998). *Basics of Qualitative Research: Techniques and Procedures for Developing Grounded Theory*. Thousand Oaks, CA: Sage Publications, Inc.

Thoonen, E. E. J., Sleegers, P. J. C., Oort, F. J., & Peersma, T. T. D. (2014). Building school-wide capacity for improvement: the role of leadership, school organizational conditions, and teacher factors. *School Effectiveness and School Improvement: An International Journal of Research, Policy and Practice, 23*(4), 441–460. doi:10.1080/09243453.2012.678867

Tiller, T. (2006). *Aksjonslæring - forskende partnerskap i skolen* [Action learning – research partnerships in school]. Kristiansand: Høyskoleforlaget.

Timperley, H., Wilson, A. Barrar, H., & Fung, I. (2007). *Teacher Professional Learning and Development: Best Evidence Synthesis Iteration*. Wellington, New Zealand: Ministry of Education.

Virkkunen, J., & Newnham, D. S. (2013). *The Change Laboratory. A Tool for Collaborative Development of Work and Education*. Rotterdam: Sense Publishers.

Vygotsky, L. S. (1978). *Mind in Society. The Development of Higher Psychological Processes*. Cambridge: Harvard University Press.

Vygotsky, L. S. (2000). *Thought and Language*. Cambridge, MA: MIT Press.

Wertsch, J. V. (1991). *Voices of the Mind. A Sociocultural Approach to Mediated Action*. Cambridge, MA: Harvard University Press.

Zwart, R. C., Wubbels, T., Bergen, T., & Bolhuis, S. (2009). Which characteristics of a reciprocal peer coaching context affect teacher learning as perceived by teachers and their students? *Journal of Teacher Education, 60*(3), 243–257. doi:10.1177/0022487109336968

3 Young refugees meeting another road safety culture
Development work in bridging a road safety gap

Eva Brustad Dalland

Introduction

According to the World Health Organization (WHO), road accidents represent a major health problem. In 2016 alone, 1.35 million people died in road accidents throughout the world. Road traffic injuries are now the leading cause of death for children and young adults between 5 and 29 years old, and the problem is highest among those living in low- and middle-income countries (WHO, 2018). To address this growing problem, the Norwegian government created a white paper titled "The National Transport Plan (2002–2011)", which presented the Vision Zero, a road safety approach outlining an official vision for a future without road traffic fatalities and serious injuries (Ministry of Transport and Communications, 1999). Based on this vision, Norwegian authorities and natives have gradually built a road safety culture, and these efforts have positively influenced the country's road safety as Norway now has the lowest number of road fatalities per million inhabitants in the world (Adminaite, Calinescu, Jost, Stipdonk, & Ward, 2018).

However, research shows that there are still high-risk groups, pointing out that immigrants coming from the Middle East and Africa are involved in more road accidents than other individuals even when they have a Norwegian driving licence (Berg, Vassenden, & Gjerstad, 2008). As a result, researchers recommend that immigrants should be encouraged to do more road safety training. Public road safety authorities have described some initiatives that can be implemented to increase road safety training among immigrants, which are mostly related to providing *information* to immigrants (Directorate of Public Roads, 2014). There is a lack of research on immigrants and refugees in their road user roles as pedestrians, passengers, or cyclists shortly after they arrive in Norway. In a holistic perspective, drivers start building their attitudes when they are in other road user roles (e.g., as pedestrians, cyclists, and passengers). We, the researchers in this project, could not find any research on *how* to teach refugees or immigrants about road safety themes when they first arrive in their new country. However, our pre-understanding in this project is that merely providing information is not enough and that a deeper educational approach is needed. Thus, the content of this chapter is guided by the following research question: *How can communities work to integrate refugees into their road safety culture?*

The aim of this study is to develop a pedagogical approach to integrate refugees and immigrants into the road safety culture in their new country based on their actual roles as vulnerable road users. The primary objectives are to find a way to communicate with newly arrived refugees about road safety and to identify some pedagogical methods and tools to do so. In addition, this study aims to gain more knowledge about young refugees' previous experiences as road users, their perceptions of their role as road users, their interactions as road users with others in their community, and their needs as roads users to improve interactions within the road safety culture.

This study uses cultural-historical activity theory (CHAT) as the theoretical framework (Engeström, 2001) in a development work research (DWR) project done in collaboration between a university and a refugee centre. This chapter first presents the Norwegian road safety culture inside an activity system where natives and the public interact to build this culture. In terms of road safety, contradictions arise when refugees and immigrants move into this activity system. After this discussion, the DWR project is presented. The findings reveal that most refugees lack experience of common cultural artefacts used by the natives in their new community, which influences road safety, and the need for pedagogical teaching to help them interact and be a part of the road safety culture. Some of the findings and experiences in this study indicate boundary crossing (Akkerman & Bakker, 2011). In this context, boundary crossing happened when the refugees showed they had taken new knowledge into themselves about road safety at the end of the project; for example, when they argued for the use of new cultural artefacts inside the road safety culture of their new community and when they reflected about cultural differences in their interactions with drivers as pedestrians.

A culture of road safety within the activity system

Within CHAT, Engeström visualizes and presents the notion of an *activity system*, a tool to describe, analyse, and understand human activity and complex connections in society and to analyse the development and interconnections of a focused activity (Engeström, 1999a; 2007). Within this perspective, Norway can be described as an activity system with a road safety culture in the community, as presented in the Vision Zero. Norway, as a society, could not accept fatalities and serious injuries due to road traffic. As a result, the Vision Zero is deeply rooted in three pillars – *ethics, science,* and *responsibility* (Ministry of Transport and Communications, 1999) – and emphasizes that all Norwegian road users, authorities, and road safety organizations have the collective responsibility to improve road safety. In Figure 3.1 presented below, Norway is seen as an activity system emphasizing road safety in which tensions arise when immigrants and refugees who come from cultures where road safety is not a focus, are expected to interact with natives about the object: road safety.

In Figure 3.1, the subjects in this activity system emphasizing road safety consists of road users, such as pedestrians, cyclists, and vehicle drivers, who interact to

28   E. B. Dalland

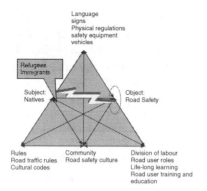

Figure 3.1 Tensions in an activity system emphasizing road safety
Source: Illustration based on Engestroms' (1999a, p. 31) model of the activity system

achieve the official goal of reducing serious road accidents. The division of labour represents interactions in the community between actors who are responsible for road safety, such as police, driving teachers, and employees from official administrative organizations and the Ministry of Transport and Communications.

CHAT comprises five main principles (Engeström, 2001). The first principle is that individuals are members of collective artefact-mediated and object-oriented activity systems that have network relationships with other activity systems. The second principle is the multi-voicedness in the activity system as individuals have different historical backgrounds, traditions, interests, and views and work together in different roles. The third principle is historicity, which reflects how historical changes are an important aspect for understanding activity theory and individual actions in the system. The fourth principle is that contradictions or tensions in the system are seen as sources of change and development. Finally, the fifth principle focuses on the possibility of expansive transformations in the activity system (Engeström, 2001).

Cultural artefacts in the activity system are essential for individuals' development as humans and can be both physical and linguistic in character, including language, signs, and symbols (Engeström, 2001). Road signs and symbols, traffic lights, cars, buses, motorcycles, bicycles, reflective equipment, PowerPoint slides, computers, and blackboards are all cultural artefacts (Dalland, 2018). Tensions in the activity system represent the power to change and develop (Engeström, 1996, 1999b, 2001). Inner tensions occur in the activity system when problems and disturbances arise, and these contradictions or tensions are illustrated in specific conceptual models based on the general model of an activity system (Engeström, 2001, 2007). Tensions arise when immigrants and refugees from countries with much higher rates of road accidents are expected to interact about road safety with natives in their new community. In 2015, an increasing wave of refugees came into Norway, which could have increased the tensions in the system of road safety culture and necessitated research and development to integrate young refugees into this culture of road safety.

The influence of lifelong learning on road safety

The third principle in CHAT is about how historicity and historical changes are important for understanding the culture and individual actions in the activity system (Engeström, 2001). The process of developing a road safety culture in Norway is connected to historical changes over time, during which natives have developed ownership in this road safety culture. In the community, individual road users and public institutions share responsibility for road safety. There are learning activities for natives throughout different stages of their lives: from the time they are babies seated in the car to later learning opportunities in the school system. Natives are involved in the entire learning process, and the community and natives influence each other in building a road safety culture. The Norwegian Council for Road Safety strongly recommends that road safety should be a natural part of children's education. Thus, starting in nursey and primary school, children learn how to act and understand signs, understand certain risks, and interact in their roles as pedestrians and cyclists in real road traffic with their parents. During this stage, the use of protection like reflective equipment and helmets is highlighted by adults.

A development work research project

The fifth principle in CHAT focuses on the possibility of expansive transformations in the activity system when inner contradictions or tensions arise and somebody starts asking critical questions about established norms (Engeström, 2001). In this study, we – the researchers – started to ask critical questions about how the community helps refugees and immigrants to integrate into the road safety community, which led to the presented research question. To answer this research question, we organized a DWR project, in which a research group from a university collaborated with a refugee centre. Figure 3.2 presents the research group and refugee centre as two activity systems collaborating around an object – namely, road safety in the community – and how to develop ways to teach and coach refugees to be a part of this road safety culture.

Figure 3.2 illustrates the subject in the first activity system – the research group from a university – where we, the two researchers, interact with two supervisors and six driving teacher students. Inside those activity systems, the second principle in the CHAT about multi-voicedness is topical and interesting. Individuals' different historical backgrounds, traditions, interests, and views influence interactions in the activity system (Engeström, 2001). One of the students has an immigrant background himself, and another previously worked in an asylum centre. In the second activity system, the subjects are two interpreters, the centre leader and one employee, and eight young refugee boys coming from Afghanistan, Eritrea, and Syria as learners for the practical pedagogical solutions tried out in the project. The employees became discussion partners and organized the practical solutions in the project. Two interpreters connected with the refugee centre helped to conduct interviews and implement the practical solutions.

30 E. B. Dalland

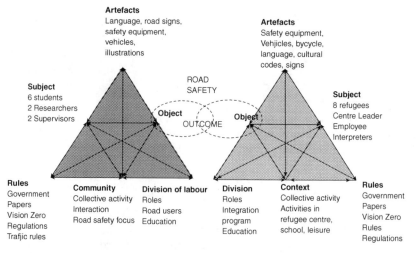

Figure 3.2 Two activity systems in collaboration in a DWR project
Source: Illustration based on Engeström (2001, p. 6)

The development work focuses on how to teach and guide young refugees to be full members of the road safety community soon after their arrival in the country. The project focuses on how to find ways to meet refugees in their *zone of proximal development* (ZPD) (Vygotsky, 1978), defined as "the distance between the actual developmental level as determined by independent problem solving and the level of potential development as determined through problem solving under adult guidance or collaboration with more capable peers" (Vygotsky, 1978, p. 86). When a learning process is going on, it is essential to stay together in context and communicate with people providing guidance. Mental processes unfold in learners at an external interpersonal level until they think and behave independently. At this point, learners absorb and own the new knowledge at an inner intrapersonal level and are able to consider this knowledge using inner speech to make independent decisions (Vygotsky, 1978). Akkerman and Bakker (2011) describe this change of becoming independent in the learning process as boundary crossing. They also suggest that boundary crossing occurs when a learner goes from being a peripheral participant to a full member of a community.

This DWR project is based on the theory of expansive learning (Engeström, 2001; Engeström & Sannino, 2010). According to this theory, an initial simple idea is transformed into a complex object and a new form of practice (Engeström, 1987, 1999b; Engeström & Sannino, 2010). Figure 3.3 illustrates the process in the development work based on the model of the expansive learning cycle, (Engeström, 1999b, 2001; Engeström & Sannino, 2010).

Figure 3.3 illustrates the development process, which starts when researchers and practitioners begin to ask critical questions about an existing practice, conduct historical and theoretical searches about the problem, and then model new solutions. A group comes together to plan and interact in the project before they try out real situations. In this way, the process runs in inner cycles from Point 3 to

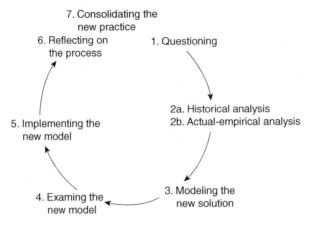

Figure 3.3 Sequences of epistemic actions in an expansive learning cycle
Source: Engeström, 1999b, p. 384

Point 6 until a new model arises and can be consolidated in the system. In some cases, a new thoroughly discussed change and collective view emerge in the activity system as a result of this process (Engeström, 2001).

Planning and trying out solutions in a real context

After Points 1 and 2 in the expansive learning cycle – the phases involving questioning and searching for official documents and previous research – we, the researchers in this DWR project, held meetings with leaders of refugee centres to discuss the problem that initiated this project. The refugee boys had received information and clear directions to use seat belts in cars and to use reflective equipment in darkness, but the boys did not use their reflective equipment as recommended. Even though the employees had walked with the refugees from the centre to their school, other road users in the local community reported the refugees' unstructured behaviour when walking to and from school.

The research group organized short workshops to discuss the young boys' concrete needs as road users and ideas about what learning tools and methods the group could try out to meet these needs. The group decided to meet with refugees soon after they arrived in the country and to do practical road safety demonstrations, but we were aware that language could be a great challenge during this stage. To ensure the quality of the practical demonstrations, the researchers, supervisors, and students drove into the practical area together to discuss the methods and learning activities and conducted demonstrations with the refugees in darkness. The group held constructive discussions in this context to point out some risk situations that the refugees may have been unaware of at the time. This development work of pedagogical tools and methods can be described as four small inner cycles inside the larger expansive learning cycle (Engeström, 1999b) when modelling and trying out different solutions.

In the first small inner cycle, the theme was about how to behave as a pedestrian and a passenger and the risk of not using seat belts, and the sequence was a short classroom lesson combined with a practical session in the car. Due to the language challenges, the research group used clear illustrations and simple examples to explain how to interact with other road users and what risks the refugees may face. In the subsequent car session, the focus was on how to properly use a seat belt and headrest to ensure one's own safety.

In the second small inner cycle, the focus was on wearing reflective equipment in darkness, and the team conducted a practical demonstration to show the dangers of moving in darkness without reflective equipment. The driving teacher students' role was to drive and explain risks as well as safety in the demonstrated situations, and they were supported by the supervisors and interpreters. The researchers' role was to simulate vulnerable road users (i.e., wearing/not wearing reflective equipment) and provide a high-quality demonstration. For example, one part of the demonstration showed the drivers' difficulty in determining whether young people were playing in the snow, at which point one young person ran into the road without reflective equipment. This scenario was created because it reflected one of the worries messages the refugee centre had received about the refugees.

In the third small inner cycle, the focus was on road signs and markings related to pedestrians, common risks that could appear in traffic situations, and proper ways to interact with drivers based on simulations by the students in context. The lesson also focused on drivers' need for additional breaking distance on slippery road conditions and the need for pedestrians to determine whether a driver is really able to stop.

In the fourth small inner cycle, half a year after the first one, the refugee boys participated in Road Safety Day at the university's campus. The students in the research group guided the refugees throughout the day and let them try different cultural artefacts related to road safety. One activity was to sit in a simulator of a truck cab as it overturned so they could get a real sense of what it felt like to hang upside down in a seat belt. Another activity was to stay inside a bus as simulated smoke came in, the focus of which was to teach the boys how to act in the dangerous situation and evacuate the bus.

Methodology and methods

The study presented in this chapter relates to the DWR project. The research team used a case study methodology, defined as a qualitative approach in which a case is explored over time (Creswell, 2007). This study focuses on eight refugee boys living in a refugee centre for half a year. In one way, the study duration is short related to processes in the expansive learning cycle (Engeström, 2001); in another way, however, this duration was necessary to influence the refugees' road safety thinking as fast as possible and to finish the work before the driving teacher students completed their education.

To get nuanced descriptions from the participants' perspective (Merriam, 2009), we held two focus group interviews both before and at the end of the development work (one in each for language group of the refugee boys) to obtain data about their prior experiences as road users and their current experiences with their new culture. The data from the first interviews formed the basis of the development work. In interactions, researchers and participants construct meaning about and a unique understanding of a topic (Kvale & Brinkmann, 2015; Merriam, 2009). For the current study, we decided to do group interviews instead of single interviews because we felt the young refugees would most likely feel more comfortable in a group setting instead of being alone. In any interview, researchers must act in a way that earns participants' trust so that participants are open and honest in the dialogue. We had to be very careful to avoid asking questions that could invoke traumatic memories in the young refugees. In interviews characterized by cultural differences and language problems, the quality of the data material can be reduced, compared to an interview situation in which the researcher and the interviewee have a shared language and cultural background. For the current study, we compensated for some of these challenges by using two interpreters, and the data material was strengthened further as the interpreters knew the boys through earlier work in the asylum centre. The computer pictures also supported communication and strengthened the quality. Having two researchers in context and having discussions with the research group about the findings and their experiences further strengthened the research quality as the data material could be seen from different views and could complement the findings.

The group composition was related to the refugees' first language. We decided not to record the interviews because the status of the refugees' residence permits was unclear, and they may have felt more anxious about their responses with a microphone on the table. The two researchers collaborated in the interviews: one asked question while the interpreter translated and the other took notes. To ensure that the refugees understood the specific traffic concepts and regulations mentioned in the questions, we used slides with illustrations. For instance, if the question was about how to use a crosswalk, we showed a picture of a crosswalk on the computer.

Participant observations (Patton, 2002) were conducted when trying out the demonstrations in context. As the demonstrations were in darkness, we, the researchers, had discussions together with the research group about the refugees' responses during the demonstrations and made notes afterwards. To analyse the data material from the group interviews, participant observations, and notes from the four cycles, the constant comparative method of analysis was used (Postholm, 2010; Strauss & Corbin, 1998), which Postholm (2010) claims can be used in all qualitative studies with substantial coding and categories. We did open coding in a dynamic process (Strauss & Corbin, 1998). During the analysis process, the researchers organized the data into groups of categories and subcategories with shared meaning and gave them suitable names. Categories arising from the data include the following main categories and sub-categories:

- Refugees' lack of awareness about risks as road users
- Refugees' shared reflections about cultural differences related to road traffic
    - Cultural differences in interactions between pedestrians and drivers
- Refugees' unfamiliarity with common cultural artefacts related to the road safety culture
    - Use of reflective equipment
    - Use of seat belts
    - Focus as bus passengers
    - Use of bicycles
- Educational tools and methods leading the refugees to deeper understanding

In this analysis process, the researchers both reduced the material and made connections between findings to create meaning. In the following the analyses and discussion of the findings are woven together with the researchers' theoretical knowledge and cultural framework (Merriam, 2009).

Findings and discussion

In the Norwegian community, natives see themselves as road users and part of the road traffic system. None of the refugees mentioned vulnerable road users or themselves as part of the road traffic concept, neither as passengers, pedestrians, nor cyclists. The young refugees' understanding of the road traffic concept was about vehicles, police, and accidents, and they explained that traffic rules and signs were mainly needed to avoid chaos.

Refugees' lack of awareness about risks as a road user

The findings in this study show that after arriving in Norway, the eight refugee boys did not think about the risks associated with road accidents at all. For them, it was a safe place to live even when moving in the road traffic system. In one way, they are right because Norway has the lowest death rate for road accidents in Europe (Adminaite et al., 2018). In another way, one of the major reasons for this great statistic is the responsibility road users feel when interacting in the activity system to build the road safety culture, one of the pillars of Vision Zero (Ministry of Transport and Communications, 1999). Natives are an integral part of the road safety system in the community and interact with others to build the road safety culture. Not only is the low rate of fatalities connected to drivers' competences, but it is also a result of interactions in the activity system (Engeström, 1999a; 2001) both between different road user groups and between authorities and road users. Thus, refugees and immigrants need to be more aware of their roles as road users when interacting in the road safety culture as the young refugees did not see themselves as vulnerable road users in the road traffic system.

High speed is a common cause of road accidents and represents a risk of serious accidents. The boys from Syria and Eritrea said the road traffic moved too slowly in Norway. Neither of the two groups could see any risk of being vulnerable road users on a European road with a high- speed limit. There are seldom vulnerable native road users moving there. In contrast to the refugees, Norwegians have built knowledge about road safety through lifelong learning about road safety and thus understand risk, which influences their choices about where to move in the road system. In another view, the young refugee boys had passed a period in their lives involving war, an unregulated traffic culture, and probably a risky flight, which likely makes their acceptance of risk higher than natives.

Refugees' shared reflections about cultural differences related to road traffic

The young boys reflected on Norwegian drivers' willingness to help them and described an event that happened on their way home from school one day:

> Some of us were pushing and joking on the way home from school, like a fight. A driver stopped and got out of his car and came to stop our fight. He thought it was a serious fight! It was a good feeling that somebody wanted to stop our fight! It was nice that he showed interest and cared about us – even though we are refugees!

The boys did not expect this kind of protection from a strange driver, and it became a positive road traffic experience for them related to cultural differences. They mentioned that this type of event would never happen in their home countries. The way they described this event also revealed their feeling of being outsiders in the community when they said, "even though we are refugees". Other road users cared about the refugees' behaviour as pedestrians as they contacted the refugee centre to report the young refugees' unstructured and unregulated behaviour along the local road.

In addition, the boys from Syria claimed it was no problem for teenagers to borrow a car there and to drive without a licence. One of them explained that he started to drive a car when he was 13 years old. The whole group claimed that, in their opinions, it would be much safer for them to drive a car without a driver licence than to ride a bicycle on a major road in Syria. If an accident happened when they were driving, however, they had to leave because they could be charged for the accident. Compared with the community in Norway, this is a very different practice. Indeed, leaving from an accident in Norway would lead to the opposite consequences because providing first aid in road accidents is required by law. This represents a clear cultural difference because helping others who are hurt is deeply rooted in the culture in their new community.

Cultural differences in interactions between pedestrians and drivers

The young refugee boys' understanding was that pedestrians in Norway have very strong rights compared to those in their home countries. They reflected on some differences related to the road safety culture in Norway, particularly pointing out that Norwegian drivers were more respectful than drivers in their home countries and that all drivers stopped when they used crosswalks. This finding corresponds to research describing cultural differences among immigrant drivers in high-risk groups from the Middle East and Africa, who think that vulnerable road users are less important and have fewer rights in the road system (Berg et al. 2008). In one way, the refugees' experiences show that Norwegian drivers follow traffic rules and take care of pedestrians in the community, and in another way, they show that those positive experiences can lead to a false sense of safety, which can increase road accidents. Natives in the activity system know that there is a risk if drivers do not stop even in crosswalks regulated with traffic lights. In childhood, they learn to check for cars when crossing the crosswalk. In this community, natives act to reduce accidents even though they have strong rights as pedestrians.

Refugees' unfamiliarity with common cultural artefacts related to the road safety culture in the community

The refugees' knowledge, experiences, and attitudes related to cultural artefacts like reflective equipment, crosswalks, cars and buses, seat belts, and bicycles were clearly different from those of native youth in Norway. Humans construct their understanding with and through cultural artefacts, which influence their inner dialogue about how to behave. Language helps individuals overcome impulsive actions and contributes to self-regulation (Vygotsky, 1978, 1986) which is essential for road users. In the community, there seems to be a lack of understanding about refugees' and immigrants' lack of knowledge about common artefacts related to road traffic in their new community since learning programs for refugees and immigrants do not deeply focus on how to be a road user in the road safety culture for refugees and immigrants. Some of the common cultural artefacts that natives use in their daily lives were unknown to the refugees, or they had no experience using these artefacts. This lack of knowledge about common cultural artefacts influenced their understanding and attitudes as well as how they think about risks and protection related to using the artefacts.

Use of reflective equipment

The four boys from Afghanistan had never seen any reflective equipment before coming to Norway, and the four boys from Syria and Eritrea had seen such equipment before but had never used it. Employees at the centre were a bit frustrated because they had clearly told the boys to use reflective equipment, but the boys failed to do so or had lost the equipment. In an interview, the refugee boys explained that they tried to remember to wear the equipment but sometimes forgot it or could not find it. They also mentioned that they recognized that the leaders and workers in the centre always used reflective equipment in darkness.

In the project, the real-world demonstration showed the boys how much better the driver could see a walker in darkness when the walker wore reflective equipment compared to when he or she did not use the equipment. During that demonstration, the refugees became more conscious that using reflective equipment could protect them in traffic situations. They became enthusiastic, saying, "This is really dangerous" as they passed a walker without reflective equipment. Thus, the demonstration along with a deeper explanation was very useful in teaching the refugees the importance of using reflective equipment in darkness and worked better than the mere recommendation to use reflective equipment. The boys were able to see the road safety effect of using reflective equipment first-hand and got a better sense of the difficulties drivers have in identifying walkers without such equipment.

Use of seat belts

None of the boys had used seat belts in their home countries. The boys from Afghanistan were not accustomed to being passengers, and the cars they did ride in usually did not have seat belts. The boys from Syria were used to cars with seat belts, but they did not use them and argued that it could be dangerous to use seat belts if the car ended up in water. Only one boy from Afghanistan reflected that using seat belts can influence safety and protect him because he had seen a film where a person was hurt because he did not use a seat belt.

In general, natives have good attitudes about using seat belts, and these attitudes are built throughout childhood and adolescence. Knowledge about seat belts' life-protecting function is common among natives, thus motivating Norwegians to use seat belts. Knowledge about the law and required use is likely not natives' first motivation to use seat belts. In the refugee centre, the boys had learned and understood that it is obligatory to use seat belts in Norway and that they had to pay money if they did not use them. At that time, they used seat belts to satisfy other individuals, not to protect themselves. In addition, the fact that they did not see any risks from the road traffic in their new country may have influenced their decision not to use seat belts for safety reasons. In their ZPD, they were in the process of maturation (Vygotsky, 1978, 1986), but they were still novices (Lave & Wenger, 1991) as they did not argue about their own safety. However, at the university's Road Safety Day, one of the refugee boys said that when he observed his friend turning around in the simulator cab, he became very anxious because he thought that his friend had forgotten to fasten his seat belt and would be hurt. He was happy when he saw that his friend had fastened his seat belt. This boy thought about his friend's safety and realized that seat belts are meant to protect drivers and passengers. His focus had moved from mere awareness of the law requiring the use of seat belts to a consciousness about his own and others' increased safety when using them. At that point in time, he was clearly in the process of boundary crossing (Akkerman & Bakker, 2011).

A change in focus as bus passengers

An unexpected finding related to cultural artefacts was that two of the boys from Afghanistan had never seen a bus before they came to Europe, only a few mini buses. In addition, none of the four boys from Afghanistan had been bus passengers before coming to Norway. After arriving in Norway, the boys often rode buses, and their focus was on the high standards in buses, especially that passengers could watch films. They had no idea about what kind of risk situations could arise when moving outside a bus, which is often highlighted when teaching native school children about risk situations. After participating in the simulated situation with smoke in the bus at Road Safety Day, the refugee boys said that they had learned to move slowly, leave the bus as soon as possible if an accident happened, and – if necessary – evacuate by knocking out a window. Clearly, after the simulation, they would have done this to save their own and others' lives in a real situation. They became more conscious about safety inside the bus, not only the comfort artefacts. The young refugee boys were in a collective boundary-crossing process (Akkerman & Bakker, 2011) related to a new artefact as bus passengers.

The use of bicycles

The boys from Syria had learned cycling and understood the risk associated with cycling in heavy traffic in their home country. They explained that in Syria, vulnerable road users had no rights and drivers did not take care of them. The boys from Afghanistan had no experience with cycling at all as they had never learned the activity. This is an important finding because cycling is engrained the daily life in their new country and the community expects people of all ages to master cycling. Cycling can be an important part of refugees' and immigrants' integration because the activity serves important transportation, environmental, and health functions in Norway. Recommendations in public documents seem to be written under the assumption that everybody learns cycling as a child. In the National Transport Plan (2014–2023), Norwegian public authorities recommend that inhabitants ride bicycles instead of driving motor vehicles, especially in urban areas (Ministry of Transport and Communications, 2013). This recommendation is based on the report "National Bicycling Strategy – Focus on Bicycle" (Directorate of Public Roads, 2012), which states that increasing the use of bicycles will positively influence the health, economy, and emissions in Norway, and a report from Civitas (Lea, Haug, & Selvig, 2012) focusing on success criteria by increasing bicycling (Directorate of Public Roads, 2012; Lea et al., 2012). Providing refugees and immigrants the chance to learn how to cycle can be valuable for both them and the community. This will likely require large amounts of resources, and if authorities focus on this issue, there may be opportunities to organize and interact with local volunteer organizations in a larger way to make it possible for motivated refugees and immigrants to learn how to cycle.

Educational tools and methods leading the refugees to deeper understanding

Using tools in this DWR project that required the young refugees to be active, helped them make reflections, talk about their feelings, and build experiences in their learning process related to new cultural artefacts and the road safety culture. Human development is woven together with cultural artefacts, so to realize deeper and more permanent learning, language and activity need to be connected first at the social level and later at the individual level as intelligent development and independent thinking (Vygotsky, 1978).

Educators need to be aware of possible cultural differences when working to find good examples to use in lessons. Even though the development group had discussed cultural differences at length, one of the examples used in the classroom was a wake-up call. A picture was shown with the intention of having the refugees reflect on the risks and consequences of not using seat belts in a crash. In the picture, there was a high-dive platform with water below and a roof with ground below, both ten metres high, and the students asked which platform the refugees would prefer to jump from. Usually, native youth say they will jump into the water because there is a lower likelihood of getting hurt. However, the refugees gave an unexpected answer: "It is just the same; we will die in both situations." They could not swim. Thus, there were cultural differences that made this a poor example even though the illustration had text in the refugees' first language. The example did not lead to the expected reflections because it was built on cultural assumptions based on common premises in Norwegian culture.

Concluding reflections

To bridge the gap about cultural differences related to road safety among refugees and immigrants in the community, the findings and experiences in this study indicate that there is a great need to include educational processes about the road safety culture in both in the introduction program for immigrants and in other learning programs over time. It is essential to fill the gap about lifelong learning and artefacts related to road safety and risk understanding in refugees' roles as vulnerable road users. Refugees and immigrants have not taken part in the life-long learning process to build their road safety thinking and do not have ownership in this road safety culture. The obligatory official introduction program for newly arrived immigrants is regulated by law, and the curriculum for this program should include themes about road safety culture and should also be extended to later learning programs for immigrants.

In the current curriculum for the introduction program (VOX, 2012), being a road user is presented among many other themes as one bullet point about transport in the local environment and simple road traffic rules. The findings in this study highlight the need to do pedagogical work to fill the gap between refugees' or immigrants' past experiences related to the road traffic cultures in their countries and their integration in the road safety culture in their new country. There is a need to see this work in a broad perspective in the activity system and focus on how to fill the lifelong learning gap related to road safety among refugees and immigrants.

References

Adminaite, D., Calinescu, T., Jost, G., Stipdonk, H., & Ward, H. (2018). *Ranking EU Progress on Road Safety. 12th Road Safety Performance Index Report.* Retrieved from https://etsc.eu/wp-content/uploads/PIN_ANNUAL_REPORT_2018_final.pdf

Akkerman, S. F., & Bakker, A. (2011). Boundary Crossing and Boundary Objects. *American Educational Research Association, 81*(2), 132–169. doi:10.3102/0034654311404435

Berg, C., Vassenden, A., & Gjerstad, B. (2008). *Innvandrere som risikogruppe i trafikken* [Immigrants as a risk group in road traffic]. *Report – IRIS 2010/ 079.* Retrieved from https://evalueringsportalen.no/evaluering/innvandrere-som-risikogruppe-i-trafikken/IRIS-rapport%202010-079.pdf/@@inline

Creswell, J. W. (2007). *Qualitative Inquiry and Research Design. Choosing Among Five Approaches.* Thousand Oaks, CA: Sage Publications, Inc.

Dalland, E. B. (2018). Integration of Refugees and Immigrants to Road Safety Culture. In M. Susimetsä & H. Ainjärv (Eds.), *Theory and Practice in Driver Education* (pp. 85–112). Tallinn: Tallinn University Press.

Directorate of Public Roads (2012). *Nasjonal sykkelstrategi- Sats på sykkel! Grunnlagsdokument for Nasjonal transportplan 2014–2023* [National Bicycling Strategy - Highlight cycling! Base Document for National Transport Plan 2014–2023]. *VD Report No.7.* Retrieved from www.vegvesen.no/_attachment/317385

Directorate of Public Roads (2014). *Nasjonal tiltaksplan for trafikksikkerhet på veg, 2014–2017* [National Action Plan for Road Traffic Safety 2014–2017]. Retrieved from www.vegvesen.no/_attachment/598739/binary/949929

Engeström, Y. (1987). *Learning by Expanding: An Activity-Theoretical Approach to Developmental Research.* Helsinki: Orienta-Konsultit.

Engeström, Y. (1996). Developmental work research as educational research. Looking ten years back and into the zone of proximal development. *Nordisk Pedagogik*, 16(3), 131–143.

Engeström, Y. (1999a). Activity theory and individual and social transformation. In Y. Engeström, R. Miettinen, & R.-L. Punamäki (Eds.), *Perspectives on Activity Theory* (pp. 19–38). Cambridge: Cambridge University Press.

Engeström, Y. (1999b). Innovative learning in work teams: Analyzing cycles of knowledge creation in practice. In Y. Engeström, R. Miettinen, & R.-L. Punamäki (Eds.), *Perspectives on Activity Theory* (pp. 377–404). Cambridge: Cambridge University Press.

Engeström, Y. (2001). *Expensive Learning at Work. Toward an Activity-Theoretical Reconceptualisation.* London: Institute of Education, University of London.

Engeström, Y. (2007). Putting Vygotsky to work. The Change Laboratory as an Application of Double Stimulation. In H. Daniels, M. Cole, & J. V. Wertsch (Eds.), *The Cambridge Companion to Vygotsky* (pp. 363–382). Cambridge UK: Cambridge University Press.

Engeström, Y., & Sannino, A. (2010). Studies of expansive learning: Foundations, findings and future challenges. *Educational Research Review, 5*(1), 1–24. doi:10.1016/j.edurev.2009.12.002

Kvale, S., & Brinkmann, S. (2015). *Det kvalitative forskningsintervju* [Qualitative research interviewing]. Oslo: Gyldendal Akademisk.

Lave, J., & Wenger, E. (1991). *Situated Learning: Legitimate Peripheral Participation.* Cambridge: Cambridge University Press.

Lea, R., Haug, E., & Selvig, E. (2012). *Klimaeffekt av økt sykling og gåing, og suksesskriterier for økt sykling* [Climatic effects when expanding bicycling and walking, and success-criteria to expand bicycling]. Retrieved from www.regjeringen.no/globalassets/upload/sd/vedlegg/sykling_rapport_130222_civitas.pdf

Merriam, S. B. (2009). *Qualitative Research. A Guide to Design and Implementation*. San Francisco: Jossey-Bass.

Ministry of Transport and Communications (1999). *Stortingsmelding nr.46 (1999–2000), Nasjonal transportplan 2002–2011* [White paper no. 46 (1999–2000). The National Transport Plan 2002–2011]. Retrieved from www.regjeringen.no/no/dokumenter/stmeld-nr-46-1999-2000-/id193608/

Ministry of Transport and Communications (2013). *Stortingsmelding nr. 26 (2012–2013). Nasjonal transportplan (2014–2023)* [White paper no. 26 (2012–2013). National Transport Plan 2014–2023]. Retrieved from www.regjeringen.no/no/dokumenter/meld-st-26-20122013/id722102/

Patton, M. Q. (2002). *Qualitative Research & Evaluation Methods*. Thousand Oaks, CA: Sage Publications Inc.

Postholm, M. B. (2010). *Kvalitativ metode. En innføring med fokus på fenomenologi, etnografi og kasusstudier* [Qualitative method. An introduction with the focus on phenomenology, ethnography and case studies]. Oslo: Universitetsforlaget.

Strauss, A., & Corbin, J. (1998). *Basics of Qualitative Research. Techniques and Procedures for Developing Grounded Theory*. Thousand Oaks, CA: Sage Publications Inc.

VOX (2012). *Læreplan i norsk og samfunnskunnskap for voksne innvandrere* [Curriculum in Norwegian and Society knowledge for adult immigrants]. Retrieved from www.kompetansenorge.no/contentassets/f6594d5ddc814b7bb5c9d2f4564ac134/laereplan_norsk_samfunnskunnskap_bm_web.pdf

Vygotsky, L. S. (1978). *Mind in Society. The Development of Higher Psychological Processes*. London: Harvard University Press.

Vygotsky, L. S. (1986). *Thought and Language*. Cambridge, MA: The MIT Press.

WHO (2018). *Global Status Report on Road Safety 2018. World Health Organization report*. Retrieved from www.who.int/violence_injury_prevention/road_safety_status/2018/en/

4 Inspired by the concept of boundary objects in arts education

Nina Scott Frisch

Introduction

The arts have been articulated as subjects in Norwegian education, from early childhood education to master's degrees, as one field of experiences, expressions, research, and learning. In national curricula, such as early childhood education and care (ECEC) at the bachelor level, the subject is defined as 'Arts, culture and creativity,' encompassing music, drama, and arts and crafts (Norwegian Directorate for Education and Training, 2017). Internationally, the arts are presented as a unified body in distinguished research journals, such as *The International Journal of Education & the Arts* and *Journal of Aesthetic Education*.

However, there are challenges and implications with the constructed unity of merged arts, as well as with different art disciplines being distinguished in early childhood education in Norway. In a bachelor teaching programme with in-depth pedagogical arts studies as part of its profile in a Norwegian university college specialising in early childhood education, a multimodal project in arts education as part of a toddler festival is used as a case to shed light on the arts as separate and merged entities in arts education, and by that to help answer the research question: *How can the concept of boundary objects be used as a thinking tool to identify common grounds for music, drama, and arts and crafts in arts education in ECEC teachers training?*

One motivation for this case study is to shed light on the arts as separate units or subjects, seen in this text as music, drama, and arts and crafts, with their art activities, with their labels and societal uses as within boundaries in society, here separate subjects in ECEC teachers' training. When merged in ECEC education as one arts subject, 'Arts, culture and creativity,' it is of interest to see how these three subjects are put into play in teaching/learning in the classroom. The purpose of this case study, then, is to explore the arts as separate units or subjects as seen by students, and then used in an arts project involving various multimodal installations, thereby merging the arts as subjects.

This study focuses on art made by students (grown-up university students) *for* children (Moe, 2018). The experience of making cultural expressions or installations for toddlers by third-year bachelor students arranged as a toddler festival at a university college in Norway is a case of exploring the arts – music, drama, and arts and crafts – and their possible boundary object-inspired themes in ECEC education. The study could help university and college arts education teachers determine how their respective arts subjects (music, drama, arts and crafts) can be used in multimodal expressions, that is multiple, simultaneous experiences with different modes of art, and thereby prioritising what to teach within an often limited timeframe, as the arts are not always given priority in Western education.

The concepts of *boundary object* (Akkerman & Bakker, 2011) and *artefact* (Cole, 1996) within a sociocultural context clarify the boundaries, and thereby the objects, that can facilitate the merger of art subjects' boundaries and their common grounds in multimodal arts expressions made by students. These artefacts are in this text defined as boundary objects. The concept of boundary objects can help teachers 1) visualize the students' conceptions of essential artefacts, here understood as signs and tools defined by Cole (1996) as artefacts (see *Methodology and Theoretical Framework* for further definition of boundary objects and artefacts) within their arts subjects' boundaries, used in this case with a focus on multimodal expressions, and therefore 2) focus on quality within a chosen segment of the subject rather that 'a little bit of everything.' This study could, then, help identify those artefacts functioning as boundary objects used in multimodal art expressions according to the intentions of the Norwegian national curriculum.

This chapter will first present the chosen methods and useful theories to analyse the case. The findings will be presented as multiple data sources in a narrative and simultaneously analysed. They will then be discussed in order to point out the possible implications for the study of arts education, aimed at the area of early childhood.

Methodology and theoretical framework

Methodology

The case study approach was used as a methodology in the realisation of an arts project among students in early childhood education, specialising in the arts. The case study approach is one of the most used research approaches in qualitative research (Creswell, 1998; Postholm, 2010; Stake, 1995; Yin, 1988) and is often chosen because it is a study of an event with a beginning and an end, an example of something, or an issue (Gudmundsdottir, 1998, 2003). Wilson and Gudmundsdottir (1987, p. 42) stated that a case study should be used when one is studying processes that are limited or bounded in time and place, as education often is. This understanding of a case study is also supported by Merriam (1998), Ragin (1992), and Hannula, Suoranta, and Vadén (2005), the latter of whom used the case study when researching artistic events, as is the case here.

Data collection

The case study featured students specialising in different art disciplines, working together on an arts installation for toddlers. Toddlers from nearby ECEC institutions were invited to experience the students' artworks during a one-day toddler festival. Data was collected using multiple methods and data sources, such as observations and a focus group interview with students. Because of a lack of time, with the students being busy during their last year, focus group interviews was used as a research strategy (cf. Creswell, 2016). The inquiry should not be time-consuming for them. The interview protocol was given to them in advance, with five questions encompassing the research focus; the interview lasted 47 minutes and was transcribed into 19 pages.

Focus group interview – the participants

The group interviewed was selected from the initial 19 third year early childhood education students specialising in the arts by first mapping their arts preferences and competences, and then asking a person who knew the class well (the teacher responsible for the class the year before in their second year). She helped me identity three students who would be good participants, representing each of their art disciplines. The interview was conducted a few weeks after their toddler festival arts project, which the students chose to name 'Playing with Light.'

Elisabeth (all participants are anonymised) had a specialisation in art from senior high school, where she also took photography courses, and was then asked to exhibit at the prestigious Nordic light festival of photography (Nordiclightfestival, 2019). The second suggested student was Mary, with a background in music. She took singing lessons during her childhood, sang in a gospel choir in high school, and was part of a band. The third, Suzan, with her arts specialisation in drama before starting her kindergarten teachers' training, has a mother who is a theatre liaison. During her childhood, she accompanied her mother to the theatre, and while she conducted guided tours on the theatre premises, Suzan played in the corridors and fell in love with drama. She specialised in it during senior high school and took a year afterwards to attend a course in actor techniques.

Apart from their separate arts competences presented, they have almost three years of specialisation in arts education at a bachelor level, aimed at the arena of pre-schools/kindergartens. These three students were asked and agreed to be part of a focus group interview with questions like: What would you say characterises your specific art discipline? What would you say are your specific tools and agencies within the boundaries of your art discipline? Can you give some examples from your art discipline work that you experienced as well pedagogically well-functioning? How did you experience the toddler festival as a joint arts project? How did the children experience the project, and can you describe and give examples?

Other data sources

As part of the data material, I included their bachelor curricula in the arts subjects as a background and reference to justify the focus of the event and of this research. I also conducted participant observations with photoshoots focusing on the students' makings. Notes made after the toddler festival about the implementation of the arts subjects and the students' own evaluations in class after the toddler festival event were also included in the data.

Analyses and ensuring quality

The notes, photos, and transcription were analysed using coding (Creswell, 2016), looking for themes covering my understanding of possible boundary objects used in these multimodal installations for toddlers, including the students' views on what artefacts they used within the boundaries of their respective art field. The identified themes became the foundation for the narrative presented below as *Findings and Analysis*. Ethical considerations were taken, the research project has been approved by the NSD (in English: Norwegian Centre for Research Data). Securing the quality of the research was done through member checking and triangulation (Postholm, 2010), and reciprocity towards the students participating in the focus group interview was implemented; they were given the transcripts on paper to check over, but also to give back something for their time and interest in my study (Creswell, 2016). Their own reflections could later be of use to them in their own studies.

Theory

Applying Cultural Historical Activity theory (CHAT) (Engeström & Miettinen, 1999) and Vygotsky's (1978, 1995) thoughts and ideas on the field of the arts (Frisch, 2006, 2010) can help anchor the disciplines in their historical functions in Western society in order to see how the arts differ in tools of mediation, experience, and active creation, which can limit or expand understanding of the arts as one unit. Therefore, the study's theoretical lenses, how the theory is used, and the understanding of the main concepts of the study (boundary objects and artefacts) must be grounded and clarified in a common sociocultural academic tradition.

CHAT is derived from Lev Vygotsky's (1896–1934) theoretical legacy. He is regarded today as one of the most important contributors to post-modern constructivism, a part of the constructivist paradigm in pedagogy, or the 'third way.' This third way is the explanatory space for human development and learning between positivism and cognitivism, referred to by Kozulin as 'constructive principles of higher functions,' or developing and using signs and tools, the core understanding of 'higher functions' (Kozulin, 1997, pp. xxii–xxvii). Vygotsky's interdisciplinary theoretical contributions within the paradigm of constructivism can be detected not only in pedagogy but also in philosophy, sociology, psychology, semiotics, anthropology, and arts interpretation (Holland, Lachicotte, Skinner, & Cain, 1998; Strandberg, 2006).

Activity theory developed from Vygotsky's research and thoughts, is today understood as sociocultural theory, from the more action-oriented CHAT to more language-focused theoretical traditions (Cole, 1996; Kozulin, 1997, pp. xliii–lvi). The essence of sociocultural theory is that individuals and their historical and social contexts are inseparable. One cannot be understood without the other. Humans are shaped by their social and cultural past and present, at the same time creating and changing their social and cultural world (Vygotsky, 1995). The development of knowledge is a social, cultural, and historical phenomenon, and a main feature of the development of mankind is the use of tools and signs (Vygotsky, 1978, 1995), or what is called mediated activity.

The Vygotskyan concepts presented by Cole (1996) explain the term *culture* as the synthesis of all tools and signs that are labelled as artefacts (Cole, 1996) available to a group of people. The term *signs* includes verbal language, body language, sounds, and visual language, while the term *artefact* covers the aspect of human existence activated when man is interacting with his physical and social environment. In arts education it involves all human creations used to mediate artistically; from tools such as for example music instruments, costumes and masks, looms, hammers, IT soft and hardware, needles and thread - to the ideas, rules, principles and articulated physical, emotional and mental skills and knowledge thought out in the arts. All human activities that use artefacts are mediated or indirect (Vygotsky, 1978, p. 54), later called mediated actions by Wertsch (1998).

'To mediate' is defined in the dictionary as 'to act as a go-between' (Hornby, Gatenby, & Wakefield, 1963, p. 611), or, to put it in sociocultural terminology, to work or communicate through artefacts. We can also understand artefacts as 'go-betweens' for humans to be understood and experienced by 'the other/ others' (Hopperstad, 2002; Matthews, 2004). Hence, mediation in this inquiry is understood as the communication of meaning from one person to 'the other' that makes persons master an understandable common cultural visual, auditory, physical, or verbal language. The person making the signs should ensure that their purpose or drive to self-express and communicate is understood by others in context. This does not, however, imply that there is no individual-psychological dimension in the making of signs in the arts – quite the opposite.

The word *artefact* is a general concept for signs (signalisation) and tools. Our interaction with the world is mediated through artefacts. Vygotsky (1978) elaborated on 1) the common features of signs and tools, 2) their differences, and 3) how they are linked together. As mentioned above, signs and tools have a mediating function in common and are both aspects of the world that people use when interacting with their physical and social environment. The most essential difference between a sign and tool, and the basis for the real divergence between them, is the different way that they orient human behaviour. The tool's function is to serve as the conductor of human influence on the object of activity, it is externally oriented, and it must lead to changes in the object. It is a means by which human external activity is aimed at mastering life. The sign, on the other hand, changes nothing of the object's psychological operation. It is a means of internal activity aimed at mastering oneself; the sign is internally oriented (Vygotsky, 1978, p. 55). For example, tools, such as the use of pencil and paper are externally oriented to draw a flower for the external world to see. The sign, for example a drawing of a flower, is internally oriented, to make us think and emotionally connect internally to other pleasant experiences with flowers. The distinction between signs and tools is still the subject of theoretical discussions. Skodvin (2004) referred to Vygotsky's emphasis on this distinction (blurred by Cole's (1996) use of artefacts) as an expression of the times this theory was written in (the 1920s–1930s in the earlier Russia – the Soviet Union). The third condition Vygotsky examined is how signs and tools are linked together. Signs and tools together help humans master and alter nature while, at the same time, through signs and tools, the altered nature alters humans (Vygotsky, 1978, 1995).

Boundary objects as artefacts

The awareness of the arts as fields of mediating with cultural tools and signs in a sociocultural understanding of human activity is important to emphasise in this context. It is useful to see the arts through these sociocultural lenses in order to analyse signs and tools, that is, artefacts, (Cole, 1996) and, through this, what overarching competences are at play when the three fields of the arts manifest as one unit. The concept of boundary objects can be understood in this context as common signs and/or tools – a connection between the arts disciplines as separate entities, which is Cole's (1996) understanding of the overarching concept *artefacts*.

The use of the concepts of signs and tools in arts- education-related research:
Each arts discipline has its signs and tools, and often the tools make the signs: Drama with signs such as speech, movement, and tools such as space/scenes, visuals such as masks and costumes, among others. Music with signs such as sounds, notes, harmonies, rhythm, words, and tools such as instruments. Fine art with signs such as principles for form, function, composition, and tools such as pencils, paintbrushes, trace-making devices, three-dimensional matter (such as clay, wood, and stone) – the list is long, and by no means is this a full list presented here.

Wilson and Wilson (1977) were the first researchers in the post-war era to implement sociocultural theory in children's artistic signs: children's drawings. Through their ground-breaking research, they showed how socially constructed signs in popular child culture was a significant visual reference in children's drawing and learning. Thompson (2002) and Frisch (2006) followed up this research in kindergartens/preschools in qualitative studies of children's drawing processes and found the same phenomenon there also. The Norwegian researchers Hohr (2015) and Letnes (2016) and the Sweden- and England-based researchers Selander and Kress (2012) saw the arts through the concepts of signs and tools in multimodal contexts. But a study helped and guided by the inspiration of the analytical thinking tool of *boundary objects* in the field of arts education in ECEC teachers training is a new perspective.

Interdisciplinary multimodality and boundary objects – an inspiration

The word *modality* derives from the word *mode*, which in French means fashion, or a certain way of expression. We can consider art forms as different modes of expression. A multimodal expression would merge these modes into one simultaneously expressed assemblage of modes. With its concepts and understandings rooted in sociocultural theory, multimodality can also be understood as boundary objects working in a zone where multi-mediation takes place. Disciplines in the arts can establish the grounds for interdisciplinary expressions. Signs and tools from the arts as separate disciplines are used in a unity of expression often used by children in kindergarten. For example, the child's drawing and drawing process often becomes a drama told, sung, and acted out while the drawing takes place.

Inspired by the analytical framework and ontological foundation grounded in CHAT (Engeström & Miettinen, 1999), the term *boundary objects* can be considered useful (Akkerman & Bakker, 2011). It is defined by Akkerman and Bakker (2011) as the cross between activity systems with the use of boundary objects/artefacts. Often used as an example, is a student report from the activity system of the student´s own teaching practice/training (a school or a kindergarten) to the activity system of the student`s university college and his or hers pedagogical teaching. These two systems are linked together with a student report, the boundary object, which is of pedagogical use, is read and evaluated by both the professors at the college/university and the practice teachers on the school or kindergarten arena responsible for the student. The report becomes an artefact that is 'crossing borders' or boundaries between the two activity systems. Can similar artefacts of border crossings (boundary objects) be found if we, inspired by CHAT, regard the arts as separate disciplines of signs, tools, skills, and functions in early childhood arts education, the boarders between then being crossed by boundary objects with multimodal functions as overarching 'go-betweens,' or as common artefacts?

The case of making cultural expressions or installations for toddlers by third-year bachelor students, arranged as a toddler festival at a university college in Norway, is an opportunity to explore art made for small children and the possible boundary object-inspired themes inherent in the activity, and is presented below.

Findings and analysis

The findings are composed of my descriptions, constructed as narratives, that were analysed to answer the research question: *How can the concept of boundary objects be used as a thinking tool to identify common grounds for music, drama, and arts and crafts in arts education in ECEC teachers' training?*

A case of arranging a toddler arts festival in a black box on campus

It was a Monday morning in October of the fall semester of 2018, and the start of the students' preparations for the annual self-managed arts pedagogical event. The university college of early childhood education, arranged its yearly toddler festival involving all third-year students (about 300) inviting the town's kindergarten toddlers to campus. A maximum of 600 toddlers are allowed into campus to enjoy and be challenged by the different arrangements made for them by the students. This event has been going on for the last 18 years or so and has become a tradition. It is, in other words, a popular happening among kindergarten staff, the target group being toddlers, who are not often considered as the audiences or agents of artistic cultural events.

This event is managed by the students and is the starting point for the class of 19 students in their last or third year of their early childhood teacher's training at the bachelor level, with a special emphasis in arts education as part of their chosen early childhood education profile. They met me, an arts and crafts teacher, as well as their teachers in music and drama, in a classroom to be inspired and briefed on the possibilities this event can encompass. Some were interested and skilled in music, others in drama, and again others in fine art. Together they formed a foundation of competence to work on a one art-form basis and on a multimodal artistic basis. They had three days to arrange and create a space in a black box on campus that could engage the toddlers, using their skills as arts education students. They were grouped into five then found their spaces in the black box and started to make their installations in each of their corners with one main theme, 'Playing with Light.'

The teachers presented the students with earlier works or solutions from previous classes as inspiration. The students also visited kindergartens in the local town/community that are known for their avant-garde, artistic, and innovative solutions when making aesthetic and pedagogical spaces for children. This was their starting point for completing the arts installations. The festival lasted for a day, from about 10 a.m. to 12:30 p.m. I visited the black box in intervals and took notes on how I perceived the children playing on the day of the festival.

The 'history' of the participants

Three students who had 'a history' when it comes to the three art forms were the focus (see methodology section above). When characterising what they regarded as the essential tools, or artefacts, within their art subject community as early childhood teachers in training, their answers can be summed up within their art discipline, as follows:

To see with your eyes and to use your hands to explore materials: Elisabeth, with arts and crafts as her field of competence, responded to the question of what she regarded as the essence of visual art. 'It is important to me,' she said, 1) 'to use my sight, my ability to see, to use my eyes as tools,' 2) 'the essential artefact being to make things with my hands, to use my hands' (the techniques), and further throughout the focus group interview she emphasises the importance of knowing the art field's artefacts, for example, the laws of visual aesthetics, such as colour theory, and to know how, for example, a camera works. She also highlighted the experience and laws of working and making with materials (such as clay) as an essence within boundaries of arts and crafts.

To use your voice; to dare to sing; to dare to express feelings: Mary, with music as her field of competence, also answered that to be in touch with her feelings was important to her. Music expresses feelings; therefore, music interested her. She also discussed the challenge of making music, like daring to sing with your own voice as a tool to make signs, such as meaningful sounds, and singing words as artefacts within the boundaries of music.

To play; to use body and room: Suzan, with drama as her field of competence, highlighted the aspects of play and make believe, to mediate with your voice; and to tell stories with figures. 'Drama in our bachelor studies is playing for grown-ups,' she said. Art and music are more technical; drama is freer and more playful. 'You do not have to know how to do a guitar grip or how to use the brush while painting,' she said. 'In drama, your voice and your body are essential tools. You can easily make figures and give them life or use one of the children's

50 N. S. Frisch

shoes and make it a character in a story.' To mediate is what she said she regards as the essence within the boundaries of drama.

These self-defined essential artefacts were seen by the students as part of their 'toolkit' in their respective art field while they have been part of arts classes in ECEC teachers training.

Playing with light: the installations

Chosen as a strategy to help shed light on the research question, a selection of observations made of three installations and the focus group interview, involving the arts disciplines in multimodal installations, are presented in order to look for boundary objects when arranging a toddler arts festival in a black box on campus. Below, the installations are presented in Figure 4.1 as spaces constructed in corners of the black box.

Figure 4.1 Photos of installations from the toddler festival 'Playing with Light'. Figure 4.1a the blue space above, Figure 4.1b the iPad space (responding to movement [a touch] with shapes, colour, and sound), and Figure 4.1c the stocking space
Source: Photos by Nina Scott Frisch

Inspired by the concept of boundary objects 51

Figure 4.1b (Cont.) The iPad space

The blue space

Elisabeth was an observer when her classmates constructed and tested the installation called the blue space. The light was made bluish green, like an aquarium or the sky. Textiles in various shades of blue were hung from the ceiling, and the floor was covered with light fluffy textiles for children to float and crawl in. The cool bluish colouring was used as an artefact (colour theory) and the space was used as artefact with knowledge of the materials and textiles to function as a playground for toddlers (see Figure 4.1a). After the festival, the group who made this installation felt that they should have been more prepared to meet the children with activities, maybe some water in bowls to play with to keep them there for a while. They also suggested that they themselves could have played roles or characters in simple costumes fitting with the theme of being under water or in the sky.

The iPad space

The students installed the app BLOOM from Apple on an iPad and projected it onto a large screen (approximately 1.5 x 2 meters) at the far end of the black box (Apple,

Figure 4.1c (Cont.) The stocking space

2019). In the dark room, the iPad reflection had quite an impact (see Figure 4.1b). The students pointed out how multimodal this installation was; the children pointed and pressed their fingers on the iPad and by that made different geometrical shapes in various colours connected to sounds projected on a large screen. There was a large space between the iPad/projector and the screen. The most fun for the toddlers was playing in this in-between space, spontaneously seeing their own shadows on the screen, making figures, and adjusting the size of the shadows of their bodies in their own compositions of sounds, shapes, and colour.

The stocking space

Elisabeth and Suzan were part of a group making the stocking space installation. They used old stockings and pantyhose to hang different shapes of lightweight flashlights from the ceiling (see Figure 4.1c), which swung when touched. They used long strips of translucent cloth and old ready-to-throw-away umbrellas and hung these upside down from the ceiling so that the toddlers could walk through, being tickled and surprised by what could be on the other side. They dressed themselves with tights on their heads, the legs functioning as ears, and with lights tucked inside the legs. As part of this installation, they acted as characters, looking almost like rabbits. The colours were in blues and greens, the lights made a significant impact in one corner of the dark black box, and the students used the visual aesthetic principles of contrasts, such as light and dark. Elisabeth and Suzan related that a few times this was a little too much for the toddlers without an activity to explore in the installation that could involve them, like some clay, construction, or sound-making, or one of the students singing or playing an instrument. Without these activities, the installation was a little scary for some children; instead, the students thought they needed something from the field of music or arts and crafts to get the children involved. At the same time, they interacted with the toddlers using their body language, voices, and sensitivity. They had also rehearsed different possible playful interaction scenarios beforehand.

Evaluating the event

The event 'Playing with Light' was evaluated when the students summed up their experiences after 'packing up' the toddler festival; evaluation was also an important theme during the focus group interview. First, the students were very clear on the positive learning aspect of the event, seeing how the toddlers in Norwegian ECEC institutions could respond to the arts in multimodal settings. What they as adults could actively make and do to engage the youngest in artistic experiences was an important part of the event for them as preschool teachers in training. What they had planned and pulled off made a difference for the children. Everything from the artistic installations in the black box made by them, to the canteen, restrooms, and the larger public areas inside and outside the campus (including a beautiful park), made accessible by other third-year early childhood education students, was integrated to meet the toddlers' needs and interests as an age group. They also emphasised the importance of being well prepared, for example, having 'waiting activities' if there was a line of children waiting to experience an installation. Making a system for taking turns as students in the installations and greeting the children with roleplaying, music, and movement was important for them but also for the children's experiences. Since there were many children (at most, there were about 30 children at one time, with maybe 10–15 accompanying adults) and 19 students involved, the installations required a structure for organising the children's sensing of the installations (not too many children and adults at the time), as well as waiting activities. This made the experience a good one for most of the children, accompanying adults, and the students. They divided themselves into three 'shifts' when interacting with the children.

The case study, then, has helped the three students chosen for the focus group interview come to an awareness of their respective arts artefacts and how they were used in the toddler festival installations as multimodal expressions, as well as what they would do differently next time.

Boundary objects as inspiration

The concept of boundary objects as inspiration to find common grounds for arts education in ECEC has helped me as a researcher and teacher to identify themes in the data that play a crucial role in the makings of multimodal art installations for toddlers. The idea of arts subjects (music, drama, and arts and crafts) in society as *within* their respective boundaries and separate analytical entities is often how these subjects are organised in education in general. How to reach out to, or go between, other art forms and connect *through* boundary object-inspired themes is presented. The results of the case study, 'Playing with Light,' can be understood in the three categories presented below. Inspired by the concept of boundary objects or artefacts, they can be adapted as common grounds in the respective arts subjects and when planning, be specified according to the pedagogical learning goals for the students making, in this case, to make arts installations for toddlers, learning about toddlers as arts recipients.

Techniques and technical tools

The use of the voice and vocal techniques is crucial in music, roleplaying, and storytelling in drama. To dare use your voice and your body is also a matter of owning musical techniques. Techniques as cultural artefacts in arts and crafts are also crucial for producing with materials, such as scissors and textiles, like with the installations. The technical tools (for example arts relevant IT-products) used here merge the subjects using all three art disciplines: music, drama, and arts and crafts. A focus on techniques and technical tools can be seen as subject matter that functions as boundary objects, with purposeful interdisciplinary use in making expressions in music, drama, and arts and crafts in ECEC teachers' training. In the installations as expressions, it merges the disciplines together and, at the same time, is useful in the subjects as separate themes of teaching.

The room as stage for arts pedagogy

The staging of arts experiences and activities can be seen as a boundary object linking the arts together. Scene-making in drama and making rooms and playgrounds as visual and musical aesthetic experiences for children links the theme of 'the room' as an overarching subject matter inspired by the concept of boundary objects.

Aesthetic principles

Fundamental theories of aesthetic expression found in music theory, visual theory, and drama theory can be seen as themes inspired by the concept of boundary objects, as manifested in the scene for expression and interaction in the black box. For example, the principles of contrasts (quantitative and qualitative), colour and texture, rhythm and repetition, high and low, dark and light, stillness, movement and loudness.

Discussion and conclusion

As seen above, an elaboration of the disciplines of music, drama, and arts and crafts within the understanding of CHAT can stage their common ground and make visible what teachers in higher education, such as teachers teaching on a bachelor level in the arts in early childhood education, can emphasise in their everyday teaching in order to get the most out of multimodal teaching experiences. Choices must be made within limited time frames of teaching, but with boundary objects as a thinking tool, teachers can find specific common foci within the respective art disciplines and coordinate these to function as boundary objects when needed, such as in multimodal installations for toddlers. Boundaries are necessarily present when the subjects are separate entities of expression in society, but interdisciplinary work is required by the national curriculum in Norway, as stated in the introduction. Looking for common themes inspired by the concept of boundary objects (Akkerman & Bakker, 2011) is, therefore, a matter of implementing the national curriculum.

To conclude, the study presented based on student interviews and teacher's observations can give teachers and curriculum developers, especially those in interdisciplinary arts studies in early childhood education who often face tight timeframes, a tool to help analyse what skills and knowledge are required when making artistic installations for the children. Within each art subject in the curriculum, the teaching could focus on the themes inspired by the concept of boundary objects, thereby meeting the requirements of the national curriculum and the toddlers' own artistic mediations, which are often multimodal. To prioritise and operationalise the themes inspired by the concept of boundary objects – 1) techniques and technical tools, 2) the room as stage for arts pedagogy, and 3) aesthetic principles – teachers of music, drama, and arts and crafts could make specific choices within these themes in the college universities teachers training in ECEC arts education. They will then be using teaching time and organise their arts subjects' lessons within the boundaries of their respective art subjects to build a competence useful in artistic expressions made for children when the arts merge in multimodal interdisciplinary expressions. Installations for toddlers in a black box, just like the one presented in this case, is the event that made it possible to explore the arts as separate entities and the arts with their common artefacts of interest inspired by the concept of boundary objects in ECEC arts education.

References

Akkerman, S. F., & Bakker, A. (2011). Boundary crossing and boundary objects. *Review of Education Research*, *81*(2), 132–169. doi:10.3102/0034654311404435

Apple (2019). Retrieved from https://itunes.apple.com/no/app/bloom/id292792586?mt=8

Cole, M. (1996). *Cultural Psychology: A Once and a Future Discipline*. Cambridge, MA: Harvard University Press.

Creswell, J. (1998). *Qualitative Inquiry and Research Design. Choosing among Five Traditions*. Thousand Oaks, CA: SAGE.

Creswell, J. W. (2016). *30 Essential Skills for the Qualitative Researcher*. Thousand Oaks, CA: SAGE.

Engeström, Y., & Miettinen, R. (1999). Introduction. In Y. Engeström, R. Miettinen, & R. Punamaki (Eds.), *Perspectives on Activity Theory* (pp. 1–16). Cambridge: Cambridge University Press.

Frisch, N. S. (2006). Drawing in preschools. A didactic experience. *The International Journal of Art and Design Education*, 25(1), 74–85. doi:10.1111/j.1476-8070.2006.00470.x

Frisch, N. S. (2010). *To See the Visually Controlled* (Doctoral thesis). NTNU, Trondheim, Norway.

Gudmundsdottir, S. (1998). Kasusstudier i lærerutdanning [Case studies in teachers' training]. *Norsk Pedagogisk Tidsskrift*, 3, 150–157.

Gudmundsdottir, S. (2003). Kasusstudier av undervisning og læring i klasserommet. Et sosiokulturelt perspektiv [Case studies in teaching and learning in class. A sociocultural perspective]. In T. Pettersson & M. B. Postholm (Eds.), *Klasseledelse* [Leading the class] (pp. 21–31). Oslo: Universitetsforlaget.

Hohr, J. (2015). Kunst og estetisk oppdragelse [Art and aesthetic education]. *Nordisk tidsskrift for pedagogikk og kritikk*, 1, 1–11. doi:10.17585/ntpk.v1.113

Holland, D., Lachicotte, Jr., W., Skinner, D., & Cain, C. (1998). *Identity and Agency in Cultural Worlds*. Cambridge, MA: Harvard University Press.

Hannula, M., Suoranta, J., & Vadén, T. (2005). *Artistic Research – Theories, Methods and Practices*. Academy of Fine Arts, Finland and University of Gothenburg, Gothenburg, Sweden: Art Monitor.

Hopperstad, M. H. (2002). *Når barn skaper mening med tegning. En studie av seksåringers tegninger i et semiotisk perspektiv* [When children create meaning with drawing. A study of six-year-olds' drawing processes seen in a semiotic perspective] Dr. polit avhandling [Ph.D. thesis]. Trondheim: Norwegian University of Science and Technology.

Hornby, A. S., Gatenby, E. V., & Wakefield, H. (1963). *The Advanced Learner's Dictionary of Current English*. London: Oxford University Press.

Kozulin, A. (1997). Vygotsky in context. In L. S. Vygotsky, *Thought and Language* (pp. xi–lvi). Cambridge, MA: MIT Press.

Letnes, M. A. (2016). *Barns møter med digital teknologi, Digital teknologi som pedagogisk ressurs i barnehagebarns lek, opplevelse og læring* [Children's interaction with digital technology. Digital technology as pedagogical resource in kindergarten children's play, experience and learning]. Oslo: Universitetsforlaget.

Matthews, J. (2004). The art of infancy. In E. W. Eisner & M. D. Day (Eds.), *Handbook of Research and Policy in Art Education* (pp. 253–298). London: Lawrence Erlbaum Associates.

Merriam, S. B. (1998). *Qualitative Research and Case Study Applications in Education*. San Francisco, CA: Jossey-Bass Publishers.

Moe, J. (2018). Barns møte med kunst og kultur [Children's encounters with art and culture]. In N. S. Frisch, M.-A. Letnes, & J. Moe (Eds.), *Boka om kunst og håndverk i barnehagen* [The book of art and crafts in kindergarten] (pp. 77–126). Oslo: Universitetsforlaget.

Nordiclightfestival (2019). *Nordic Light Festival of Photography*. Retrieved from www.nordiclightfestival.no/

Norwegian Directorate for Education and Training (2017). *Framework Plan for Kindergartens – Content and Tasks*. Oslo: Ministry of Education and Research. Retrieved from www.udir.no/globalassets/filer/barnehage/rammeplan/framework-plan-for-kindergartens2-2017.pdf

Postholm, M. B. (2010). *Kvalitativ metode. En innføring med fokus på fenomenologi,etnografi og kasusstudier* [Qualitative methods. An introduction with focus on phenomenology, ethnography and case studies]. Oslo: Universitetsforlaget.

Ragin, C. C. (1992). Introduction. In C. C. Ragin & H. Becker (Eds.), *What is a case? Exploring the Foundation of Social Inquiry* (pp. 1–17). Cambridge, UK: Cambridge University Press.

Selander, S., & Kress, G. (2012). *Læringsdesign: i et multimodalt perspektiv* [Designs for learning: in a multimodal perspective]. Fredriksberg: Frydenlynd.

Skodvin, A. (2004). Innledning [Introduction]. In L. S. Vygotskij, *Tenkning og tale* [The Norwegian version of Vygotsky's Thought and language] (pp. 7–21). Oslo: Gyldendal Akademisk.

Stake, R. (1995). *The Art of Case Study Research*. Thousand Oaks: SAGE.

Strandberg, L. (2006). *Vygotskij i praktiken* [Vygotsky in practice]. Stockholm: Norstedts Akademiske Förlag.

Thompson, C. M. (2002). Drawing together: Peer influence in preschool-kindergarten art classes. In L. Bresler & C. M. Thompson (Eds.), *The Arts in Children's Lives, Context, Culture and Curriculum* (pp. 129–138). Norwell, MA: Kluwer Academic Publishers.

Vygotsky, L. S. (1978). *Mind in Society. The Development of Higher Psychological Processes*. Cambridge, MA: Harvard University Press.

Vygotsky, L. S. (1995). *Fantasi og kreativitet i barndomen* [Imagination and creativity during childhood]. Gøteborg: Daidalos.

Vygotsky, L. S. (2005). *Concrete Human Psychology – An Unpublished Manuscript by Vygotsky 1926*. Retrieved from http://communication.ucsd.edu/MCA/Paper/Sovjet%20Psych/Sovjet%20Psych.pdf

Wertsch, J. (1998). *Mind as Action*. New York: Oxford University Press.

Wilson, S. M., & Gudmundsdottir, S. (1987). What is this a case of? *Education and Urban Society*, 20(1), 42–54.

Wilson, B., & Wilson, M. (1977). An iconoclastic view of the imagery sources in the drawing of young children. *Art Education*, 1, 5–11.

Yin, R. K. (1988). *Case Study Research. Design and Methods*. Thousand Oaks, CA: SAGE.

5 Cultural-historical activity theory as the basis for mentoring student teachers in triads

Janne Madsen

Introduction

Practice has been referred to repeatedly as an important element of teacher education (e.g. Korthagen, Loughran, & Russell, 2006; Skagen, 2009). Furthermore, students acknowledge that practice is an advantageous arena for learning. Student teachers in Norway scored 4.1 on a scale from 1–5 on the question 'How satisfied are you with the professional challenges in the period of practice?' and 4.0 on the question 'How satisfied are you generally with the practice education?' (Bakken, Pedersen, & Øygarden, 2018, pp. 30–31). This suggests that these student teachers agreed with the notion that practice is an arena for learning. However, it seems that establishing a connection between learning theory and learning through practice remains a challenge. According to Solstad (2010), students experience the campus and practice parts of their education as 'two different worlds'. Researchers have also found the connection between theory and practice to be important, but challenging (see e.g. Finne et al., 2011). Steering documents for teacher education stress this connection between theory and practice (Gloppen, 2013; NOKUT, 2006). Therefore, in addition to the governmental framework, all three parts of the triad – student teachers, teacher educators in the field of practice (hereafter called practice mentors) and teacher educators who teach theory (hereafter called subject teachers) – support that practice is a useful arena for learning. This inspired me to explore mentoring communication, collaboration and mutual learning in triads of student teachers, practice mentors and subject teachers with the aim of proposing interventions. In this research, I, the researcher also have the role of subject teacher.

Meetings involving student teachers, practice mentors and subject teachers have a long tradition, but as Korthagen et al. (2006) writes, 'The routine was familiar, the rationale had long been forgotten, and cooperation was anything but close' (p. 1035). In this study, I caught the situation at the very beginning of a five-year-long run of teacher education and operated on the assumption that not only student teachers and practice mentors, but also subject teachers as educators need to improve their professional actions. When these three groups meet as a triad, the boundaries between their fields are crossed with learning and collaboration as a possible result (Engeström, 2001; Yamazumi, 2006). With the three parts of this triad sharing the context of student teachers' practice, I explored the possibilities of collaboration within the triad.

This shaped the following research question: *What does an analysis using cultural-historical activity theory (CHAT) uncover about the communication, collaboration and mutual learning in triads in teacher education?* Traditional teacher education is primarily directed at the teacher students' learning. In this research, I was seeking possibilities for increasing the learning for all parts of the triad. The findings of this research will inform interventions, and the next phase of this research project will focus on the design of a research-based intervention.

The combination of schools, classrooms and mentoring relations is a complex context to research (Roald, 2010). In the next section, I shall describe this context. Then a literature review will follow before I present the theoretical fundament of CHAT and boundary crossing. Subsequently, I will describe the research method before presenting the analysis including three examples of the students' practice in schools, which show very different approaches to the triad meetings across boundaries. Finally, I will discuss these three approaches and propose a framework for a research-based intervention.

Context

This research investigated the first period of practice in a five-year-long master's programme in teacher education at a university in Norway. For many of the practice mentors and all of the students, this was a new, unknown setting in which they were searching for their role and function. Most of the practice mentors in this research have some education in mentoring and all are experienced in guiding pupils in classrooms; thus, they were at least somewhat prepared to mentor the teacher students. The students were divided into small groups of two to four participants and were practising in 12 different schools. For the triad meeting, the subject teacher visited the schools where the students had been in their first practice situation for about a week.

The administration of the teacher education passed quite a lot of written information to the practice mentors. Only one page was related to the content of the triad meeting and another page presented part of the curriculum with descriptions of the expected learning outcomes for the period of practice. There was no information about the subjects that the students had been taught previously. While the expected learning outcomes for the period of practice were listed, there was only a link to information on a webpage about the expected learning outcomes for the following years and the expected outcomes, more generally, of the education of professional teachers.

The schools, represented by headmasters and practice mentors who are familiar with the local setting, were responsible for pre-organising the triad meetings, and the meetings, as could be expected, were very different. In many of the 12 schools, separate meetings were carried out with students and practice mentors. The students were concerned about practical elements of their education and their assignments. They referred to numerous events, which they seemed to have difficulty describing and understanding. Many of these meetings quickly began to resemble lectures with the subject teacher answering the students' many questions. Some practice mentors also asked practical questions. The meetings with practice mentors in some schools also developed into transfers of information; the subject teacher sometimes even 'lectured' the practice mentor. This appeared as though it might reflect the status of the participants.

The participants were all informed about the expected framework of the period of practice through handouts from the university administration. The subject teacher did not receive any information about the schools, the practice mentors or the classes beforehand, but she had met all of the students and some of the practice mentors in other educational settings. The involved parties knew each other at very different levels. In a traditional setting, such a framework would support ordinary, linear communication: subject teacher ↔ students ↔ practice mentor. The participants knew neither about each other's motives nor about their goals.

In some schools, a meeting with all parts of the triad took place, but, as shown below, it was difficult overall to establish a triad as an arena for mutual learning. This first part of the interventional research project, therefore, was aimed at exploring and analysing to define relevant interventions for the next period of practice coming up about four months later.

Literature review

The aims of teacher education are to shape professional, competent teachers who can work in an extremely complex context, organise for a coherent school and educate pupils to a professional level prescribed in the national curriculum. Then, it seems obvious that this education also ought to coherently congregate the corresponding main elements to prepare the students as future teachers. Nevertheless, teacher education is criticised for being fragmented and lacking coherence, with only tenuous connections between the different subjects and between the subjects and the practice (Korthagen et al., 2006; NOKUT, 2006). Indeed, the teaching profession comprises vast and diverse subjects and fundaments of knowledge (Munthe & Haug, 2010). This might be a reason for teacher educators not to be able to handle the challenge, which has been present for almost a century, as Dewey (1916) described the problem in the early 1900s.

Korthagen et al. (2006) characterise teacher education as fragmented because the theory and methods are disconnected from the practice. They also question the relevance of its organisation: 'Teaching practice is usually seen as the opportunity to apply previously learned theories and lecturing appears to be viewed as an appropriate form of teaching about teaching' (p. 1021). Further, they highlight the increasing pressure on teacher education: 'this theory-into-practice view of teacher education is increasingly being challenged for its many limitations and inadequacies' (p. 1021). The situation ought to be changed for the better.

There could be a coherent connection between the theoretical and practical aspects of teacher education, but although the actors seem to agree about the importance of this connection, this is not what teacher educators and students experience (Briseid & Werner, 2013). According to Grimen (2008), teacher education has many different goals, and these goals represent clashes of interests. The relationship between theory and practice is an example of such a clash. On one hand, theoretical knowledge should be useful. On the other hand, some theoretical knowledge does not apply in practical settings. However, according to Grimen, practical approaches create coherence and are of fundamental significance to the teaching profession. Drawing clear distinctions between the concepts in education for professionals serves no purpose; instead, one should see the concepts as connected.

Munthe and Haug (2010) study integration in teacher education. According to them, answering the following questions can determine whether there is a connection between theory and practice: To what extent do teacher educators face the field of practice in their approach to teacher education? Are the teacher educators concerned about what happens on the practical side of teacher education? Lastly, does the teaching in teacher education integrate factual knowledge into theory and practice? (p. 190). They find that teacher educators are more concerned about practice now than ever before (p. 198). However, it seems that the student teachers' point of view differs from that of the teacher educators as the former, as compared to the latter, have reported experiencing far less of a connection between theory and practice (p. 200).

Learning about and practising teaching strategies could allow for creating coherence between theory and practice in teacher education. In a triadic setting where the practice mentors are the experts on teaching in practice, one would expect them to present good examples of teaching for the students to observe and learn. Yet it seems as if practice mentors in the Western world do not always model teaching as expected. In Edwards' (1997) study, the student teachers did not often observe their practice mentors. Norwegian teacher education has been through several reforms in recent years. In the new curriculum (Ministry of Education, 2016), the first period of practice is labelled as 'observation practice', where the students are acquainted with some theory of observation. These observations are combined with dialogue and reflection. The trend described by Edwards (1997) seems to be changing, and observation of practice mentors modelling seems to be more common.

According to Briseid and Werner (2013) and Solstad (2010), the combination of observation and reflection changes the period of practice from an arena of undertaking teaching to one of developing a professional role as a teacher. To establish this arena, the theoretical part of the education must be relevant for performing teaching (Briseid & Werner, 2013; Ministry of Education, 2016).

Kvernbekk (2011) finds that theory in practice is not based on research. She refers to 'weak theories', which are mainly unarticulated and unsystematically based on experience, in contrast to 'strong theories', which are systematic and general, not rooted in practice. This might also explain why Solstad (2010) finds that practice mentors only to a limited degree use theoretical knowledge when mentoring student teachers. If strong theory and practice are not related in a useful way for both theoreticians and practitioners, it is unlikely that they will enlighten and support each other. To support their mutual utility, collaboration between the field of practice and the theoretical field seems critical. Thus, the importance of triads that comprise students, subject teachers and teacher mentors seems to be growing.

According to Korthagen et al. (2006), 'the transfer from theory presented during teacher education to practice in schools is often meagre' (p. 1021). These researchers adopt an international perspective representing three different continents. I will now present some of their research on the inner connections between theory and practice in teacher education. From the perspective of my research, a hypothesis could be that the theory is not experienced as relevant in the field of practice. Therefore, increased dialogue between theoreticians and practitioners might enhance the relevance of the theory.

Korthagen et al. (2006) argue for stronger emphasis on practice, but not if it 'boils down to learning the tricks of the trade, without much deepening through theory' (p. 1021), while working towards adopting 'reflective practices' (p. 1025). They stress the need for teacher educators and student teachers to learn through a combination of reflection and experience, guiding advice for change and development more generally (p. 1022). They are also concerned with talking and reflecting on their experiences: 'Helping student teachers recognize and respond to the competing demands in their learning to teach is one way of helping them to learn in meaningful ways through experience' (p. 1027). This will support the student teachers in understanding the complexity of the field, maybe even to decrease the gap between theory and practice.

If one organises for 'a more process-oriented view of knowledge, and break with traditional ways to introduce theory into teacher education programs' (Korthagen et al., 2006, p. 1027), they argue, 1) the theory created will be closely linked to known practical settings, 2) the student teachers will gain experience and knowledge of knowledge creation, which is useful for them as future teachers, and 3) the student teachers will be prepared to take a different approach to theory in their teaching of pupils in the classroom. However, it is not only the student teachers who need to explore their own situation and take actions to improve; the whole triad is interpreted here as a learning unit. All participants in the triad should own the challenges, ideas and solutions (Madsen, 2010).

Theoretical foundation: CHAT as a frame for triad meetings

This study is based on CHAT (see e.g. Engeström, 1987, 1999, 2001; Säljö, 2001; Vygotsky, 1978). As such, the empirical data are understood through the lens of CHAT. According to this understanding, the participants act within a shared system situated in a historical and cultural setting. Through their actions, the participants, as subjects, express their goals and motives. Language is an important tool when acting and collaborating in this system. The different nodes in the system influence each other, representing a systemic approach (Bateson, 1972). This is characteristic of an activity system covering a large or small part of the whole life of the participants (Engeström, 2001). The participants interpret their experiences to construct their understanding. As a whole, the participants in the triad influence each other and the system so that the education, workplace and teaching and learning in the classroom are all in an ongoing, changing, interacting movement (Yamazumi, 2006). The collaboration and communities are constantly under construction and reconstruction (Hanssen & Østrem, 2007).

With CHAT as the basic theoretical foundation, mentoring, meetings, talks and learning are understood as dialogic, cooperative processes with active participants exploring new understandings (Engeström, 1987, 1999, 2001; Gillies, 2016; Mercer & Hodgkinson, 2008; Mercer & Littleton, 2007). Korthagen et al. (2006) show an awareness of the importance of talking and reflecting together for the student teachers to understand the thoughts behind the teaching. According to them,

> [t]alking aloud … is one way of doing this, but at the heart of this principle is the need for student teachers to see into their teachers' thinking about teaching so that they can access the ideas and feelings associated with taking risks and learning about teaching in meaningful ways.
>
> (p. 1037)

Discussion, reflection, learning and development are understood as intertwined processes in CHAT (Engeström, 2001). When mentoring is understood on this theoretical basis (Madsen, 2015), research can then be understood as a fundament for interventions (Yamazumi, 2006).

Within teacher education, the tradition of mentoring starts with an expert who disseminates knowledge to novices. The subject teachers and practice mentors are experts in their respective fields and the students are novices in both fields. The two groups of teacher educators have not yet developed traditions for collaboration; in other words, there is a gap between the fields of theory and practice (Lillejord & Børte 2014; NOKUT, 2006). The fields are encircled by boundaries that the students cross to become carriers of knowledge across the different contexts and fields of knowledge, but neither schools nor universities have traditionally crossed these institutional boundaries (Jakhelln, Lund, & Vestøl, 2017).

According to Akkerman and Bakker (2011), a boundary 'can be seen as a sociocultural difference leading to discontinuity in action or interaction' (p. 133). Student teachers experience this discontinuity when they cross boundaries in the process of developing from novices to experts and when moving from learning theory in university to practising in a school. 'All learning involves boundaries', state Akkerman and Bakker (2011, p. 132). Practice mentors, teacher students and subject teachers crossing their boundaries taking some steps towards establishing a new activity system could involve mutual learning for all parts of the triad.

The following six nodes exist in the activity system covering the triad: results, artefacts, subjects, objects, rules of the shared community and division of labour (Engeström, 1987). These nodes are part of the analysis and interpretation and some of them will be discussed below. The upcoming interventions in this project will be connected to the aims of minimising the gaps and increasing collaboration across boundaries in order to establish arenas for mutual learning to enhance all three groups of participants. In this chapter, however, the situation is mapped for planning the first interventions.

Research method

This chapter builds on empirical data gathered from mentoring meetings with student teachers in their first year of teacher education. These meetings occur when the students are in their first period of practice in different parts of Norway. The practice mentor and subject teacher, the latter is also the researcher, were present for some of the meetings, while a group of two to five students and the subject teacher (the researcher) were present for some other meetings.

A qualitative case study (Creswell, 2013) was used as an approach to study communication, collaboration and mutual learning between the participants with the intention of suggesting qualitative improvements for future mentoring meetings.

The empirical data were collected by observing the meetings in groups. I, the researcher, both observed and participated as the subject teacher, thereby acting in an observer-as-participant role (Gold, 1958). The mentoring sessions were audio-recorded, transferred to NVivo, partly transcribed and analysed using elements of the constant comparative analysis method (Strauss & Corbin, 1998) while being systematically coded and categorised. In the categorising process, I put weight on themes (Braun & Clarke, 2006). The findings will later be used in other triads as mirror data (Cole & Engeström, 2007). Then the participants will be able to discuss the examples presented. They can use the experiences, research findings and their evaluations of the mirror data as the basis for development. The analysis and interpretations were done from the perspective of CHAT (Engeström, 1987). The categories developed during the analysis were *communication* and *collaboration*, both theory-driven, and *mutual learning* which was empirically driven.

The content of the three categories leads to the division of the schools into three groups: schools 'not expecting communication', schools 'open to communication' and 'collaborating schools'. Each section covers data from more than one school, and the descriptions are constructs based on empirical data exemplifying the three approaches that emerged during the analysis. The participants have been anonymised and are all described as women in this text. The quotations were transcribed and translated from the audio-recordings and are marked with *italics*.

Findings

The three categories communication, collaboration and mutual learning were analysed and this led me to three types of interaction between the students and the practice mentors in the schools and further to the findings described in the following three sections.

Schools not expecting communication

In the schools not expecting communication between the students and subject teachers, the practice mentors only to a small degree used vocabulary expressing themselves as expert teachers. They seemed unprepared for a professional talk about teaching and learning and primarily concerned about all the hindrances, problems and challenges that a teacher faces.

From the outset, the students and practice mentors at these meetings did not appear to be a team. One part of the group did not seem to know what the other part had planned and vice versa. At some schools, the participants were not even present at the agreed time when the subject teacher arrived at the school; it seemed as if they had not discussed beforehand what should happen on the day of the meeting. From a very general perspective, the two parts shared the goal of educating good teachers and directed their dispositions towards this goal. However, the participants did not seem to communicate a shared understanding of the framework for the setting that would allow for moving towards achieving this goal.

During one of the triad meetings, the students attempted to describe their situation as future teachers,[1] while their practice mentor mainly argued against the present working conditions for teachers. She found it necessary to *warn* the students about the future work content of *teaching pupils more about manners and less about the subject and always being short of time*. She also argued that *teacher education should not teach students different ways of making good observations because observation takes time and there is no time allocated for this during the teachers' working hours*. The teacher did not put forward any suggestions for how to handle a situation as described during this meeting.

In schools with limited communication, students seem to experience a feeling of not being part of the school community as they had expected. They experience themselves as reduced *to the lowest status – even lower than a supply teacher*. One student explained it like this: 'We are not heard when we suggest something, even though we might know more about [this][2] than the teachers.' The student expressed *regret* that she had tried to participate in the solution. She felt that she had invaded an arena where she was supposed to observe, not participate.

Looking at these triad meetings through the lens of CHAT, the student quoted above described this specific situation with characteristics not consistent with either shared artefact, shared understanding of the division of labour, shared understanding of the rules for students nor with the students as part of the community of teachers. Thus, the school culture seems largely to support a more traditional, hierarchical organisational structure. Interventions in the schools in this group could be focussed on building a shared understanding among the parts to increase communication and perhaps even collaboration to achieve shared goals. All of these participants could be involved in the movements to place all involved parts in a mutual learning arena.

Schools open to communication

In the schools that were open to communication with the subject teacher from the university, the practice mentors were concerned about their identity as experienced and reflexive teachers and their assessment of the students' capability of establishing appropriate relations to groups of collaborators, such as colleagues and parents.

In these schools, the participants appeared to function as a team with members undertaking different functions. They shared plans, showed mutual respect and fostered a pleasant situation by including the visiting subject teacher from the university. The practice mentors and teacher students independently described a high degree of learning during this period of practice. Both groups also described a situation with experienced practice mentors who reflect on what they consider to be good, professional actions and clearly communicate this to the students.

The information that the practice mentors conveyed to the students was not always formulated as answers. The practice mentors appeared to take their role seriously and arranged for the student teachers to explain what they had learnt, not unlike the way that pupils are taught. They expected the teacher students (and the pupils) to learn and to work for this learning. The practice mentors clearly communicated to the students the criteria for what they defined as good teaching. For instance, some of the practice mentors described different pupils in the class for the students and told them why and how these pupils needed different teaching. According to the students, one practice mentor also modelled different ways of starting a lesson to show different reactions from the pupils and to make the teacher students reflect and discuss the pros and cons.

The practice mentors modelled their teaching and argued for their choices, but the students did not seem to actually discuss these topics. This may either be because the practice mentors closed the discussions owing to their confidence in knowing what is right and wrong: 'I know this class and these pupils', said one practice mentor. Or it may be because the students were not assuming their roles as collaborative reflectors and collaborative learners: 'We only were taught in English and Norwegian this term', the students argued in relation to why they felt like novices in the actual subject. They accepted their position as novices with little or nothing to add to the discussions.

This situation can be understood as the beginning of a movement from being peripheral participants towards being centrally placed participants (Lave & Wenger, 1991). If teacher education were organised according to an apprenticeship scheme, starting out as novices who do not participate equally in discussions would be expected. However, teacher education in most countries is organised according to schemes for academic education where groups of students change, the practice mentors change, the subject teachers change and the students are, based on their theoretical foundation, supposed to participate, but in a student role. Theoretical reflections related to relatively short periods of practice are what tie up a rather fragmentary structure of the professional master in teacher education.

Instead of interpreting the period of practice as a period of apprenticeship, I will return to the aim of establishing an arena for collaboration and mutual learning.

When interpreting the data using CHAT (Engeström, 1987, 1999), I found that the parts aimed for a shared object: education of competent, reflexive teachers. They also share an understanding of the use of some artefacts, like different ways of planning for teaching and learning. However, the students and practice mentors seem to place themselves in very different statuses: the practice mentor is the knowledgeable expert, while the students are the unexperienced novices. They do not share an arena of mutual learning.

Collaborating schools

In the collaborating schools, the practice mentors were dedicated to establishing teams including the student teachers. The members of this team filled different roles, but were expected to participate using their individual competencies. They argued for establishing educational settings where learning is scaffolded for all pupils and for situations where even the skilled practice mentors learn from new experiences with pupils and teacher students.

In some of these schools, the subject teacher did not receive a plan beforehand. However, in contrast to the non-communicating schools, the practice mentors and teacher students appeared as a team. They collaborated in formulating their plans and were open to different ways of organising the day. Furthermore, they had already prepared a shared plan ensuring inspection, teaching and learning for the pupils. The students reported having been included in a group of colleagues in the schools. In one case, they even spoke of the other teacher in the class team as a practice mentor. The students seemed to be a team of communicating and collaborating colleagues.

In one of these schools, some pupils were very challenging because they were new to the school and needed very explicit frames. The students were embraced in this work. They were allocated different work tasks, were related to certain pupils and collaborated with the practice mentor like assistant teachers while experiencing being mentored adequately. Interpreting this situation using CHAT, the primary shared goal for the teacher students and practice mentor was the pupils' social behaviour and learning. The students explained their experience of being part of a group, and they seemed to be part of an activity system that welcomed them into a community, with a transparent set of rules dividing the labour.

The practice mentor expressed her satisfaction with the situation. She had chosen to be a practice mentor, after many years of working in schools, because she 'needed some new professional inputs, and these students are competent', she said. In this way, she expressed a situation characterised by learning. Moreover, the students described collaborative learning. Altogether, this appeared to be an arena of mutual learning.

Discussion and conclusion

In this research project, all the participants in the triads are supposed to learn and develop as professionals. For me as the subject teacher and for the practice mentors the mentoring is part of our development as professional practitioners. According to

Korthagen, Loughran, and Russell (2006, p. 1030) the learning of the student teachers is only meaningful and powerful when it is embedded in the experience of learning to teach. The learning should relate to their understanding of their future professional practice. Student teachers' experiences during periods of practice should not be undervalued. In all three types of schools in this study, they appeared to receive useful professional input from practice mentors, although this input seemed to vary considerably depending on the practice mentors' different attitudes towards 'good teaching and learning', as described in the context above.

Student teachers' experiences during periods of practice should not be undervalued. In all three types of schools in this study, they appeared to receive useful professional input from practice mentors, although this input seemed to vary considerably depending on the practice mentors' different attitudes towards 'good teaching and learning', as described in the context above.

A challenge in this research project seems to be mutual learning in the triads. The subject teacher is concerned about this. Yet some of the observed triad meetings evinced more characteristics of lecturing than of communication. The schools and practice mentors know the local setting and were responsible for pre-organising the setting for these meetings. This way of organising seems to be in line with the traditional way of thinking where one does not 'overcome discontinuity between institutions in the development of shared activities' (Akkerman & Bakker, 2011, p. 133). The intentions and plans for boundary crossing between the two fields of teacher education might not have been precise and clear enough to overcome this discontinuity. The results of this varied substantially, apparently in accordance with the levels of communication, collaboration and mutual learning in the schools. Awareness, knowledge and the vocabulary used in conversations about the basic principles that constitute a 'good teacher' seem to be important for all three parts of the triad in establishing a mutual arena for learning and should be part of future interventions.

Some practice mentors in collaborating schools discussed the expectations of the triad meetings with their students beforehand and planned out their own ideas. In addition, they were open to the subject teacher's expectations. These settings were characterised by communication, collaboration and an intention to pursue mutual learning. Other practice mentors, mainly in the communicating schools – who constituted the majority – planned without discussions, but informed the students and established a setting characterised by high levels of information and communication and some attempts at collaboration, all organised and controlled by the practice mentor. The opposite was true of the non-communication schools, where it appeared as though the participants did not reflect or plan for the triad meeting. The timetables were full, no rooms were available for the meeting or the teacher students were needed in the classroom when the teachers were meeting the subject teacher, and vice versa. Evidently, this is not only a question of teacher educators from a university being interested in, and open to, collaboration with the field of practice (Munthe & Haug, 2010). It is also about the practice mentors being open to collaboration. The traditional discontinuity between institutions (Akkerman & Bakker, 2011) must be amended to influence the traditions for communication, collaboration and mutual learning. The setting described in the last example is characterised by neither communication nor collaboration nor mutual learning.

The practice mentors were informed about the overall intentions of the periods of practice in distributed texts, verbally in meetings and in an information film about practice. The students were also informed, and assignments related to the practice were formulated to strengthen the relationship between theory and practice. In this way, Skagen's (2009) research framed the before-research interventions. However, all of this information moves *from* the university *towards* the students and practice teachers. The situation in itself, based on the teachers', students' and subject teacher's understandings of teacher education and information handed out by the university, do not seem to establish a situation of collaboration and mutual learning as this is not forwarded as a shared goal. All of the participants belong to a community with ideas of *professional teachers* as a shared goal. As a group, the participants do not seem to share strategies for becoming a 'learning group'. The actors are not prepared to cross boundaries (Akkerman & Bakker, 2011; Engeström, Engeström, & Kärkkäinen, 1995).

Most of the conversations did not appear as dialogues but as more traditional expert–novice conversations. This might relate to different understandings of the learning subject and dialogue as a learning tool (Mercer & Hodgkinson, 2008; Mercer & Littleton, 2007). Most of the participants did not exhibit shared strategies for influencing the conversation and dialogues by changing the divisions of responsibility and labour. Not even the subject teacher's intention of establishing triads for mutual collaborating and learning were clearly visible during this process.

In this research, I identified some collaborating schools where the practice mentors reflected and decided on collaboration across the traditional boundaries. They also managed to take steps forward and use strategies for mutual learning as an artefact. Nodes including rules, division of labour, inclusion of students in the community and clearly working towards shared goals seem to be important.

For later interventions, therefore, I will look into the nodes of the activity system (Engeström, 1987, 2001) to establish mutual learning in triads. In this way, I shall deploy the research findings from this part of the project to 1) organise for professional communication in the triad and 2) establish a dialogue that is based on professional discussions as part of the collaboration between the different teacher educators.

Notes

1 Part of this was not recorded because it was put forward in a very informal conversation on the way to the meeting room.
2 The quoted student proffered an example at this moment.

References

Akkerman, S. F., & Bakker, A. (2011). Boundary crossing and boundary objects. *Review of Educational Research, 81*(2), 132–169. doi:10.3102/0034654311404435

Bakken, P., Pedersen, L. F., & Øygarden, K. F. (2018). *Studiebarometeret 2017: hovedtendenser* [Main tendencies in the study barometer 2017]. Retrieved from www.nokut.no/globalassets/studiebarometeret/2018/praksis—studiebarometeret-2017.pdf

Bateson, G. (1972). *Steps to an Ecology of Mind*. New York, NY: Ballantine Books.

Braun, V., & Clarke, V. (2006). Using thematic analysis in psychology. *Qualitative Research in Psychology, 3*(2), 77–101. doi:10.1191/1478088706qp063oa

Briseid, L. G., & Werner, S. (2013). Sammenheng mellom teori og praksis i lærerutdanningen? [Relations between theory and practice in teacher education?] *Skriftserien. Universitetet i Agder*, 163(e).

Cole, M., & Engeström, Y. (2007). Cultural-historical approaches to designing for development. In J. Valsiner & A. Rosa (Eds.), *The Cambridge Handbook of Sociocultural Psychology* (pp. 484–507). New York, NY: Cambridge University Press.

Creswell, J. W. (2013). *Qualitative Inquiry and Research Design: Choosing among Five Approaches*. Thousand Oaks, CA: Sage.

Dewey, J. (1916). *Democracy and Education. An Introduction to the Philosophy of Education*. New York, NY: Macmillan Company.

Edwards, A. (1997). Guests bearing gifts: The position of student teachers in primary school classrooms. *British Educational Research Journal, 23*, 27–37. doi:10.1080/0141192970230103

Engeström, Y. (1987). *Learning by Expanding*. Helsinki, Finland: Orienta-Konsultit Oy.

Engeström, Y. (1999). Activity theory and individual and social transformation. In Y. Engeström, R. Miettinen, & R. Punamaki (Eds.), *Perspectives on Activity Theory* (pp. 19–38). Cambridge, MA: Cambridge University Press.

Engeström, Y. (2001). *Expansive Learning at Work. Towards an Activity-Theoretical Reconceptualization*. London, UK: Institute of Education, University of London.

Engeström, Y., Engeström, R., & Kärkkäinen, M., (1995). Polycontextuality and boundary crossing in expert cognition: Learning and problem solving in complex work activities. *Learning and Instruction, 5*(4), 319–336. doi:10.1016/0959-4752(95)00021-00026

Finne, H., Jensberg, H., Aaslid, B. E., Haugsbakken, H., Mathiesen, I. H., & Mordal, S. (2011). *Oppfatninger av studiekvalitet i lærerutdanningen blant studenter, lærerutdannere, øvingslærere og rektorer* [Students', teacher educators', teaching practice supervisors' and headmasters' view of quality in teacher education]. Retrieved from http://ivu.sintef.no/dok/sintef_a18011

Gillies, R. M. (2016). Dialogic interactions in the cooperative classroom. *International Journal of Educational Research, 76*, 178–189. doi:10.1016/j.ijer.2015. 02. 009

Gloppen, B. H. (2013). Trepartssamtalen – en arena for å styrke samspillet mellom høgskolens undervisning og praksis? Eksempler fra lærerutdanningen [Tripartite talks – an arena to strengthen the interaction between University College and practice? Examples from teacher education]. *Uniped, 36*(1). doi:10.3402/uniped.v36i1.20949

Gold, R. L. (1958). Roles in sociological field observations. *Social Forces, 36*, 217–223.

Grimen, H. (2008). Profesjon og kunnskap [Profession and knowledge]. In A. Molander & L. I. Terum (Eds.), *Profesjonsstudier* [Professional education] (pp. 71–86). Oslo, Norway: Universitetsforlaget.

Hanssen, B., & Østrem, S. (2007). Det levende lærerarbeidet [The vivid teaching work]. *Norsk Pedagogisk Tidsskrift, 3*, 207–219.

Jakhelln, R., Lund, A., & Vestøl, J. M. (2017). Universitetsskoler som arena for nye partnerskap og profesjonskvalifisering [University schools as an arena for new partnerships and professional qualification]. In S. Mausethagen & J.-C. Smeby (Eds.), *Kvalifisering til profesjonell yrkesutøvelse* [Qualification for professional work] (pp. 70–81). Oslo, Norway: Universitetsforlaget.

Korthagen, F., Loughran, J., & Russell, T. (2006). Developing fundamental principles for teacher education programs and practices. *Teaching and Teacher Education*, 22, 1020–1041. doi:10.1016/j.tate.2006.04.022

Kvernbekk, T. (2011). The concept of evidence in evidence-based practice. *Educational Theory*, 61(5). doi:10.1111/j.1741-5446.2011.00418.x

Lave, J., & Wenger, E. (1991). *Situated Learning*. Cambridge, UK: Cambridge University Press.

Lillejord, S., & Børte, K. (2014). *Partnerskap i lærerutdanning – en forskningskartlegging – KSU3-2014* [Partnership in teacher education – a mapping of the research]. Oslo, Norway: Kunnskapssenter for utdanning.

Madsen, J. (2010). Må lærerne eie prosjektet for at vi skal lykkes i arbeidet med å utvikle skolen? [Do the teachers have to own the project in order to succeed developing the school?] In M. Ekholm, T. Lund, K. Roald, & B. Tislevoll (Eds.), *Skoleutvikling i praksis* [School development in practice] (pp. 151–167). Oslo, Norway: Universitetsforlaget.

Madsen, J. (2015). Kulturhistorisk virksomhetsteori som bakgrunn for veiledning [Sociocultural activity theory as a base when mentoring]. In H. Bjørnsrud (Ed.), *Skolebasert kompetanseutvikling – Læring og utvikling for ungdomstrinnet* [Schoolbased competence development- Learning and development in lower secondary school] (pp. 142–161). Oslo, Norway: Gyldendal.

Mercer, N., & Hodgkinson, S. (Eds.). (2008). *Exploring Talk in School*. London, UK: Sage.

Mercer, N., & Littleton, K. (2007). *Dialogue and the Development of Children's Thinking: A Sociocultural Approach*. London, UK: Routledge.

Ministry of Education (2016). *Forskrift om rammeplan for grunnskolelærerutdanning for trinn 1–7* [Regulation for the framework plan for primary school 1–7]. Oslo, Norway: Ministry of Education.

Munthe, E., & Haug, P. (2010). En integrert, profesjonsrettet og forskningsbasert grunnskolelærerutdanning [An integrated, professionally applied and research based teacher education]. *Norsk Pedagogisk Tidsskrift*, 94(3), 188–202.

NOKUT (2006). *Evaluering av allmennlærerutdanningen i Norge 2006: Del 1: Hovedrapport* [Evaluation of teacher education in Norway 2006: Part 1: Main report]. Retrieved from www.nokut.no/contentassets/40568ec86aab411ba43c5a880ae339b5/alueva_hovedrapport.pdf

Roald, K. (2010). *Kvalitetsvurdering som organisasjonslæring mellom skole og skoleeigar* (PhD dissertation). Bergen, Norway: Universitetet i Bergen.

Skagen, K. (2009). Veiledning i praksis. Om praksisopplæring i norsk allmennlærerutdannelse. En artikkel i NYMY-prosjektet [Mentoring in practice. About practical training in Norwegian teacher education. A paper in the NYMY project]. *Acta Didactica*, 3(1/8), 15. doi:10.5617/adno.1036

Solstad, A. G. (2010). Praksisnær teori og teorinær praksis – den nødvendige relasjonen [Theory close to practice and practice close to theory –the necessary relation]. *Norsk pedagogisk tidsskrift* [Norwegian pedagogical journal], 94(3).

Strauss, A., & Corbin, J. (1998). *Basics of Qualitative Research: Techniques and Procedures for Developing Grounded Theory*. Thousand Oaks, CA: Sage.

Säljö, R. (2001). *Læring i praksis. Et sosiokulturelt perspektiv* [Learning in practice. A sociocultural perspective]. Oslo, Norway: Cappelen akademiske forlag.

Vygotsky, L. S. (1978). *Mind in Society. The Development of Higher Psychological Processes.* Cambridge, MA: Harvard University Press.

Yamazumi, K. (2006). Activity theory and the transformation of pedagogic practice. *Educational Studies in Japan, International Yearbook*, 1, 7–90. doi:10.7571/esjkyoiku.1.77

6 Encouraging working and communicating like mathematicians
An illustrative case on dialogic teaching

Vivi Nilssen and Torunn Klemp

Introduction

> You remember, we talked about what mathematicians do? Finding out something, deciding something. And they write and tell others what they have found. That is what we are going to do today. To start, you cut out the figures [from the sheet I gave you]. Then the mathematician job starts.

Through this quotation, we understand how teacher 'Pamela' tells her second graders that they are to work like mathematicians. Mathematicians explore, decide, write and tell others what they have found. We also understand that they have talked about this subject previously, revealing they are accustomed to this way of working with mathematics. In the study presented in this chapter, we explore how and why Pamela encourages the pupils to work like mathematicians.

Pamela's way of thinking about teaching mathematics is strongly advocated in the literature. To learn mathematics involves more than replicating procedures and solving isolated problems without errors (Anghileri, 2006; van Oers, 2013). Mathematical literacy contains a reflective discourse, and, as Pimm (2017) argues, 'mathematics is, among other things, a social activity, deeply concerned with communication' (p. xvii). Basic mathematical proficiency implies learning to speak like a mathematician. Thus, mathematical thinking calls for the ability to communicate with oneself or others about mathematical objects and their interrelationships (van Oers, 2013). This is mirrored in the Norwegian national curriculum (Norwegian Directorate for Education and Training, 2016) where basic oral skills in mathematics imply 'participating in conversations, communicating ideas and elaborating on problems, solutions and strategies with other pupils' (p. 4). The pupils should put discoveries and ideas into words and argue their merit by first using an informal language and later using more precise terminology, modes of expression and concepts.

Teachers play a vital role via the signals they send regarding knowledge and the value they place on methods of thinking and knowing (Anghileri, 2006). One such signal is to establish a classroom culture where explanations and discussions of strategies are more important than simply producing correct answers. In contrast to teaching that is built on teachers' explanations, social norms can be established in the classroom where the pupils themselves are expected to explain and justify their solutions (Yackel & Cobb, 1996). Consequently, the teacher's ability to develop and implement a strategy for dialogic teaching that can enhance the pupils' mathematical literacy is essential.

We still need more research into teacher proficiency in mathematical communication and the personal construction of pupils (van Oers, 2013). The literature on successful teacher strategies for facilitating dialogic interactions in the early school years has been especially scant (Muhonen, Rasku-Pettonen, Pakarinen, Poikkeus, & Lerkkanen, 2016). Thus, the aim of this case study focusing on Pamela's teaching is to explore how teachers can promote pupils' participation in a classroom community where sharing ideas is valued and mathematical ideas are reasoned and justified. We ask the following question: *How does one primary school teacher perform dialogic teaching?*

> This study of Pamela's teaching is part of a larger multilayered intervention study called *Language Use and Development in the Mathematics Classroom* (LaUDiM) in which two primary teachers and seven researchers in the area of mathematics and education collaborate. The main objective is to understand and increase pupils' proficiency in expressing mathematical ideas, reasoning and justification. Another objective is to contribute to capacity building in schools and in teacher education through joint classroom research. Creating a joint research environment for learning across boundaries (Engeström, Engeström, & Kärkkäinen, 1995) has been an important tool in LaUDiM. Following two classes over a period of three and a half years, from year two to year five, the teachers and the researchers have been involved in seven cycles of planning, each of them containing teaching and reflection of two lessons. Before designing activities for the lessons, an analysis of the mathematical content was carried out. The teachers planned in more detail and taught the lessons in their classes, and the researchers observed and video-recorded the activity in the classrooms. Between the two lessons, the researchers and the teachers met for reflections on the following: Did the lesson go as we thought? Is there a need for change of direction? After the lessons, the researchers and teachers watched the video together, discussing the didactics and the pupils' learning, thus starting the analysis.

Previous research

Sociocultural perspectives and the emphasis on use of language and dialogue have strongly influenced educational discourse in recent decades. Still, the initiation-response-feedback (IRE/F) pattern remains a dominating script in many classroom interactions worldwide (Wells & Auraz, 2006), leaving little room for 'students explaining their thinking, working publicly through an incorrect idea, making a conjecture or coming to consensus about a mathematical idea' (Franke, Kazemi, & Battey, 2007, p. 231). Mercer, Dawes, and Staarman (2009) assert that the lack of strategies for using discussions in teaching is the reason dialogic teaching has progressed so little to this point. As for the situation in Norway, Skorpen (2006) indicates that there is little room for dialogue between teachers and pupils or between pupils, and Bjørkås and Bulien (2010) shows that comments from pupils are rarely followed up.

Working like a mathematician, that is, making thinking visible and sharing knowledge, implies the need for collaboration. However, the results of research on the outcome of pupils' collaborative work are contradictory. Although Light and Littleton (1999) report compelling evidence for the benefits of collaboration, other studies are more negative and link the doubtful quality of much collaborative work to ineffectiveness in the pupils' communication (Mercer, Dawes, Wegerif, & Sams, 2004; Sfard & Kieran, 2001). To collaborate, pupils need a clear concept of both what they are expected to do and how to communicate to develop shared meaning (Mercer et al., 2004). Comparing the dialogues of a successful pair of pupils with a less successful pair, Dahl, Klemp, and Nilssen (2018) relate three features of a successful discussion: a shared goal, making thinking visible using different representations and the ability to listen to each other. A study by van Houten (2011, cited in van Oers, 2013) shows that the vocabulary ability and narrative competence of primary pupils had significant predictive value for mathematical skill.

Over the past several decades, numerous studies have pointed to valuable teacher strategies in dialogic teaching. To help pupils develop strategies, Askew, Brown, Rhodes, William, and Johnston (1997) suggest that the teacher should challenge the pupils to explain their thinking and to listen to the thinking of others, whereas Wood (1994) points to teacher interventions that clarify thinking and make explicit those aspects that are most critical to understanding. A review study by Kyriacou and Issit (2008) supports the idea that teachers' questions should elicit reasons and explanations.

Mercer, Wegerif, and Dawes (1999) assert 'that the best primary education will be achieved through a balanced integration of teacher-led, whole-class activities with structured peer group activities and individualised work' (p. 108). The benefit is a combination of intellectual guidance and active participation in intellectual communities of discourse and practice. In a review, Mercer and Howe (2012) advocate for holding back demonstrations and explanations until the ideas of some pupils have been heard, giving pupils enough time to construct thoughtful answers to questions, as well as using whole-class discussions to help pupils see the point and purpose of their topic.

Alexander (2017) presents five key principles for dialogic teaching that harness the power of talk to stimulate and develop pupils' thinking, learning and understanding: the classroom discourse must be *collective* (class or groups), *reciprocal* (listening to each other, sharing and considering alternative ideas) and *supportive* (helping each other to reach a shared understanding), and the content of the talk must be *cumulative* (building on each other's ideas) and *purposeful* (goal-directed). In addition, van Oers (2013) advocates for two basic pedagogical prerequisites in dialogic teaching. First, the teacher must really believe in 'children's potential to mathematise with their own notions of quantity, space, relation, etc., and to communicate about them with others' (p. 200). Second, communicating about any mathematical object should be constantly embedded across the curriculum, in order to foster pupils' mathematical orientation in the world.

In a recent study, Howe, Hennessy, Mercer, Vrikki, and Wheatly (2019) sum up five recurring themes in proposals about characteristics of dialogic classroom discourses that optimise pupil outcomes: 1) open questions are used; 2) participants make extended contributions elaborating and building on previous contributions made by themselves or others; 3) differences of opinions are acknowledged, probed and critiqued, bringing in the reasons they are based on; 4) integrated lines of enquiry are used for linking the different contributions and resolving differences; and 5) pupils are made aware on a metacognitive level of the value of verbal interaction (p. 4). However, Howe et al. (2019) find we still lack compelling evidence that implementation of all these characteristics optimises student outcomes. In their review, they find such evidence for characteristic 3 and 5 in pupil-pupil dialogues, whereas encouraging findings for teacher-pupil dialogues in mathematics regarding characteristic 1, 2 and 3 comes from studies that are either too small in scale or unclear regarding outcomes. The results in Howe et al.'s (2019) large-scale study is consistent with the three first characteristics; the teacher-pupil dialogues manifest high levels of pupil participation, elaboration and querying.

Theoretical framework

The point of departure for this study is cultural-historical activity theory (CHAT), a development of socio-cultural theory based on Vygotsky's thoughts and ideas. Socio-cultural theory asserts that individual learning can be understood by studying how individuals participate in social practices, this perspective can help us examine whether the teaching practice engages the pupils in purposeful and in-depth enquiry (Rogoff, 1994). One of the strengths of the theory is that it explains 'how collective understanding is created from interaction with others' (Mercer & Howe, 2012, p. 13).

For studying how Pamela, our case study teacher, encourages pupils to work and communicate like mathematicians, three levels of analyses developed by Leont´ev is used. Human processes can, according to Leont´ev (1978, 1981), be viewed from the level of overall *activity*, the level of constituent *actions* and the levels of *operations* by which the actions are carried out. The three strata may be treated as hierarchically related, but they represent different perspectives on the same event. Activities are distinguished on the basis of their motive and the objective towards which they are oriented; actions on the basis of their goals; and operations on the basis of the conditions in which they are carried out (Wells, 1999). An activity may be carried out in a variety of ways by employing different goals (with their associated actions) under different conditions (with their associated operations) (Wertsch, 1981).

To move towards the overarching goal of the activity, the individual performs a chain of goal-directed actions through a number of operations, and the 'activity' is translated into reality. The choice of actions with its operations is linked to the individual's perceptions of the goal and the situation the actions are performed in. Thus, even if all teachers are by definition engaged in the practice of education, we can observe differences in how individual teachers perform the actions that constitute the activity: 'In encouraging or restricting certain kinds of behaviour (...) the teacher is operationalizing his or her theory of education' (Wells, 1999, p.171). We can analyse events that take place in a classroom from the perspective of the teacher's (implicit) theory of education.

An action requires that the actors give it their conscious attention, whereas an operation might develop into a well-practiced routine (Leont'ev, 1981). In an intervention study such as LaUDiM, however, the particular means (operations) the teacher uses to conduct the goal-directed actions need conscious attention. Mediating tools have a central role in the theory of 'activity', connecting humans with the world of objects and with other people. Tools relate to the operation level, where methods or material objects are crystallised.

Method

The study idea originates from an analysis of whole-class discussions from the first year of the LaUDiM project (Burheim, Nilssen, & Rønning, 2017). Listening to the dialogues, we became aware of how Pamela used pupils' written work from previous lessons as tools when she conducted whole-class dialogues. We also noticed that the pupils very often used the word 'because' to justify their answers in these dialogues. Furthermore, Pamela repeatedly used the phrase 'as the mathematicians do' throughout the lessons. This inspired our research question: How does one primary school teacher perform dialogic teaching?

To answer the research question, we chose a case study methodology as it is suitable for catching complex school practices (Gudmundsdottir, 2001). In addition, single, qualitative case studies are suitable when researchers want to understand the particular practice in depth (Stake, 1995). Our study meets the criteria of such a methodology as the phenomenon under study is bounded in time and place, and there is a multitude of data material (Creswell, 2013). Based on Pamela's assertion during a planning session that working on polygons was suitable for discussions between pupils, we chose to dig into Pamela's teaching of polygons to learn more about dialogic teaching.

The data material for the case study is four video-recorded whole-class sessions; eight video-recorded dialogues from peer-work and pupils' written work, all from two consecutive lessons; three audio-recorded interviews with Pamela; and video-recordings from planning and reflection sessions connected to the two lessons.

We used Leont'ev's (1978, 1981) three levels of analyses in our study. He argues that to understand why separate actions are meaningful, we need to understand the motive, i.e. the driving force, behind the whole activity. Thus, we started to reveal the driving force behind the activity analysing Pamela's utterances in all phases of her teaching, in the planning and reflection sessions and in the interviews. We noticed key words (e.g. 'mathematicians') and phrases (e.g. 'let them present what they think'). We asked questions such as the following: 'What was she talking about when she used the word "mathematicians"?' We found that Pamela's motive and the object she acts on is to encourage pupils to work and communicate like mathematicians, which implies making thinking visible, sharing ideas and agreeing on common knowledge.

The next step was to identify what must be done, i.e. the goal-directed actions, and how it can be done, i.e. the means by which an action is carried out to move the practice towards the object. To get an overview, we watched all the videos from the classroom. As we found that Pamela built her whole-class dialogue around the work of just two groups, we transcribed these pupils' peer work and the whole-class discussion to reduce the material. Although Leont´ev's three levels guided the analysis for identifying the involved actions and operations Pamela used to guide the pupils' work, we also used analytical tools from the constant comparative method (Strauss & Corbin, 1998) throughout the process. We asked questions and compared paragraphs in the data material, drew diagrams and used the flip-flop technique, turning concepts in and out and upside down. We identified three goal-directed actions: *modelling explorative work, monitoring the pupils' work* and *orchestrating for agreement*. The involved operations are illustrated in the next section.

According to Lincoln and Guba (1985), dependability concerns whether the findings are consistent with the data collected and that the findings make sense given the collected data. To give the readers insight and show that the findings are credible and consistent with the data collected, we have chosen to illustrate our findings with a rich selection of dialogues and quotations. Thus, we aim to support the transferability and the dependability of the study. Another procedure for enhancing the credibility was member checking with Pamela.

We have followed the guidelines of the Norwegian National Committee for Research Ethics in the Social Sciences and the Humanities (NESH, 2016). We have obtained written consent from the school and all parents of the pupils involved and Pseudonyms are used to protect identities. The project plan has been approved by the Norwegian Centre for Research Data.

Findings: identifying the activity, actions and operations

The introductory quote to this article is from Pamela's presentation of the task. We have found that the object of the activity and thus Pamela's motive in her teaching of mathematics, is to encourage pupils to work and communicate like mathematicians. This implies making thinking visible, justifying solutions and agreeing on shared solutions. Regarding working with polygons, the pupils are to agree on a definition of properties of different kinds of polygons. Pamela stated she thinks working with polygons is suitable for discussions:

> Polygons are well suited [for a discussion] because they can possibly have different apprehensions, and it can be discussed and argued (…). I think it will be interesting to get them to write down a definition of what they decide it to be (…). Here I think the children really will experience that they can decide; 'I decide, and I have thought'.

Pamela believes that differences of opinion and the fact that the pupils are free to form their own definitions will motivate them to share their thinking.

As presented, we found that Pamela uses three interrelated, goal-directed actions to move her teaching practice towards the object working and communicating like mathematicians: modelling explorative work, monitoring the pupils' work and orchestrating for agreement. The modelling action and the monitoring action guide how Pamela enacts the orchestrating action. The three actions partly occur simultaneously during the two lessons but are presented according to the phase of the teaching where the action is most dominant (introduction/individual work and peer work/whole-class discussion).

Modelling explorative work

In the first goal-directed action, *modelling explorative work*, Pamela's goal is that the pupils understand how they can work to decide which polygons belong together and why. When Pamela introduces the task and the plan for the first lesson, modelling is the dominating action. Pamela shows the pupils a sheet with different polygons (including a non-example; Figure 6.1).

She explains that they first are going to work individually and cut out the figures. She continues: 'Then you are sorting. You must decide which figures belong together. Then you must decide what you want to call them.' She writes 'sort alone' on the board.

Then Pamela introduces the next step, working with peers, where the goal is to present their work to each other and agree on what to call the different groups of figures and why. The idea is that they need to compare and argue for their solution, she says. Pamela exemplifies using triangles, which are not part of the task: 'I have put these together because, in my opinion, they are triangles.' Using the pronoun 'I', Pamela puts herself in the situation of a pupil who is sorting and focusing on the need for presenting a reason. Foreseeing that the pupils might have different opinions, she continues: 'So maybe you

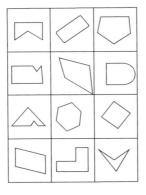

Figure 6.1 Polygon figures to be sorted

```
Dette er _____ fordi
                                                         
                                                         
                                                         
                                                         
Navn: _____
```

Figure 6.2 Sheet for naming, pasting and explaining a group of polygons (this is _____ because _____)

disagree; then you must talk together, listen to what the other has to say and tell what you think yourself. Then you must agree upon a way of sorting them.' Pamela writes 'talk together' on the board.

In the next step of the introduction, Pamela shows the pupils a form they will fill out for each group of figures (see Figure 6.2).

On the top of the sheet, she says, they name the group of figures they think belong together and then they describe why they think that these, e.g. are triangles. To clarify the content further, she once again dramatizes the situation using the voice of a pupil: 'Yes, this explanation I think we have finished; it explains what a triangle is.' Then she underlines the need to agree before the pupils can paste the figures: 'When you fully agree on what triangles are and why, then you finally are allowed to paste them on.' Pamela is now ready to complete the working plan on the board. Before writing, she introduces a new concept from the world of mathematics:

> When mathematicians work with figures like this, and when they write such explanations about what they are, they call it to write a definition. I'll write it here: 'write a definition', and finally: 'paste figures'.

This ends Pamela's modelling of working and communicating like mathematicians in the first part of lesson 1. Sort, decide, name, explain, reason, compare, argue and agree are important words in Pamela's introduction. In addition, she introduces 'definition', the concept a mathematician would use in such a situation.

The central operations are going through the working plan step by step, modelling what to say and how to act, and using the working sheets and the whiteboard as tools. Doing so, Pamela uses an example and changes between using her own guiding teacher voice and the voice of a virtual pupil. This is a kind of modelling she also uses when the pupils are working individually or with peers. In the interview, Pamela comments on her role as dialogue partner: 'I pretend that I ponder over the same things as they do (...). try to be one of them instead of being the teacher, playing ball with them.' In other cases, she follows up by modelling comparison processes by posing questions systematically to pairs of pupils to get them on track in the preferred working model (e.g. Pamela's talk with George, Frances and Knuth in the next paragraph).

Monitoring the pupils' work

Monitoring the pupils' work is the second goal-directed action in Pamela's teaching, especially defining her teaching in the part of the lesson where the pupils work individually or with peers. The recordings show that Pamela observes and talks with all the pupils. She encourages the pupils to explain to her how they have sorted and how they have come to agree on the properties of a group of figures.

Through this in-between desk work, Pamela identifies the problem of defining what edges, 'peaks' and 'lines' mean, as expressed by the pupils. In Norwegian, polygons are literally named after the number of edges by using the standard Norwegian number words, e.g. a triangle is called a 'three edge' (*trekant*), a quadrilateral is called a 'four edge' (*firkant*) and so on. What we mean by 'edges' quickly comes in to focus when discussing the properties of the different polygons. Some pairs have a shared opinion on what counts as edges and what counts as vertices. From the video-recording, e.g. we can see that Roger and Naomi both use their fingers to point to the vertices when they individually decide on which pile the polygons belong to as quadrilaterals (*firkanter*), pentagons (*femkanter*) or hexagons (*sekskanter*). When they discuss their shared solution, they have a shared vocabulary, even though it differs from conventional mathematics.

George, Frances and Knuth, the only group of three pupils, on the other hand, disagree. When Pamela comes to the table, George explains:

GEORGE: Frances says that these are edges [point to the vertices at a figure]. Those peaks?
FRANCES: Yes, these are edges.
KNUTH: No, no.
FRANCES: Yes, but, edges and corners[1] are the same as edge-corner ('*kant-hjørne*', a constructed word).
PAMELA: It sounds like you have discussed something?
FRANCES: Yes.[The pupils explain and point.]
PAMELA: So, George thinks these are edges [points at the edges] and these are corners?
[After a five-second silence, Knuth nods.]
PAMELA: Do you agree, Frances?
FRANCES: I don't know [shakes her head].

PAMELA: You don't know, okay, what do you think, then?
FRANCES: That these are the edges [point at the vertices].
PAMELA: You think that these are the edges [points at two of the vertices in a figure]; this is what they call edges?
FRANCES: Mm.
KNUTH: Then we must discuss further! [Slaps his forehead with his palm.]
PAMELA: Must agree before we can start writing how we will name them.

In this excerpt, we can see that Pamela asks a mixture of open and closed questions to understand the pupils' apprehensions of the edge concept. She clarifies the different positions for the pupils and avoids verifying any of the positions as right or wrong. When Knuth concludes that they must keep on discussing, Pamela agrees, pointing to the working plan that we 'must agree before we can start writing'. In the whole-class dialogue two days later, George points to the edges, signifying that the group has reached an agreement.

The pupils' written work shows that all working pairs named the figures based on the number of edges: 'These are pentagons because they have five edges.' However, through her monitoring, Pamela understands that behind this apparent agreement, the pupils still might comprehend the concept of an edge differently (as an edge or as a vertex).

The central operations in *monitoring the pupils' work* are to attend to the pupils and to ask questions of the pupils' work to understand each pupil's thinking. The design of the task and the organising of the pupils' work form an important basis for such monitoring. As mentioned previously, Pamela thought working with polygons was a good theme to discuss. The sorting, naming, defining and mixing of individual work and peer work are other elements in the setting that help Pamela ascertain the pupils' thinking. In an interview, Pamela confirms the importance of asking the right kind of questions when observing:

> I think they need questions that clarify their own thoughts. [The teacher] must get the pupils to justify what they have found out and believe. And maybe ask them to show with an example or to explain why they believe what they believe. How can we know? (…). Can you show me on a drawing?

Her focus is on the pupils' own thoughts, 'what they end up with before anyone has given them anything'. When monitoring the pupils work, her role is to interpret what they say and do, and then help them formulate their thinking:

> I believe that the teacher's role [in this phase] is to observe what the pupils are doing. Talk with them while they are working, trying to get them to explain what they have done, put into words what they have thought, what they struggle with or what they want to try. And not giving them any input, but maybe ask some questions that might, well, not exactly push them forward, but maybe get them to think something new or get them to pursue a thought they already had and clarify it.

Working and communicating like mathematicians 83

The hope is that the monitoring will support progress in their work. Pamela lacks this part in teaching where the pupils are told what to do. In the reflective session between the two lessons, Pamela reveals a great belief in the pupils' ability:

> The competence they have (...) [is] to try to find methods they believe in but yet haven't found a way to use. Then you achieve so much more than if you sit down and wait for someone to tell you [how to do something].

Even though monitoring the pupils' work especially defines the situation when the pupils work individually or with peers, monitoring is also part of Pamela's teaching in whole-class settings. Through all of this, she is alert to the pupils' thinking.

Orchestrating for agreement

The third goal-directed action, *orchestrating for agreement*, defines Pamela's teaching in the final phase of the learning sequence, i.e. aiming for a joint understanding of polygons and their properties. Pamela opens the whole-class dialogue by saying:

> On Monday, you worked like mathematicians; you sorted. I went around, watching, and there is something I want to know more about. All groups had made a pile and said this was quadrangles, for instance Roger and Naomi. Here is their work (comes up on the smartboard). They have written: 'This is a quadrilateral because it has 4 edges' and pasted on all the figures they have decided to be quadrilaterals. All groups have written like this. Can one of you tell me how you thought when you wrote that it had four edges? Roger, can you come and show us?

Once again, she underlines the working plan – they are 'working like mathematicians' – and they have reached a common answer: all have decided that quadrilaterals are figures 'with four edges'. Pamela presents Roger and Naomi's work on the board as an example (Figure 6.3). Without confirming their solution, she invites Roger to the board to show where they find the edges. Roger points to the four vertices as he counts to four.

The whole-class dialogue continues:

PAMELA: OK, so you counted to four. What is an edge, according to you two?
ROGER: [pointing to the vertices] It is these peaks.
PAMELA: And you agreed, Naomi?
NAOMI: Yes.
PAMELA: But I heard some groups were thinking a little bit differently about edges? Can you, George, tell us what you, Frances and Knuth talked about?
GEORGE: We did not think like one, two, three, four [points to the vertices], but one, two, three, four [points to the edges].
PAMELA: Can anyone see the difference between what Roger and Naomi thought and what George, Frances and Knuth thought?

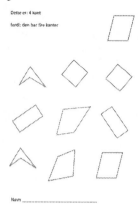

Figure 6.3 Rogers and Naomi's work on the task presented in Figure 6.2

NINA: Yes, the lines.
PAMELA: What is the difference then, Nina?
NINA: They counted by the lines, and they counted by the peaks.
PAMELA: Yes, George said one, two, three, four [points to the edges] while Roger and Naomi thought like this: one, two, three, four [points to the vertices]. Hmm?! So, we disagree on what an edge really is; some of you talk about edges in one way, these [points to the vertices], and some of you talk about edges in another way, these [points to the edges].

The way Pamela shapes this discussion follows the same explorative pattern she modelled when introducing the task. The pupils are invited to explain their thinking and reason related to the figures, she compares the solutions together with the pupils and the pupils are invited to decide whether they agree or disagree.

At this point, Pamela has made it clear to all the pupils that even if they have given the same answer, 'this is a quadrilateral because it has four edges', they think differently about edges, either as vertices or as edges. In this dialogue, Pamela engages Nina, another pupil, to analyse and highlight the difference between the work of the two groups. In the session after teaching, Pamela reveals that she deliberately invites some pupils into the whole-class discussions to get the right progress:

> I had decided who I wanted to share some of the things based on what I saw on Monday. Generally, I try to let all of them speak. But sometimes I know that some of them can give good explanations, and if there is something specific we need to highlight, I use one of them.

Pamela is orchestrating the discussion with a firm hand based on what she has planned beforehand. Based on her monitoring of the pupils' work, she has picked out and highlighted two examples to visualise that the pupils have different understandings of the edge concept. In reflection, Pamela admits that she had thought the concept was clearer to more pupils than it obviously was. Regardless, Pamela had planned to spend quite some time on the edge concept, as she explains:

> On this stage, before commenting on what is right and what is wrong, it is all about their thinking. It is important to let them tell their minds before I tell what is right. If not, they will never dare to speak, or at least they gradually will stop trying to. I always try to act in this way.

The pupils need space to share, and some pupils, according to Pamela, 'will need time to change their opinion'. In the reflective session, we find yet another reason for spending so much time on the edge concept. Talking about the different pupils' work, Nina's satisfaction when she discovered that the number of vertices and edges were equally high in all polygons came into focus. Pamela comments:

> Yes, because she did find out, didn't she, that this went for quadrilaterals, as well as for pentagons and hexagons (...) and then we can discover later, if we work with cubes, that, no, here it is something else, this only goes for [figures] which are flat.

Pamela thinks ahead and knows that agreeing on the precise naming of polygons will help the pupils in their future learning of polyhedrons.

Pamela's next teaching operation is to once again lean on "what mathematicians do":

> When mathematicians talk together, they must agree upon one thing; they must find a common explanation on what a quadrilateral is. So, the first thing we must do is to find out about the edge; [find a definition] we can agree on.

They must 'find a common explanation' like the mathematicians do. To get the children to agree on one name for the same object, Pamela keeps the discussion going by bringing in more voices. Eventually, she brings in a reference context from their everyday life, a mini-pitch (Figure 6.4). The operation is planned ahead of time, and Pamela has prepared a picture on the whiteboard that they can use for discussing edges and vertices.

Did they agree? Well, they agreed to disagree. Towards the end of the lesson, Pamela performed her last operation as she takes the pupils out walking the mini-pitch. All the pupils ran to the correct places when Pamela told them to go and stand at the *edge* of the pitch, and stand in the *hjørne* [2] of the pitch.

Discussion

The findings show that Leont'ev's three levels of analyses open up and make visible the different kinds of actions and operations seemingly necessary to

Figure 6.4 The mini-pitch

encourage pupils to work and communicate like mathematicians. On the operation level, there are tasks that cannot be fulfilled without sharing ideas, making the pupils thinking visible, which is a goal on the action level. Like mathematicians, they are tasked with finding out something, writing it down and agreeing with others.

Pamela shapes the learning environment through three actions, *modelling explorative work, monitoring the pupils' work* and *orchestrating for agreement*. Analysis of the dialogues in the three different actions gives reason to believe that sociomathematical norms (Yackel & Cobb, 1996) on working like mathematicians are developed in the class. Yackel and Cobb (1996) argue that such norms are interactively constituted by the teacher, as a representative of the mathematical community, and the pupils. As an example, they present an analysis of a classroom characterised by comparison processes that make sense of different explanations and establish 'taken-as-shared meanings' (p. 466), showing how this culture connects to a norm on what counts as an acceptable mathematical reason.

We have shown that Pamela not only explicitly refers to 'what mathematicians do' and what they say, but she also wants the children to act and communicate as mathematicians. Mathematical literacy as presented by Pimm (2017) is her guiding principle, and, working like mathematicians is valued in her class because it will add to the pupils' mathematical literacy (Anghileri, 2006). As underlined by van Oers (2013), she really believes in the pupils, that they can work like mathematicians: 'The competence they have (…) to try to find methods they believe in but yet haven't found a way to use.' Her dialogue with the pupils is inclusive; she takes all ideas seriously: 'she just has to get them to pursue a thought they already had and clarify it'.

Kazemi and Stipek (2009) identified the socio-mathematical norm that collaboration includes accountability and consensus through argumentation. We have identified a similar norm on the importance of agreeing through dialogue. The norm is presented through modelling: 'So maybe you disagree; then you must talk together, listen to what the other has to say, and tell what you think yourself. Then you must agree.' And the message seems to be internalised by at least some of the pupils. Without Pamela telling them that the dialogue makes it clear that Knuth's group disagrees on the meaning of edge, he concludes, 'then we have to discuss further'. Howe et al. (2019) describes adoption of a metacognitive perspective upon verbal interaction and the importance of learning as one of five proposed characteristics of dialogic teaching that optimise pupils' outcomes. Knuth's awareness of the need for talking together might be a first step on the way to developing the proposed perspective.

Pamela's pupils are also held accountable as in Kazemi and Stipek's study (2009). As we saw in the presented excerpt from Pamela's dialogue with George, Frances and Knuth, every pupil is asked to share their thinking in the comparison process. 'Do you agree, Frances? (…). You don't know, okay, what do you think, then?' The pupils can make up their own mind, but they are obliged to make a stand before the teacher reveals what is correct. Pamela's actions mirror what Mercer and Howe (2012) see as a valuable teacher strategy; i.e. she holds back demonstration and explanation until the pupils' ideas have been heard, giving them enough time to construct thoughtful answers to questions, rather than moving quickly on if they are hesitant.

Pamela's three actions – modelling of the explorative work method, monitoring the pupils' work and orchestrating the agreeing process – seem to be of significance for a successful dialogic teaching sequence (Alexander, 2017). Modelling the explorative working method and monitoring pupils' work help Pamela orchestrate a *collective, reciprocal* and *purposeful* discourse. Every step in the learning process is directed towards the goal – to agree on a definition of properties of different polygons – and all the steps are linked through Pamela's three actions. The process includes both dialogues in peer groups and in whole-class settings where the pupils listen to each other and become aware of the differences in how they think about the concept of edges. As supported by Howe et al. (2019), the illustrative excerpt from the whole-class discussion shows that Pamela includes open questions, and differences of opinion are acknowledged, probed and critiqued to uncover the reasons for the pupils' opinions. She also makes explicit links amongst the contributions and orchestrates an enquiry that will lead to agreement as suggested. These are characteristics of a *cumulative* classroom discourse, which is Alexander's (2017) fifth key principle. Finally, we assert that the recordings give an impression of a *supportive* classroom culture where the pupils freely share their thoughts, which is Alexander's fourth key principle for dialogic teaching.

To sum up, through the three goal-directed actions Pamela has clarified what is expected of the pupils regarding how to act and how to communicate in the collective mathematics classroom as recommended by Mercer et al. (2004).

However, these analyses are not enough to assert that Pamela's second graders have internalised this discourse.

Notes

1 The Norwegian language has no precise scientific word for "vertex". The word *hjørne* means "corner" as well as vertex. Here we use corner to mark that the pupils probably still use their everyday language.
2 Refer to the description of this term in footnote 1.

References

Alexander, R. (2017). *Towards Dialogic Teaching. Rethinking Classroom Talk*, 5th edn. Cambridge, UK: Dialogos.

Anghileri, J. (2006). Scaffolding practices that enhance mathematics learning. *Journal of Mathematics Teacher Education*, 9(1), 33–52. doi:10.1007/s10857-006-9005-9

Askew, M., Brown, M., Rhodes, V., William, D., & Johnston, D. (1997). *Effective Teachers of Numeracy: Report Carried Out for the TTA*. London: King's College.

Bjørkås, Ø., & Bulien, T. (2010). Utforskende matematikksamtaler i klasserommet [Explorative dialogues in the classroom]. In T. Guldal, C. F. Dons, S. Sagberg, T. Solhaug, & R. Tromsdal (Eds.), *FoU i praksis 2009: Rapport om praksisrettet FoU i lærerutdanninga* (pp. 23–37). Trondheim, Norway: Tapir Akademisk forlag.

Burheim, O. T., Nilssen, V., & Rønning, F. (2017). Fra å kjenne igjen til å beskrive egenskaper. Om kanter og hjørner [From recognising to describing properties. About edges and vertices]. *Bedre Skole*, 29(3), 64–69.

Creswell, J. W. (2013). *Qualitative Inquiry & Research Design: Choosing among Five Approaches*, 3rd edn. Los Angeles: Sage.

Dahl, H., Klemp, T., & Nilssen, V. (2018). Collaborative talk in mathematics – contrasting examples from third graders. *Education 3–13. International Journal of Primary, Elementary and Early years Education*, 46(5), 599–611. doi:10.1080/03004279.2017.1336563

Engeström, Y., Engeström, R., & Kärkkäinen, M. (1995). Polycontextuality and boundary crossing in expert cognition. Learning and problem solving in complex work activities. *Learning and Instruction*, 5(4), 319–335. doi:10.1016/0959-4752(95)00021-00026

Franke, M. L., Kazemi, E., & Battey, D. (2007). Mathematics teaching and classroom practice. In F. K. Lester, Jr., (Ed.), *Second Handbook of Research on Mathematics Teaching and Learning* (pp. 225–256). Reston, VA: National Council of Teachers of Mathematics.

Gudmundsdottir, S. (2001). Narrative research on school practice. In V. Richardson (Ed.), *Fourth Handbook of Research on Teaching* (pp. 226–240). Washington, DC: American Educational Research Association.

Howe, C., Hennessy, S., Mercer, N., Vrikki, M., & Wheatley, L. (2019). Teacher-student dialogue during classroom teaching: Does it really impact upon student outcomes? *Journal of the Learning Sciences*. doi:10.1080/10508406.2019.1573730

Kazemi, E., & Stipek, D. (2009). Promoting conceptual thinking in four upper-elementary mathematics classrooms. *Journal of Education*, 189(1/2), 123–137. doi:10.1177/0022057409189001-209

Kyriacou, C., & Issit, J. (2008). What characterizes effective teacher-pupil dialogue to promote conceptual understanding in mathematics lessons in England in key stages 2 and 3? *EPPI-Centre Report No. 1604R*. London: Institute of Education, University of London.

Leont´ev, A. N. (1978). *Activity, Consciousness, and Personality*. Englewood Cliffs, CA: Prentice Hall.

Leont´ev, A. N. (1981). The problem of activity in psychology. In J. W. Wertsch (Ed.), *The Concept of Activity in Soviet Psychology* (pp. 37–71). Armonk, NY: M. E. Sharpe.

Light, P., & Littleton, K. (1999). *Social Practices in Children's Learning*. Cambridge: Cambridge University Press.

Lincoln, Y. S., & Guba, E. G. (1985). *Naturalistic Inquiry*. Newbury Park, CA: Sage Publication.

Mercer, N., & Howe, C. (2012). Explaining the dialogic processes of teaching and learning: The value and potential of sociocultural theory. *Learning, Culture and Social Interaction*, 1(1), 12–21. doi:10.1016/j.lcsi.2012. 03. 001

Mercer, N., Dawes, L., & Staarman, J. K. (2009). Dialogic teaching in the primary science classroom. *Language and Education*, 23(4), 353–369. doi:10.1080/09500780902954273

Mercer, N., Wegerif, R., & Dawes, L. (1999). Children's talk and the development of reasoning in the classroom. *British Educational Research Journal*, 25(1), 95–111.

Muhonen, H., Rasku-Pettonen, H., Pakarinen, E., Poikkeus, A.-M., & Lerkkanen, M.-K. (2016). Scaffolding through dialogic teaching in early school classrooms. *Teaching and Teacher Education*, 55, 143–154. doi:10.1016/j.tate.2016.01.007

NESH (2016). *Guidelines for Research Ethics in the Social Sciences, Humanities, Law and Technology*. Retrieved from https://ahrecs.com/resources/norway-guidelines-for-research-ethics-in-the-social-sciences-humanities-law-and-theology-nesh-guidelines-2016

Norwegian Directorate for Education and Training (2016). *Mathematics 2P subject curriculum (MAT5–03)*. Oslo, Norway: Author.

Pimm, D. (2017). *Speaking Mathematically. Communication in Mathematics Classrooms*, 2nd edn. London: Routledge.

Rogoff, B. (1994). Developing understanding of the idea of communities of learners. *Mind, Culture, and Activity*, 1(4), 209–229.

Sfard, A., & Kieran, C. (2001). Cognition as communication: Rethinking learning-by-talking through multi-faceted analysis of students' mathematical interactions. *Mind, Culture and Activity*, 8(1), 42–76. doi:10.1207/S15327884MCA0801_04

Skorpen, L. B. (2006). Kunnskapstypar og arbeidsformer i matematikk i begynnar-opplæringa [Knowledges and methods in early mathematics]. In P. Haug (Ed.), *Begynnaropplæring og tilpassa undervisning, kva skjer i klasserommet?* (pp. 115–151) Bergen, Norway: Caspar Forlag.

Stake, R. (1995). *The Art of Case Study Research*. Thousand Oaks, CA: Sage Publications.

Strauss, A. L., & Corbin, J. M. (1998). *Basics of Qualitative Research. Techniques and Procedures for Developing Grounded Theory*, 2nd edn. Thousand Oaks, CA: Sage Publications.

van Oers, B. (2013). Communicating about number: Fostering young children's mathematical orientation in the world. In L. D. English & J. T. Mulligan (Eds.), *Reconceptualizing Early Mathematics Learning, Advances in Mathematics Education* (pp. 183–203). Dordrecht, Netherlands: Springer. doi:10.1007/978-94-007-6440-8_10

Wells, G. (1999). *Dialogic Inquiry. Toward a Sociocultural Practice and Theory of Education*. New York: Cambridge University Press.

Wells, G., & Auraz, R. (2006). Dialogue in the classroom. *Journal of the Learning Sciences*, 15(3), 379–428. doi:10.1207/s15327809jls1503_3

Wood, T. (1994). Patterns of interaction and the culture of mathematics classrooms. In S. Lerman (Ed.), *Cultural Perspectives on the Mathematics Classroom* (pp. 149–168). Dordrecht, Netherlands: Kluwer.

Yackel, E., & Cobb, P. (1996). Sociomathematical norms, argumentation, and autonomy in mathematics. *Journal for Research in Mathematics Education, 27*(5), 458–477. doi:10.2307/749877

7 Realizing data-driven changes and teacher agency in upper secondary schools through formative interventions

Lise Vikan Sandvik and Anne Berit Emstad

Introduction

In this chapter, we present a development work research (DWR) project aiming to understand the professional development of assessment literacy in Norwegian upper secondary schools. Over the last few decades, developing assessment literacy in and across schools has been an international concern, involving policy and practitioners, and different professional development programs have been developed and implemented to develop assessment literacy (Laveault, 2016). Due to the central role assessment plays in student learning and the key role teachers play in educational assessment (Black & Wiliam, 1998a; Wiliam & Thompson, 2007), there is a growing interest in assessment literacy as an integral part of teacher professionalism (DeLuca & Johnson, 2017; Laveault, 2016). Despite these compelling benefits, research shows that many teachers struggle to interpret assessment policies and to implement assessment practices related to contemporary policies and assessment theories (DeLuca & Johnson, 2017; Hopfenbeck, Flórez Petour, & Tolo, 2015; Popham, 2009).

The first challenge seems to be the complexity of the knowledge and skills being assessed. Assessment literacy involves a basic understanding of educational assessment as well as the related skills to apply, such as the various reliable measures of student achievement and how to use this information to facilitate valid instructional designs (DeLuca & Johnson, 2017; Popham, 2009, 2013; Stiggins, 2010; Xu & Brown, 2016). Second, the development of expertise among teachers and school leaders in assessment seems to be challenging (Laveault, 2016) when it comes to professional development and to generating change at the school level (Hill, 2016).

A major challenge in the Norwegian education system when it comes to implementing Assessment for Learning (AfL) programme – a government-initiated programme seen as a top-down implementation – has been the low accountability and transparency on the one hand and the high level of decentralization and autonomy among the teachers on the other (Hopfenbeck et al., 2015). The capacity to use assessment information appears to be a real challenge for teachers when the purpose is to support learning (Hopfenbeck, Tolo, Flórez Petour, & Masri, 2013; Laveault, 2016; Mausethagen, Prøitz, & Skedsmo, 2018).

Research recommends using professional development (PD) as a component of policy enactment (Laveault, 2016; Postholm, 2018), and bottom-up implementation processes characterized by trust, dialogue and high levels of teacher agency are considered important to resolve tensions in educational reforms to realize teacher-driven improvements in schools (Donohoo & Velasco, 2016; Hopfenbeck et al., 2015; Leahy & Wiliam, 2012). Also, the role of school leaders to facilitate and follow up the improvements is crucial, as is the university researchers who function as trainers or facilitators (Datnow & Hubbard, 2016; Postholm, 2015). Shared transformative agency happens when a group of teachers search collaboratively for a new form for productive activity (Virkkunen, 2006), but it also needs a form of collaboration that crosses established organizational boundaries (Kotter, 1996).

This chapter reports on a DWR project focusing on the school-based professional development of assessment literacy in 20 upper secondary schools (year 16–18) in Norway. The DWR project concerns the challenges related to the large-scale implementation of the AfL programme, and it is an attempt to link school development and teacher learning in classroom assessment practices. This goal is based on the assumption that learning occurring in school in cooperation with other teachers and a school administration that supports social learning is the best way for teachers to develop their own teaching, which, in turn, can lead to benefits for the students' learning (Postholm, 2018).

In this DWR project, the expansive learning cycle (Engeström, 1987) (see Chapters 1 and 2) stimulates teacher agency in school development processes. The purpose of this research is to explore how this project using an expansive learning approach (Sannino et al., 2016) would enhance teachers' assessment literacy and to build capacity in schools for more data-driven assessment practices. There is an increasing need for interventions that support not only teachers' involvement in transforming the system in which they are involved but also their development into a collective subject of change.

Assessment for learning implementations

There are numbers of examples of how the implementation of AfL programmes has been done successfully in small-scale projects in which the motivation to join the project is based on special arrangements (Baird, Hopfenbeck, Newton, Stobart, & Steen-Utheim, 2014; Black & Wiliam, 1998b; Hayward & Spencer, 2010; Hodgson & Pyle, 2010). Enacted as large-scale policy, however, there have been difficulties in their implementation (Hopfenbeck et al., 2013; Tam & Lu, 2011; Thompson & Wiliam, 2008).

When a school develops its assessment practice, well-established teaching routines can be challenged by new ideas. The literature discusses concerns about the lack of subject content knowledge and assessment skills among teachers and also calls for a broader understanding of the complexity of AfL programmes and the wider context of education (Black & Wiliam, 2018; Carless, 2005; Hodgson & Pyle, 2010; Nordenbo, Larsen, Tiftikçi, Wendt, & Østergaard, 2008; Thompson & Wiliam, 2008).

Another implementation concern is related to whether teachers are part of a whole-school commitment to the implementation and whether AfL communities have been created to generate change at the school level (Hill, 2016). The school's overall assessment literacy is a crucial aspect of such processes and includes the ability of teachers and school leaders to investigate students' achievements, to develop action plans based on assessment results to raise learning outcomes and to participate in the public debate on the use and abuse of such data (Black, Harrison, Lee, Marshall, & Wiliam, 2010; Fullan, 2001).

There are a number of models for how school development can take place, and according to Kennedy (2005), they can be categorized on a spectrum from the pure transfer of knowledge to more transformative-oriented and inquiry-based development models. In the transfer model, also called the 'cascade' model for school development, the existing knowledge introduced into the school has been dominant and also within the assessment field (Hutchinson & Hayward, 2005). New school development models, in contrast, emphasise an investigative and school-based approach to the professional learning of teachers and school leaders (Cochran-Smith & Lytle, 2009; Jiang & Hill, 2018; Timperley, 2011) in close collaboration with experts (Datnow & Hubbard, 2016). Successful school development processes, therefore, require knowledge, good relationships, trust, and meaningful collective experiences (Fullan, 2001). To establish and sustain AfL communities, creating professional learning communities has been recommended as a strategy (Birenbaum, Kimron, & Shilton, 2011; Hargreaves, 2013; Timperley, Wilson, Barrar, & Fung, 2007).

The Norwegian context

Norway, like many other countries, has been inspired by the AfL movement, and in 2006, the country underwent new curriculum reforms focusing on learning outcomes descriptions. A national AfL programme was launched in 2010 (and concluded in 2014) to develop assessment skills at school, especially AfL terms. Schools were motivated to participate through government funding. The national initiative was based on the four research-based principles of the AfL programme (Assessment Reform Group, 1999), which are also emphasised in the Norwegian Education Act as a student's right to receive assessment that promotes learning (Regulations of the Education Act, 2006).

The Norwegian authorities assumed that the relationship between policy and practice was quite simple. If the teachers received information about new ideas and the opportunity to reflect on them along with some tools for school development, the implementation would be relatively problem free. The idea was that some teachers would hear a little about the desired changes, and then they would spread these ideas or practices in their own classroom, among their own colleagues and to other schools. Experience from AfL programme in Norway shows that the transfer model (Kennedy, 2005) has good intentions but also several shortcomings in its practical implementation (Hopfenbeck et al., 2015). Furthermore, the cascade model does not consider the complexity of a school as an organization and how teachers learn with it (Hutchinson & Hayward, 2005; Sandvik & Buland, 2014).

The context of the DWR project

A county municipality in Norway and a university have entered into an agreement to undertake a DWR project aimed at school-based professional development of assessment literacy. The agreement covers all upper secondary schools in the county and lasts four years (20 schools and two years in each school), where the schools enrol in groups of four during the four-year period. The purpose of this DWR project is to develop the school's overall knowledge and understanding for the professional development of assessment literacy in a community of practice. A key objective is to help develop assessment literacy through inquiry-based teaching practices within the school subjects – that is, the teachers develop the capacity to do development work research (DWR) related to their teaching and assessment practices. This DWR emphasises school-based professional development (Cochran-Smith & Lytle, 2009), which implies that the school, including management and all participants in the competence initiative, actively participates in the development process within its own workplace (Bennett, 2011).

Researchers collaborate with the schools for a period of two years (see Figure 7.1 below). The university researchers, as collaboration partners, stress that they do not own the DWR project. The school and the school leadership are at the front of this school-based project. The first half year is used to assist the school leadership in anchoring the project among teachers. In addition, it involves a mapping phase to gain knowledge about the school's assessment literacy and experience with PD before starting the development work. Also, the school leadership often needs to gain more knowledge about how to lead PDs during the project. The expansive learning cycle (Engeström, 1987, 2001) (see Chapters 1 and 2) forms the basis for the work on assessment and PD, both for teachers and leaders; it stresses the use of data to investigate both the assessment practices and

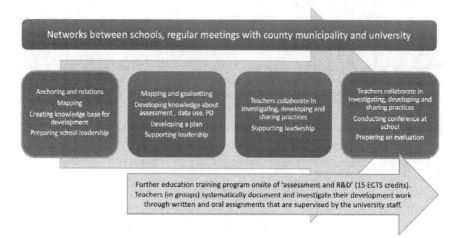

Figure 7.1 DWR model for PD and literacy assessment

the outcome of their DWR. The school leaders and teachers receive professional support onsite, and the university collaboration partners also give guidance and supervision between school visits to support the DWR. There are also established networks between schools, where school leaders have the possibility to share experiences, discuss problems, and learn from each other. Additionally, DWR could be both teacher training and further education in a flexible model. The further education training program 'assessment and R&D' awards participants 15 ECTS credits upon completing the program. This means that teachers in groups of three or four collaborate in the different phases of the expansive learning cycle (Engeström, 1987, 2001). In the further education programme, the teachers systematically document and investigate their practice in assignments, which are supervised by university researchers; the teachers also receive extra lectures and training in different but related topics. The university researchers also offer available resources, model texts, and writing frames to meet the various phases of the expansive learning cycle (Engeström, 1987, 2001). Figure 7.1 below gives an overview of the different processes in this DWR project.

In this chapter, we analyse data from two of the 20 participating schools. School 1 was a small upper secondary school (200+) with vocational studies, and School 2 was a large (700+) urban upper secondary school. These two schools were chosen as case schools because they chose different ways of working within the DWR project. School 1 chose the further education programme, whereas School 2 decided on teacher training without ECTS credits. Furthermore, School 1 is a school with vocational studies, and School 2 educates students for university studies. The following research question frame our research: *How can expansive learning enhance teachers' professional learning to develop data driven assessment practices in upper secondary school?*

Theoretical and methodological framework

This study is based on the cultural history activity theory (CHAT) (Wertsch, 1991). In this study, assessment is understood as situated social practice, which means that what is seen as legitimate knowledge and practice in the classroom is influenced by both traditions and the institutional discourse on assessment (Pryor & Crossouard, 2008). This approach to assessment may identify tensions and conflicts within the social practice where the assessment takes place. Black and Wiliam (2009) have applied CHAT to analyse how formative assessment may change what the teacher expects of her students and how different assessment tools can be used to change the assessment practice. Furthermore, studies giving greater insight into the effect of formative assessment has significant importance for how the teacher uses the knowledge she gains about the students' learning. Pryor and Crossouard (2008) have applied CHAT to study how the teacher's role as teacher, examiner, subject expert and learner affects the division of work and how the rules are formed in relation to the students. They claim that by being aware of the different roles, the students will find it easier to understand switching between them, which, in turn, will help them develop critical awareness of the educational discourse and its construction. These are examples of how CHAT could be applied in analysing assessment cultures on the macro level. On the micro level, Thorne (2004) has used CHAT to study how co-student assessment functions in a classroom and to examine the changes that are required to improve this assessment practice. On a more organizational level, Postholm et al. (2013) have used CHAT to understand how school-based competence development may contribute to developing professionalism in lower secondary school. In a review of studies based on CHAT, Roth and Lee (2007) emphasise the advantages of the theory in development-oriented studies, and the authors call for studies that use the theory on both the organizational and individual level.

Engeström introduced formative interventions as a way of putting teacher agency in the front in the design of research (Engeström, 2011; Sannino et al., 2016). A DWR project is a 'formative intervention' methodology (Engeström & Sannino, 2010), which promotes positive change in practices using a participatory, collaborative design. It also offers the following: a) interventions based on design done by the teachers or leaders; b) a collective design effort based on an expansive learning process, including participatory analyses and implementation phases; and c) insight into the capacity building work of schools as well as the differences in context-specific knowledge needs in the individual school's activities concerning data use. Within formative interventions, the expansive learning cycle (Engeström, 1987, 2001) is a model that could stimulate inquiry-based teaching practices and data use. The model is presented in detail in Chapters 1 and 2.

Formative interventions could also contribute to the development of theories, practices and tools that can be used in other schools and in teacher education to develop further knowledge about professional development in data-poor and autonomous contexts (Engeström, Sannino, & Virkkunen, 2014).

Teacher agency

In today's working life, teachers are expected to be creative, present initiatives and contribute to innovative solutions. They are expected to critically reflect on and develop their work practices; however, they are also expected to be committed and loyal to the school and as well as its policy. The desired agency is, therefore, to be considered participative, development oriented, innovative and compliant. Implementing the nationwide AfL programme showed that teachers were not fully committed or engaged in the top-down programme (Hopfenbeck et al., 2015; Sandvik & Buland, 2014). Practices developed mostly individually, and collaboration that crossed established organizational boundaries did not succeed.

Agency in CHAT is not the starting point (Virkkunen, 2006). The starting point is activity, and activity always has a creative and transformative aspect to it, which comes from its inner contradictions and movement. According to Virkkunen (2006), agency in CHAT boils down to the following question: how do participants become authors of their activity and give direction and shape to the activity? Within CHAT, studying agency means going to the roots of how agency emerges (Virkkunen, 2006).

The expansive learning cycle is the model used in this DWR project to stimulate teacher agency, question today's practice, analyse it, develop new solutions, investigate them and then make decisions about future practice (Engeström, 1987, 2001). The cycle is also used as a theoretical framework to understand the processes in the two schools analysed.

Boundary crossing and boundary objects

In this DWR project, the schools and the university collaborated to improve assessment literacy among teachers and school leaders, and 'in-service training' was introduced and created as the new boundary object. As Bowker and Star (1999) explain, 'Boundary objects are those objects that both inhabit several communities of practice and satisfy the informational requirements of each of them' (p. 297). In order to facilitate DWR, the university could provide teacher training and further education in a flexible model. The in-service training had two forms. In School 1, it took form as further education with exams giving 15 ECTS, whereas in School 2, only teacher training without exams and ECTS was chosen as DWR.

The in-service-training was intended to lead to profound changes due to assessment literacy in the two schools, as we examined the learning that took place for the participants – that is, teachers across departments and their leaders crossed community boundaries and engaged in the joint enterprise of teaching and learning mediated by the in-service training. The object was to improve literacy assessment across boundaries.

Boundary-crossing involves going into unfamiliar territories and requires cognitive retooling. New elements are introduced from one community of practice to another via boundary crossers, or 'brokers' (Wenger, 1998). These elements, referred to as 'boundary objects' (Star, 1989), often lead to the creation of new tools. Akkeman and Bakker (2011) argue that not only people but also objects can play an essential role in crossing boundaries.

Boundaries may be challenging, but they may also give opportunities for innovation and renewal, as crossing boundaries forces the teachers to reflect on their practices and assumptions, which can contribute to deeper learning (Wenger, McDermott, & Snyder, 2002). Boundary crossing within work gives opportunities to realize and explicate differences between practices and, thus, to learn something new about their own and others' practice (Akkerman & Bakker, 2011). In our case, two activity systems collaborated – the community of each participating school and the university. The collaboration intended to acquire expertise across boundaries.

Methodology and methods

A case study approach (Creswell, 2013) was used to investigate the DWR projects conducted in the two schools. We have used different sources of data, and all data reported in this chapter informs the study. Audio-recorded data from focus group interviews with school leaders (12 leaders: seven from School 1 and five from School 2) and teachers (40 teachers: between three and five in each focus group interview) before and after the interventions were used for this study. The interviews were transcribed by a researcher assistant and then analysed.

Other sources of data for this study included the following: school plan documents, teacher documents about the DWR (historical analysis, questions to investigate practice, theory and methods informing the DWR, and analyses of the results of the DWR), and field notes and observations from meetings and workshops with teachers and leaders during the intervention phase.

To analyse the data, we coded the data from each school using directed content analysis (Wenger, McDermott, & Snyder, 2002). We focused on how teacher collaboration in developing professional assessment practices were affected by the use of the expansive learning cycle as a model to follow in the DWR project and on how expertise was acquired across boundaries to bring the practice towards the object and to develop assessment literacy across boundaries. Then, we interrogated the coded data through theoretical categories suggested by the construct of the expansive learning cycle (Engeström, 1987, 2001), teacher assessment literacy in practice as conceptualized by Xu and Brown (2016) and of teacher transformative agency occurring through boundary objects (Wenger, 1998).

Findings

Four main findings were identified in relation to teacher collaboration and assessment literacy: 1) commitment and school leadership; 2) participation in community activities; 3) developing the assessment knowledge base; and 4) using data to inform and develop practice. In the table below (Table 7.1), we present how the two schools followed the different phases of the expansive learning cycle.

The role of commitment and school leadership

At School 1, they had organised their work in collaborative teams, and they were used to share and plan teaching with other teachers. Also, the leaders were used to be close to their teachers. They had expressed expectations that the actions should be integrated in their daily work, and they used much effort to anchor the project within the teachers. Also, as they expressed, they 'showed an open interest in the teachers' different projects, and the leaders participated in activities with the teachers.

In School 2, the situation was different. The school leadership had addressed challenges associated with an organization that was not used to such collaborative work between teachers or between leadership and teachers. At the closing meeting with the university, one of the leaders said the following: 'I am even more certain that we need to be closer to the teachers as leaders. I have learned that I have to be patient, be close on the coordinators, asking for their progress without telling them what to do.' However, one of the leaders felt they had succeeded in developing more collaboration within the teams:

Table 7.1 The DWR seen through the lens of the expansive learning cycle

	School 1 (further education programme, 15 ECTS credits)	School 2 (teacher training programme, without ECTS credits)
Questioning	Leadership expressed the need to further develop assessment literacy based on the student survey and needs expressed by the teachers. Even though the project was initiated by the municipality county, this initiative was based on a need expressed by the school leaders. Clear expectations were expressed by school leaders. Time to use and the teachers' role in the project were negotiated in meetings with the local representatives for the teacher's union at the school and in meetings with the university and the school, where the teachers defined their roles in the project. The words used included, positivity, engagement and willingness to collaborate and change. The teachers chose groups themselves.	Leadership expressed the need to further develop assessment literacy based on the student survey. Even though the project was initiated by the municipality county, this initiative was based on a need expressed by the school leaders. Clear expectations were expressed by school leaders. Time to use in the project was negotiated in meetings with the local representatives for the teacher's union at the school. Information about the project was given by the leaders and in meetings with university and school. The leaders set the groups in which the teachers should collaborate.
Historical empirical analyses	Obligatory working demands. In teams, they planned an action based on historical analysis. The plans were submitted for feedback from the university researcher several times during the process. The groups used theory in planning action. Teachers implemented and evaluated actions – gathering data and analyse.	Mandatory working demands. In teams, they planned an action based on experiences. Only a few groups based their plans on historic analyses. The plans were submitted for feedback from the university researcher once. Only a few groups used theory in planning action.
Modelling new solution Examining the new model	All the groups planned and implemented interventions. The groups used student data to plan and evaluate, and to work systematically with planning, implementation and evaluation. There was ongoing interaction between university and school community, including guidance on skype, written feedback, workshops and mini-conferences. The university and school had regularly contact. The leaders facilitated and supported interaction between university and school at the teacher level.	All the groups planned and implemented interventions. Only two of the groups used data in planning and evaluation. The university met leaders regularly and gave written feedback to teachers at two mini-conferences. The university did not meet all teacher teams.

	School 1 (further education programme, 15 ECTS credits)	School 2 (teacher training programme, without ECTS credits)
Implementing the new model Reflecting on the process	Teachers presented the results on a conference at school. Teachers wrote written assignments as exam for the further education. Teachers had developed new practices they would use directly in their teaching practices or would further develop. The leaders had a closing meeting with school and university.	Teachers presented the results on a conference at school. Teachers didn't come up with written work for documentation. Some teachers had developed new practices they would use directly in their teaching practices or would further develop. The leaders had a closing meeting with school and university.

There has been close cooperation between department head, subject coordinators and teachers. And we're not done yet. It is a development that will continue. We had great doubts and we had a bad start. But we have come very well into our goals. We didn't want small stunts. We wanted to have long-term development work.

Participation in community activities

The teachers at the two schools had different experiences connected to collaboration; also, the local values and rules concerning collaboration were totally different. Some teachers at School 2 worried about the development projects coming from outside the school. One teacher asked: 'Why do we need to collaborate more? Does it mean I'm not doing a good job?' However, as the project gradually got settled, many teachers found that the project had been important considering the community of practice of the different departments and that they had increased knowledge about assessment. They found they actually could discuss pedagogical practices with colleagues they never had talked to before.

At School 1, this project stimulated more systematic collaboration; sharing between groups was especially valuable for the teachers. One important thing for the systematic work was how the leadership put the collaborative work on the time schedule for teachers – one hour per week was dedicated for this work. Some of them also had the opportunity to present their work for teachers at other schools, and one teacher said this was 'extremely motivating and stimulating'.

Developing the assessment knowledge base

The main difference between the projects in the two schools was that in the School 1, almost every teacher wanted to go through the project and finish the education programme, including all of its obligations and assignments. Many of the teachers at School 1 had not finished a master's degree because they came from other occupations as mechanists, healthcare professions or other occupations taught in the school. Therefore, they felt a need for more formal education. At

School 2, the situation was different. Most of the teachers had a master's degree and were teachers at a school preparing students for university studies. They did not feel the same need for this formal competence.

At School 1, the teachers worked hard to develop relevant research questions; they read assessment theory, chose research methods fitting their research questions and wrote written assignments. During the whole process, they interacted closely with the university, as they got feedback, support and theoretical advice from university members during the different phases of the DWR. This is what one group wrote in its assignment:

> We believe that as a group we are left with a great benefit from the work. We developed our assessment expertise, both through practical actions and the theoretical knowledge through the project. This will affect our teaching and assessment practices to a large extent in the future.

At School 2, the work developed in other directions. The university mainly interacted with the leaders but not with the teachers. The teachers planned their work alone in groups and did not want much interaction with the collaboration partners from the university to investigate the practice, neither for theory nor for methods. It is not clear how much the leaders interacted in the processes either.

The leaders from School 2 reported from their meetings with the student council. The students had experienced various practices concerning assessment for learning – something that the students found very confusing and unfair. They had clearly expressed to the leadership that they wanted teachers who can use assessment criteria in their teaching practice. It appears that assessment has generated more interest among the students through the project.

Using data to inform and develop practice

The expansive learning cycle suggests that the teachers and researchers (collaboration partners from the university) should use data about the participants' learning to inform the project – both in the historical and actual-empirical analysis as well as in the evaluation phase. At School 1, two of the groups reported that they found the evaluation gave useful information about the students' learning processes that they reported, which would be used to develop this project even further. Other groups based their information on the teachers' experiences and shared their reflections on what they had tried. Data were also collected and used by the teachers in order to evaluate the influence of their DWR projects in their classrooms and to write the report that served as the exam of the further education. At School 2, data use was a new turn in their collaboration and sharing practices; the project challenged the way collaboration was done. One teacher expressed the use of data this way: 'it has totally changed how I teach and assess my students work'. However, only a few of the groups evaluated the influence of their DWR projects on student learning.

Discussion

Teacher agency

The findings indicate that DWR projects can contribute to transform teachers' agency using an expansive learning approach and enable them to understand the importance of data use to enhance students' learning (Sannino et al., 2016; Virkkunen, 2006). This project with the further education programme followed by most of the teachers in School 1, seem to have stimulated a change in the activity system at the school level. The further education programme created a closer relationship with the university, as there were obligatory tasks to be delivered and upon which to receive feedback. This specialization may have led to increased understanding and, thus, increased commitment, as the teachers find that this has significance for improving their own practice.

This capacity to go into DWR seems to depend on the teachers' openness and willingness to do inquiries into their own and others' practices. The further education programme – having clear expectation tasks to be done as well as access to the expertise provided through feedback by the university (Postholm, 2016) – may also have strengthened the commitment to the project and created a collective motive to act on the object (Engeström & Sannino, 2010).

Creating a culture in schools that encourages the using of data to inform practice is a goal (Robinson, 2011). Our findings indicate that teacher agency is transformative, and the changes in schools seem to be durable when commitment to the activity is established. In School 2, the school leaders where more reluctant to stress the use of data or to express clear expectations, and because of this reluctance, it seems that the teachers continued their habit of just sharing experiences about practice without properly exploring it. They were operating as reflective practitioners but not going into a more inquiry-based teaching practice (Hutchinson & Hayward, 2005; Kennedy, 2005). The expertise of the university became not a part of the progression of the DWR, as it was in School 1. Expansive learning is a way to develop new activity, a new form of collective practice. This development seems to happen if the commitment to the activity is established. Specialization can lead to increased understanding and commitment when the teachers find that it can improve their practice.

The school leaders are responsible for establishing and developing a shared understanding and interaction practice (Robinson, 2011). In the schools that have had success in developing an inquiry-based assessment culture, the leaders have managed to establish a culture in the school where learning and development are pervasive characteristics of the school culture.

Data use and PD

This study further illustrates how collaborative learning activities in PD act as a trigger of self-awareness and are an important source of feedback on professional learning achievements among teachers (Hill, 2016). These activities give insight into the capacity building work of schools and highlight the differences in the knowledge needs of the schools concerning PD and data use when developing assessment literacy (Hopfenbeck et al., 2015; Mausethagen et al., 2018).

Teachers at School 1 are more collectively motivated towards the object; they also have increased interaction with the university when planning and investigating their teaching. The school leadership established new arenas for collaboration; the teachers experienced the demands as stimulating, and they felt inspired by having access to external expertise. In contrast, at School 2, the teachers were less committed to interventions and were unwilling to do a thorough analysis or use data in their investigations.

Using interviews and written reports as research data has clear limitations, as their conclusions may be a result of compliance with the perceived expectations for the work the teachers are supposed to do, and not truthful accounts of their collaborative learning processes. However, given our conceptualization of this DWR project as boundary crossing, these data could also be considered boundary objects (Akkerman & Bakker, 2011; Star & Griesemer, 1989) designed specifically to assist teachers and researchers in navigating between new borders.

Our study shows that commitment is important when development projects are initiated from outside the school, and simply to start with the needs of the schools and teachers is not enough in order to engage the teachers in DWR. Similarly, school leaders cannot simply identify the school's needs for development based on a student survey in order to gain teachers commitment to engage in DWR. Our data indicates that further education as a collective activity may lead to increased commitment, as it strengthens the need for interaction and for the use of expertise across boundaries, and this may transform teacher agency. When there is collective motivation towards the common object and when needs are thoroughly investigated, DWR can support the development of PD within schools that are driven by teachers. The study can contribute to the development of theories, practices and tools to be used to develop further knowledge about professional development and data use in data-poor and autonomous contexts, where DWR projects, expansive learning and transformative agency are the main characteristics of these methodological and theoretical foundations.

References

Akkerman, S. F., & Bakker, A. (2011). Boundary crossing and boundary objects. *Review of Educational Research*, 81(2), 132–169. doi:10.3102/0034654311404435

Assessment Reform Group (1999). *Assessment for Learning: Beyond the 'Black Box'*. Cambridge: University of Cambridge School of Education.

Baird, J.-A., Hopfenbeck, T. N., Newton, P., Stobart, G., & Steen-Utheim, A. T. (2014). State of the Field Review Assessment and Learning. In *Report for the Norwegian Knowledge Centre for Education*. doi:10.1016/j.celrep.2015.12.030

Bennett, R. E. (2011). Formative assessment: A critical review. *Assessment in Education: Principles, Policy & Practice*, 18(1), 5–25. doi:10.1080/0969594X.2010.513678

Birenbaum, M., Kimron, H., & Shilton, H. (2011). Nested contexts that shape assessment for learning: School-based professional learning community and classroom culture. *Studies in Educational Evaluation*, 37, 35–48. doi:10.1016/j.stueduc.2011.04.001

Black, P., & Wiliam, D. (1998a). Assessment and classroom learning. *Assessment in Education: Principles, Policy & Practice*, 5(1), 7–74. doi:10.1080/0969595980050102

Black, P., & Wiliam, D. (1998b). Assessment and classroom learning. *Assessment in Education: Principles, Policy & Practice*, 5(1), 7–74. doi:10.1080/0969595980050102

Black, P., & Wiliam, D. (2009). Developing the theory of formative assessment. *Educational Assessment, Evaluation and Accountability*, 21(1), 5–31. doi:10.1007/s11092-008-9068-5

Black, P., & Wiliam, D. (2018). Classroom assessment and pedagogy. *Assessment in Education: Principles, Policy & Practice*, 1–25. doi:10.1080/0969594X.2018.1441807

Black, P., Harrison, C., Lee, C., Marshall, B., & Wiliam, D. (2010). *Assessment for Learning: Putting it into Practice*. London: Open University Press.

Bowker, G. C., & Star, S. L. (1999). *Sorting Things Out. Classification and its Consequences*. Cambridge, MA: MIT Press.

Carless, D. (2005). Prospects for the implementation of assessment for learning. *Assessment in Education: Principles, Policy & Practice*, 12(1), 39–54. doi:10.1080/0969594042000333904

Cochran-Smith, M., & Lytle, S. L. (2009). *Inquiry as stance: Practitioner research for the next generation*. New York: Teachers College Press.

Creswell, J. W. (2013). *Qualitative Inquiry & Research Design: Choosing among Five Approaches*, 3rd edn. Los Angeles: Sage.

Datnow, A., & Hubbard, L. (2016). Teacher capacity for and beliefs about data-driven decision making: A literature review of international research. *Journal of Educational Change*, 17(1), 7–28. doi:10.1007/s10833-015-9264-2

DeLuca, C., & Johnson, S. (2017). Developing assessment capable teachers in this age of accountability. *Assessment in Education: Principles, Policy and Practice*, 24(2), 121–126. doi:10.1080/0969594X.2017.1297010

Donohoo, J., & Velasco, M. (2016). *Collaborative Inquiry for Educators: A Facilitator's Guide to School Improvement*. Thousand Oaks, CA: Corwin, A SAGE company.

Engeström, Yrjö. (1987). *Learning by Expanding*. Helsinki: Orienta-Konsultit Oy.

Engeström, Y. (2001). *Expansive Learning at Work. Toward an Activity-Theoretical Reconceptualization*. London: Institute of Education, University of London.

Engeström, Yrjö. (2011). From design experiments to formative interventions. *Theory & Psychology*, 21(5), 598–628. doi:10.1177/0959354311419252

Engeström, Yrjö, & Sannino, A. (2010). Studies of expansive learning: Foundations, findings and future challenges. *Educational Research Review*, 5(1), 1–24. doi:10.1016/j.edurev.2009.12.002

Engeström, Yrjö, Sannino, A., & Virkkunen, J. (2014). On the methodological demands of formative interventions. *Mind, Culture, and Activity*, 21(2), 118–128. doi:10.1080/10749039.2014.891868

Fullan, M. G. (2001). *Leading in a Culture of Change*. San Francisco: Jossey-Bass.

Hargreaves, A. (2013). Assessment for learning and teacher learning communities: UK teachers' experiences. *Teaching Education*, 24(3), 327–344.

Hayward, L., & Spencer, E. (2010). The complexities of change: formative assessment in Scotland. *Curriculum Journal*, 21(2), 161–177. doi:10.1080/09585176.2010.480827

Hill, M. F. (2016). Assessment for learning community: Learners, teachers and policy-makers. In D. Wyse, L. Hayward, & J. Pandya (Eds.), *The SAGE Handbook of Curriculum, Pedagogy and Assessment* (pp. 772–789). London: SAGE.

Hodgson, C., & Pyle, K. (2010). *A Literature Review of Assessment for Learning in Science*. Slough: NFER.

Hopfenbeck, T. N., Flórez Petour, M. T., & Tolo, A. (2015). Balancing tensions in educational policy reforms: Large-scale implementation of assessment for learning in Norway. *Assessment in Education: Principles, Policy & Practice*, 22(1), 44–60. doi:10.1080/0969594X.2014.996524

Hopfenbeck, T. N., Tolo, A., Flórez Petour, M. T., & Masri, Y. El. (2013). Balancing trust and accountability? The assessment for learning programme in Norway: A governing complex education systems case study. *OECD Education Working Papers*, No. 97, OECD Publishing, Paris. doi:10.1787/5k3txnpqlsnn-en

Hsieh, H.-F., & Shannon, S. E. (2005). Three approaches to qualitative content analysis. *Qualitative Health Research*, 15(9), 1277–1288. doi:10.1177/1049732305276687

Hutchinson, C., & Hayward, L. (2005). The journey so far: Assessment for learning in Scotland. *Curriculum Journal*, 16(2), 225–248. doi:10.1080/09585170500136184

Jiang, H., & Hill, M. F. (2018). Teacher learning and classroom assessment. In H. Jiang & M. F. Hill (Eds.), *Teacher Learning with Classroom Assessment* (pp. 1–17). Singapore: Springer.

Kennedy, A. (2005). Models of continuing professional development: A framework for analysis. *Journal of In-Service Education*, 31(2), 235–250. doi:10.1080/13674580500200277

Konkola, R., Tuomi-Gröhn, T., Lambert, P., & Ludvigsen, S. (2007). Promoting learning and transfer between school and workplace. *Journal of Education and Work*, 20(3), 211–228. doi:10.1080/13639080701464483

Kotter, J. P. (1996). *Leading Change*. Boston, MA: Harvard Business School Press. Retrieved from www.hbs.edu/faculty/Pages/item.aspx?num=137

Laveault, D. (2016). Building capacity: Professional development and collaborative learning about assessment. In D. Laveault & L. Allal (Eds.), *Assessment for Learning: Meeting the Challenge of Implementation* (pp. 131–143). Cham, Heidelberg, New York, Dordrecht, London: Springer.

Leahy, S., & Wiliam, D. (2012). From teachers to schools: Scaling up professional development for formative assessment. In J. Gardner (Ed.), *Assessment and Learning* (pp. 49–71). doi:10.4135/9781446250808.n4

Mausethagen, S., Prøitz, T., & Skedsmo, G. (2018). Teachers' use of knowledge sources in 'result meetings': thin data and thick data use. *Teachers and Teaching*, 24(1), 37–49. doi:10.1080/13540602.2017.1379986

Nordenbo, S. E., Larsen, M. S., Tiftikçi, N., Wendt, R. E., & ØstergaardS. (2008). *Lærerkompetanser og elevers læring i barnehage og skole. Et systematisk review utført for Kunnskapsdepartementet, Oslo*. Aarhus: Universitetet i Aarhus.

Popham, W. J. (2009). Assessment literacy for teachers: Faddish or fundamental? *Theory into Practice*, 48(1), 4–11. doi:10.1080/00405840802577536

Popham, W. J. (2013). On serving two masters: Formative and summative teacher evaluation. *Principal leadership*, 13(7), 18–22.

Postholm, M. B. (2015). Methodologies in cultural–historical activity theory: The example of school-based development. *Educational Research*, 57(1), 43–58. doi:10.1080/00131881.2014.983723

Postholm, M. B. (2016). Collaboration between teacher educators and schools to enhance development. *European Journal of Teacher Education*, 39(4), 452–470. doi:10.1080/02619768.2016.1225717

Postholm, M. B. (2018). Teachers' professional development in school: A review study. *Cogent Education*, 5(1), 1522781–1522781. doi:10.1080/2331186X.2018.1522781

Postholm, M. B., Dahl, T., Engvik, G., Fjørtoft, H., Irgens, E. J., Sandvik, L. V., & Wæge, K. (2013). *En gavepakke til ungdomstrinnet? En undersøkelse av piloten for den nasjonale satsingen på skolebasert kompetanseutvikling*. Oslo: Akademika forlag.

Pryor, J., & Crossouard, B. (2008). A socio-cultural theorisation of formative assessment. *Oxford Review of Education*, 34(1), 1–20. doi:10.1080/03054980701476386

Regulations of the Education Act (2006). *Regulations of the Education Act*, paragraph 3.

Robinson, V. (2011). *Student-Centred Leadership*. San Francisco: Jossey Bass.

Roth, W.-M., & Lee, Y.-J. (2007). "Vygotsky's Neglected Legacy": Cultural-Historical Activity Theory. *Review of Educational Research*, 77(2), 186–232. doi:10.3102/0034654306298273

Sandvik, L. V., & Buland, T. (2014). *Vurdering i skolen. Utvikling av kompetanse og fellesskap. Sluttrappport fra prosjektet 'Forskning på individuell vurdering i skolen' (FIVIS)*. Trondheim: NTNU.

Sannino, A., Engeström, Y., & Lemos, M. (2016). Formative interventions for expansive learning and transformative agency. *Journal of the Learning Sciences*, 25(4), 599–633. doi:10.1080/10508406.2016.1204547

Star, S. L., & Griesemer, J. R. (1989). Institutional ecology, 'translations' and boundary objects: Amateurs and professionals in Berkeley's Museum of Vertebrate Zoology, 1907–1939. *Social Studies of Science*, 19(3), 387–420. doi:10.1177/030631289019003001

Stiggins, R. J. (2010). Essential formative assessment competencies for teachers and school leaders, In H. L. Andrade & G. J. Cizek, (Eds.) *Handbook of Formative Assessment* (pp. 233–250). New York, NY: Taylor & Francis.

Tam, H. P., & Lu, Y. J. (2011). Developing assessment for learning in a large-scale programme. In R. Berry & B. Adamson (Eds.), *Assessment Reform in Education: Policy and Practice. Education in the Asia-Pacific Region: Issues, Concerns and Prospects, Vol. 14*, (pp. 185–196). London: Springer.

Thompson, M., & Wiliam, D. (2008). Tight but loose: A conceptual framework for scaling up school reforms. In C. Wylie (Ed.), *Tight but Loose: Scaling up Teacher Professional Development in Diverse Contexts* (pp. 1–44). Princeton, NJ: Educational Testing Service (ETS).

Thorne, S. L. (2004). Cultural historical activity theory and the object of innovation. In O. St. John, K. van Esch, & E. Schalkwijk (Eds.), *New Insights into Foreign Language Learning and Teaching* (pp. 51–70). Frankfurt: Peter Lang Verlag.

Timperley, H., Wilson, A., Barrar, H., & Fung, I. (2007). *Teacher professional learning and development*. Ministry of Education, University of Auckland.

Timperley, Helen. (2011). *Realizing the Power of Professional Learning*. New York: Open University Press. doi:10.1111/j.1467-8535.2012.01297_6.x

Virkkunen, J. (2006). Dilemmas in building shared transformative agency. *Activités*, 03(3–1). doi:10.4000/activites.1850

Wenger, E. (1998). *Communities of Practice, Learning, Meaning and Identity*. Cambridge: Cambridge University Press.

Wenger, E., McDermott, R., & Snyder, W. M. (2002). *Cultivating Communities of Practice*. Boston, MA: Harvard Business School Press.

Wertsch, J. V. (1991). *Voices of the Mind. A Sociocultural Approach to Mediated Action*. Cambridge, MA: Harvard University Press.

Wiliam, D., & Thompson, M. (2007). Integrating assessment with instruction: What will it take to make it work? In C.A. Dwyer (Ed.) *The Future of Assessment: Shaping Teaching and Learning* (pp. 53–82). Mahwah, NJ: Erlbaum.

Xu, Y., & Brown, G. T. L. (2016). Teacher assessment literacy in practice: A reconceptualization. *Teaching and Teacher Education*, 58, 149–162. doi:10.1016/j.tate.2016.05.010

8 A study of case-based problem-solving work in groups of principals participating in a school leadership programme

Kirsten Foshaug Vennebo

Introduction

International research has documented a variety of strategies for fostering the professional development of school leaders (Lumby, Crow, & Pashiardis, 2008; Young, Crow, Murphy, & Ogawa, 2009). In leadership development programmes, case-based instruction is a widely used strategy (Taylor, Cordeiro, & Chrispeels, 2009). The goal of using case-based instruction is to challenge students to struggle with multifaceted issues of the cases. This chapter explores problem solving among groups of principals when working on a problem situation concerning school practices presented to them by a case. Empirical research on case-based instruction indicates that discussing cases and their attributes provides a potentially viable approach for increasing leadership knowledge and skills (Avolio, Reichard, Hannah, Walumbwa, & Chan, 2009; Yukl, 2010). First, case-based or experiential learning allows leaders to make sense of complex, unfolding situations, to understand the expectations of followers and to formulate visions and new practices (Mumford, Peterson, Robledo, & Hester, 2012). Second, case-based knowledge appears to be relatively easily acquired, such as through narratives that present actors who are engaged in problem solving (Kolodner, 1997). Third, evidence also indicates that how case methods facilitate learning depends on the content, organisation and application of cases in leadership development programmes (cf. Mumford et al., 2012). However, existing research has paid little attention to problem-solving work when casedbased instruction is utilised as a strategy for school leadership development in formalised leadership education. A possible explanation for this is that the research on case-based instruction in leader education typically relies on surveys and interviews and not on observations or micro-analyses of what is really happening when professionals work in authentic situations (Mumford et al., 2012).

This chapter reports on how groups of principals *do* problem-solving work based on a case narrative and addresses the following research questions: *What characterises problem solving in groups of principals when working on a problem situation concerning school practices presented to them by a case?* Empirically, the chapter is grounded in a larger study of case-based instruction that was used in a National School Leadership Programme in Norway, situated at a university, for newly appointed school leaders

(Hybertsen et al., 2014). The case concerns complex issues related to accountability. It was shaped and illustrated by a narrative about a combined primary and secondary school, the Blueberry School.

The chapter begins by introducing The National School Leadership Programme and the case narrative, after which I discuss cultural-historical activity theory (CHAT) as an analytical approach for investigating problem-solving work in the context of case-based instruction within the school leadership programme. In the next section, I provide an overview of the methodological approach before presenting an analysis of the research findings. This is followed by a discussion with some concluding remarks.

The National School Leadership Programme

Norwegian authorities, influenced by the OECD project, 'Improving School Leadership', launched a nationwide education programme in 2009 for newly appointed principals; here, the goal was to improve their qualifications as leaders and to support national policies. The National School Leadership Programme was built around five curriculum themes that the Norwegian Minister of Education and Research tendered for: students' learning, management and administration, cooperation and organisation building, development and change, and the leadership role (Hybertsen et al., 2014). According to Timperley (2011), one of the fundamental principles of professional learning is having multiple opportunities to learn and apply information. A process of ongoing reflection and discussion that challenges the current way of thinking is valuable in building new practices. In the programme, case-based instruction and group coaching have been used to influence practice and build leadership capacity, including developing ethical considerations (Aas, 2016; Aas & Vavik, 2015). In the current chapter, I draw on video data from problem-solving work performed by groups of principals based on the case narrative of the Blueberry School.

The school case narrative – Blueberry School

Blueberry School is a combined primary and secondary school with 548 students, 57 teachers and 24 assistants. The leadership team consists of the principal and three designated leaders who lead the teaching teams (Grades 1–4, Grades 5–7 and Grades 8–10). Three years ago, it was decided that the secondary school should merge with the new primary school. A newly appointed principal has been leading the school for two years, and the school is waiting for new buildings to be constructed because the classrooms are located on different sites. However, due to weak local government finances, the buildings will not be completed for at least two years. Given the poor student performance, change is needed. The principal has stated that the teachers in Grades 5–7 are willing to change, while the teachers in Grades 8–10 are satisfied with their instruction and are therefore reluctant to change. In a meeting with the superintendent, the principal was confronted with the students' performance results, which were lower than expected, especially in Grades 8–10. He was also informed that the superintendent had received two phone calls from parents with complaints about bullying and poor well-being among the pupils. In addition, the superintendent pointed out that the employee survey showed that satisfaction among the staff was lower compared to the previous two years. The principal was concerned about the situation, and on behalf of the superintendent, he had to be informed about the situation and prepare an action plan for improvement by their next meeting. The principals in the National Leadership Programme were invited to discuss how to best handle the situation and what to include in a concrete plan for action.

A CHAT perspective on problem-solving work in the context of case-based instruction

Problem-solving work related to organisational issues involves challenging, ambiguous and open-ended negotiations (Engeström, 1999, 2011). It can be assumed that although such work based on case-based instruction may be driven by the overriding purposes of those designing the cases, the collective negotiation and instantiation of such purposes involves demanding discussions that are often imbued with tensions (cf. Vennebo & Ottesen, 2014).

The interplay between overriding purposes and negotiations between practitioners working together to realize them thus becomes crucial to understanding how problem solving emerges in the context of case-based instruction within school leadership programmes. Therefore, to grasp how groups of school principals are working on the problem situations presented to them by a case concerning school practices, it is important to explore the purposeful work through which the interplay emerges and takes shape. CHAT provides the conceptual tools required to examine situated work activities in depth and will therefore be used in the present study.

Work related to case-based instruction, such as the work of the groups of principals explored in this study, may be seen as taking place in an *experimental setting* in CHAT (Van der Veer & Valsiner, 1991). To experimental settings the participating subjects always bring their own set of conceptual tools, mediating means, that the instructors cannot control externally in any rigid way. As such, the experimental setting becomes a context of investigation in which the instructors can introduce the participants to uniquely framed objects to be solved and can manipulate their structure in order to trigger, but not 'produce', the participants' *framing and constructions of solutions* to the objects. In experimental settings, the partners' interests converge during negotiations over *the objects and conceivable outcomes*, against their shared responsibility (cf. Engeström, 2011).

Although uniquely framed objects may motivate and give meaning to situated work activities, such objects are ambiguous and open to interpretation and contestation. At any moment in the evolving activities, objects may be specified, modified or adjusted in the local instantiation of the object. In discussions, and incidental to the work process or issues emanating from their experiences, the groups' members direct their attention to different aspects of the object. Upon analysing (more or less systematically) the situation, the groups could end up with an object (i.e., a narrower problem framing) that suggests a direction for the problem situations at hand (cf. Engeström, 2008). However, the objects do not guide the actors in predetermined directions; rather, they set up a 'horizon for possible actions' (Engeström, 1999, p. 381). Within these horizons, the creation of potential solutions to the problems are closely related to the 'search actions' of object construction and redefinition, often set in motion by agentive individuals in the form of performing open-minded and future-oriented questioning actions.

Work on problem situations is enacted in processes associated with the redefinition and adjustment of objects, often in the form of problem finding/definition and problem solving (Engeström, 1999). Problem finding/definition refers to the sequential and interactional modes of actions in the form of questioning and analysing in relation to the situations at hand in order to determine the causes or explanatory dynamics of the emergent tensions inherent in the problems and challenges of practices. Problem-solving is premised on these kinds of actions, informed contextual analysis, as well as on interpretations of the problems and participants' capacities to make these interpretations explicit through the internalisation and externalisation of perspectives (Edwards, 2009; Engeström, 1999). Perspectives are *'views from somewhere'* and refer to 'the understanding participants construct about themselves in relation to the context in which they find themselves' (Holland & Reeves, 2001, p. 273). Perspectives are participant- situated interpretations of the problems at hand, which build on their experiences, histories and knowledge. In object-oriented activity, participants give voice to distinct perspectives as *potential resources* to the activity. This means that work on problems of practice is collective and collaborative in nature; it occurs in the interactions between individuals and the use of resources involved, as intertwined kinds of interactions consisting of problem framing/ definition and problem solving. As such, the participants in this study drew on their perspectives (their respective bodies of experiences, histories and knowledge) from a diverse set of educational practices as well as educational information activated by the representations in the case (understood as information given in the case) as resources for the actual problem solving. In this sense, the uniquely framed object is the assignment on behalf of the superintendent, the perspectives are the respective bodies of knowledge the principals bring into the work on the object, and the representations are, for example, information about the challenges of practice.

It is important to note that although work activities may share common ground and be motivated by common objects, they are not integrated wholes in which the parts move in harmony; the common objects that link purposefully working participants are multi-voiced and include different motives and resources that potentially may be contradictory (cf. Miettinen, 2005). Thus, although participants work towards common purposes, the valuation of the resources brought together for problem framing/definition and problem solving may vary because motives and needs differ among the participants. This could provoke tensions and sometimes lead to struggles and contesting positions.

Tensions and contradictions can be springboards for the expansion of organisational routines and the transformation of tools and practices. However, it is important to note that they do not necessarily trigger innovative resolution efforts or the expansive construction and redefinition of the problems being worked on. Thus, when exploring how groups of principals are working on the problem situations presented to them by a case concerning school practices, the question of whether tensions occur, and the subsequent ways in which the tensions are recognised and worked on, are of particular interest. In addition, we cannot abstract the situated actions and interactions from the socio-cultural contexts in which they take place. This layer adds a socio-historical aspect to the interaction. We cannot reduce the context to something that simply 'surrounds'; instead, the context is interwoven in actions and interactions. Socio-historical contexts both afford space for and constrain the practitioners' actions (cf. Edwards, 2010; Engeström, 1999). Thus, in order to understand how problem-solving emerges in groups of principals in the context of case-based instruction within school leadership programmes, it is necessary to study the interplay between group members and the nature of the problems they work on, as well as to consider the cultural-historical resources in use. CHAT offers conceptual and methodological tools to aid the analysis of work on problem situations. These tools enable researchers to unveil and explain the complexity of the actions and resources brought together for problem solving and the solutions involved in the work. To date, these kinds of actions and resources have received modest attention in empirical research that has investigated case-based problem-solving work among principals participating in leadership development programmes.

Methodology

As explained in the introduction, the study this chapter builds on is part of a larger study. This study was conducted as a qualitative observation study of 12 groups which were composed of five principals representing different school levels, school size and geographical location in Norway. Each group discussed, about 60 minutes in length, the Blueberry School case and various assignments to be worked on. The 12 group discussions were video recorded, and the resulting material consisted of 12 hours of video data. This chapter is based on video data recordings from four of the group discussions, which were based on the case and the assignment referred to in this chapter (four group discussions with about one hour from each discussion, for a total of four hours). All students agreed that the group discussions could be video recorded, and that the video data could be used in research. The data were analysed by using the Videograph software programme and were then transcribed into text that, in sum, comprised 41 A4 pages.

The dataset covers the entire problem-solving trajectories of the four groups. The video data recordings made it possible to go through the principal groups' unfolding interactions repeatedly during the video analysis. This allowed me to follow the principal groups' interaction in terms of what they performed in relation to the case narrative. In the analysis, I focused on how the participants performed as the principal groups gradually arrived at a resolution and direction. In order to illustrate what characterises the problem-solving work of groups of principals, I chose selected sequences from one of the group discussions about these kinds of problems. The reason for selecting these data was that the selected sequences constitute instances of recurring 'scripts' that are representative of the way the problem situation concerning the school practices are worked on and how the group of principals gradually arrived at a resolution and direction for the problem at hand. The selected excerpts constitute the basis for close-up analysis and were chosen because each, in different ways, constitutes turns in attention, actions and interactions towards the common object, and the use of resources. I have labelled them as follows: 1) Revealing and framing challenges, 2) Examining challenges, 3) Further examining of challenges and suggesting directions, and 4) Following up activities and further directions.

I used interaction analysis to analyse the video data (Jordan & Henderson, 1995). This kind of analysis is well suited for studying actions and interactions within and between settings. Moreover, it is particularly useful for studying interactions between participants (like members of a group of principals) and the case representations that came into play in different ways by paying close attention to what is performed and done.

One limitation of the study must be noted. The study represents a cognitive approach to leadership development and reflects the principals' perceptions, not their actual leadership activity (Mumford et al., 2012). On the other hand, there are indications that the subject matter is recognisable to them, and that they relate their reflections to similar problems and possible activities in their own practices.

Problem-solving work in groups of principals

The problem-solving work started with the instructor/researcher reading the case loudly for the group before she handed out the written case narrative to each of the group members. Then, she emphasised that the principal of the Blueberry School was concerned about the critical situation and had to prepare an action plan for improvement for the next meeting with the superintendent within a short time. Finally, the instructor/researcher reminded the groups about their task and the time allocated to the work: Imagine yourself in the role of the leadership group at the Blueberry School and discuss how to understand and go about the critical situation and what the principal should include in a concrete plan for action to be presented for the superintendent shortly within a frame of one hour.

In the analysis of the problem-solving work that follows, you will meet the principals Sara, John, Steven, Ann and Karen, who led the problem-solving work trajectory.

Revealing and framing challenges

As the problem-solving work in the group started, Karen pointed out how to lead the work, first in a way that encouraged the group members to 'think loud' about the critical situation at the Blueberry School and to identify and sort out the challenges at hand. Excerpt 1 below illustrates how the group of principals identified and framed challenges as a part of the initial problem-solving work.

Excerpt 1

1:	Karen	Yes, maybe we need to start with sorting out what the challenges here are. A new principal is in place in a relatively new school. What exactly are his challenges? Should we try to sort them out a bit? Mm.... A new elementary school and an old secondary school.
2:	Steven	It's bullying issues.
3:	Karen	Yes
4:	Steven	Weak academic results.
5:	Karen	Yes
6:	Sara	Low employee satisfaction.
7:	Karen	Yes, well-being
8:	Ann	Yes, and then it is a huge difference in the willingness to change.
10:	Karen	Mmm
11:	John	Weak community
12:	Karen	Yes, yes and innovative thinking
13:	Sara	Is anything written about the buildings?
14:	John	Yes, something is written about the buildings. The school classrooms are located on different sites.
15:	Steven	There is probably a lot of uncertainty about the buildings too? Because they do not know when to move in.
17:	Karen	Yes, our task, the way I understood it, is to take the role of the leadership group, and to think about what the principal should do in this situation. And then it might perhaps be wise to focus on the challenges that are on the agenda after the meeting with the superintendent. To focus on and be able to identify what the problem really is about.

Here, Karen initially suggests that the group has to sort out existing challenges simultaneously as she gives a few remarks on the situation by activating the case. Then, the group members give voice to and frame five main challenges: a) bullying (2), b) weak academic results (4), c) low employee satisfaction and well-being (6, 7), d) huge differences in willingness to make changes and a low degree of innovative thinking (8, 11) and e) uncertainty about moving into a new school building. It became evident that each group member brought his or her own perspectives on challenges into the problem-solving work through sequential and interactional modes of action in the form of questioning and analysing in relation to the situation at hand by beginning to retrieve the information collected in the case. Similarly, it was Karen, positioned to lead the work, who supported and acknowledged the contribution of each group member by nodding and expressing 'yes' and 'mm' and reminding them about their task by expressing loudly how it would be smart to proceed further: 'to identify what the problem really is about' (7). It was through Karen's support of each member's contribution and her perspective that attention was given to the assignment at a collective level and that the contour of the trajectory of the problem-solving work took form. As we have seen in Excerpt 1, the group of principals has taken the first step in constructing the object by framing challenges and expressing what to focus on further, as raised by Karen, which may give a potential direction to the work.

Examining challenges

In the continuation of Excerpt 1, the group of principals talks about the meeting between the principal at the Blueberry School and the superintendent and states that the superintendent had confronted the principal with three arenas for improvement. Then, they talk back and forth about what they would have mapped to get insight into the situation. They mention, for example, mapping the competence among the teachers and the school culture. Further, they continue their examination by questioning and analysing the challenges at hand by retrieving further information collected in the case, which supports Karen's initial proposed direction for their work. In this part of the trajectory of the problem-solving work, a turn towards what they know about the challenges take place, as shown in Excerpt 2 below, which starts with a statement from Steven.

Excerpt 2

18:	Steven	There is no information about whether they have a bullying programme. What is written is that the school has received complaints but has not taken the complaints seriously when the bullying has been reported ...
19:	Sara	Is everyone at the school aware of the academic results and the weak development that has been, especially in mathematics?
20:	Karen	Yes, and what about reading? How have they worked with test results over the last three years at least?
21:	Ann	Is it known within the school that it is the tenth grade that is the 'hard' core, whether it is a known issue, or is it only the principal and those in the leadership team who experience it in this way?
22:	Sara	Yes, this is a question about culture.
23:	Steven	Then, it could be interesting to know for what reason the annual employee satisfaction survey conducted the two past years showed increased well-being. In the first two years with a new principal, there was increased well-being; after, well-being has deteriorated.
24:	John	But, can we sort out these things? For example, something about anti-bullying and the students' psychosocial environment, something that revolves around the student's academic achievements, and something about employee well-being?
25:	Karen	Let us see (is writing). Can you please repeat?
26:	John	The students' psychosocial environment, the academic – well, results and development, and employee well-being.

A potential direction 'to identify what the problem really is about' was set as part of the problem-solving work (see Excerpt 1). In Excerpt 2, there were two patterns of interaction: *questioning and analysing the challenges* (18–21, 23) and *interpreting and categorising challenges* (22, 24–26). It is typical in problem-solving work to question and analyse the challenges in relation to the situation at hand in order to determine the causes inherent in the problems and challenges of practice. By analysing the information collected in the case, Steven (18, 23) ascertains the information they have about the challenges identified: bullying and low employee satisfaction. Whereas others in the group pose questions (19–21) related to some of the other challenges identified by the group members, which Sara (22) in turn interprets and frames as cultural questions. As such, she posits school culture as a possible cause of the challenges up to the collective level. Moreover, there is another interesting aspect that becomes evident in this part of their trajectory. John poses an open question: 'but can't we sort these things?', followed by his interpretation of 'these things', which he categorises as anti-bullying and the students' psycho-social environment, as something that centres around the students' academic results, and as something that is about job satisfaction among the employees. By looping back and using the prior framed challenges as resources, he tries to sort out, concretise and summarise what the challenges 'really are about', and in this way he makes the challenges into problem situations to be solved. Karen responds to John's initiative by expressing 'let us see, can you repeat' and by writing down what John repeats. By using the term 'us', she invokes the others in the group and thus makes a bid for collective attention to the problem situations.

Further examining of challenges and suggesting directions

The group continued to examine and analyse the challenges; however, they now focused on finding explanations for and causes of the challenges they strived to frame and understand. The building process and the uncertainty about moving into a new school building, was used as one explanation. Moreover, they talked about what to do internally at the school. One option mentioned by a participant was to arrange a meeting with all the staff and have 'such a meta-communication' to create collective awareness of the challenges. Whereas another participant of the group recommended conducting an organisational analysis and a point-of-view analysis (digital analysis tools provided by the Norwegian Directorate of Education for use in schools), which he referred to as reasonably good tools if they could manage to use them. In this part of the trajectory of the problem-solving work, a turn towards how to set a direction became evident. As shown in Excerpt 3 below, Ann blurts out a question:

Excerpt 3

27:	Ann:	But should we go concretely into each of the three areas; what do we want to do as the principal?
28:	Karen	I think if we should relate to the assignment of the superintendent, then it is to inform about the situation. And we have somehow clarified a little about what the situation is about, i.e., what the challenges are, and we have some questions, we do not know everything. We may need to, yes, describe a little first, and put in some terms, yes, conditions?
29:	John	What do you think to describe, then?
30:	Karen	I think we can clarify. We do not know if the school has a bullying plan
31:	Ann:	I think first we have to clarify what is in place, what they have plans for
32:	John	I think first that we have to clarify what is in place, what they have plans for.
33:	Sara	Probably there is a plan in a drawer at least. Yes, for sure. That's something known to use.
34:	Karen	But now when we have to present a proposal for a concrete plan for the superintendent, I think we need someone to take responsibility for taking notes. Since I'm going to lead the conversation, it will be fine if someone else can take notes.
35:	Ann	I can take notes

In this excerpt, there are two patterns of interaction. There is the *question for further* (focus, summing up, hypothesis) *direction* (27, 28, 32, 33, 34, 35), followed by *further examinations statements* (30, 31). It is interesting to see how the prior concretising of the three problem spaces contributes to setting one possible further direction for the work trajectory, thus leading John (29) to question the direction suggested by Karen. At the same time, Karen (30) follows up her suggestion by giving voice to a perspective stating further direction: to clarify if the school has a bullying plan. Her initiative is supported by Ann (31), who states that they have to clarify what they have plans for, which in turn leads to a hypothesis (32) and Sara's perspective (33) that confirms that a plan exists, at least in a drawer. By using 'we know', Sara anchors her confirmation in the group members' experiences. Karen then follows up, again reminding the group about the assignment on behalf of the superintendent to be worked out, and encouraging someone to take notes as, at the same time, she positions herself as the leader of their conversation.

In this excerpt, the object is acted upon in a chain of perspectives put forward by the different principals. It is in the interaction of their perspectives that a conclusion is reached, what I will call a tool to be used further in their problem-solving work. It is clear that all members of the group made efforts to bring the conclusion up to a collective level (27, 32, 35). According to conventions for leadership actions, Karen is the one who sums up consecutively (28, 34). Similar to what we saw in Excerpt 2, it is John who gives voice to perspectives that suggest further directions. As we can see, John's perspective is used as a resource by Ann (27) for promoting a further direction, and John articulates (32) a way forward that turns Karen's attention towards the object of their work. Karen responds by referring to their assignment on behalf of the superintendent. By expressing the need for someone to take notes as she leads, Karen again invokes the others in the group and thus makes a bid for collective attention to the object to be worked on, which implies establishing a division of labour and the creation of a tool to be used (notes). However, they still have not found a way to respond to the assignment.

Following-up activities and further directions

In the continuation of Excerpt 3, the group talks back and forth about what could be done at Blueberry School. They make links to what they had talked about earlier. For example, the use of tools for mapping the situations at Blueberry School again become a point of focus. Further, in this part of the trajectory, they talk about how to organise the work at the school for dealing with the challenges. They conclude that the designated leaders of the teaching teams would be important in the process. Then, their conversation turns towards how to make good routines for dealing with bullying. In the wake of this, they turn their attention towards how to deal with the challenge framed in Excerpt 2 as 'anti-bullying and the students' psychosocial environment'. Excerpt 4 starts with John putting forward a suggestion for how to proceed.

Excerpt 4

36:	John	Shall we think, that a group is composed to examine the psychosocial plan consisting of the three designated leaders, and some teachers and the counsellor?
37:	Ann	So, a group from each department?
38:	John	Yes, who gets the responsibility to evaluate and revise the plan that exists.
39:	Karen	Actually, I have experience with – I have almost been in the same situation just now. I came to a school where there was a thin document that was made a very long time ago. So, it was enough for people in the school to say they had a plan, but the plan was not active. Therefore, during the last year, we have worked out a concrete plan. It's called the 'Well-being action plan'. And really, it is about both the student's and the teacher's environment, even though it is the students who naturally are in focus. But we started out last year at this time, with a group. We connected to the parents; we used the advisory bodies ...
40:	John	The superintendent will also have an action plan for improvement, should we set some deadlines?
41:	Karen	Yes

There are four patterns of interaction in this extract. There is *preparation work of following-up activities at the school* (36, 37, 38), *sharing prior experiences with the follow-up activities* (39), a further *direction statement suggestion* and finally a *confirmation statement for further direction* (41). These four interaction patterns are tightly interwoven, where institutional practices, participants' experiences and individual agency are brought up to the level of collective problem-solving work. John, for example, brings in procedures from school settings (36, 38) as he suggests following-up activities. Whereas Karen (39) refers to experiences with relevance to the procedure suggested by John as well as to the object of their activity: to respond to the assignment on behalf of the superintendent, which involves making a plan. With Karen's prior experiences with the object of their work as a resource, John puts forward a perspective pointing to an alternative way to go forward, which in turn Karen confirms and endorses. Clearly, John again brings his individual agency up to a collective level, and Karen continues to include his initiatives in the overall problem-solving work (36, 38, 40).

Excerpt 4 led to talk about how to work with the plan, first with attention to milestones and who should be involved in the work. Then, the group turned its attention towards how to create ownership of the plan among the teachers. They also payed attention to the necessity to raise challenges, and what the causes of the challenges could be in the information to be given to the superintendent. At that point of their trajectory, the instructor/researcher provides the following information, 'now you have 10 minutes left to discuss and I will remind you about the assignment, to prepare an action plan that you can present to him in your next meeting shortly'. After this break, they continued to discuss challenges to be raised and their causes – for example, that low employee satisfaction and well-being could be attributed to the ongoing and never-ending building process and to the uncertainty about moving into the new school building. In this part of the trajectory, John breaks in and turns attention to what they need to do.

Excerpt 5

42:	John	*I feel we have to be more concrete (Yes, commented from the others in the group). We beat around the bush in a way, we talk about a lot of things.*
43	Karen	Yes
44	Steven	Yes, I suggest we focus on subject sections across the grades. Right, subjects are at all grades.... So, showing that we are going to work with a subject content, and then organising in subject sections can be a way to do it.

In this excerpt, there are two patterns of interaction: *a need statement for further direction* and *preparation work of following-up activities at Blueberry School*. When I look at and listen to this turn (on the video recording), it seems John is feeling a bit discouraged, as is evident in his low tone, slow speech and body language. In (42), his need statement opens with the words 'I feel', indicating that he is building on previous moments of actions to initiate further direction of action: to become more concrete, which in turn becomes endorsed by all in the group. This indicates that the group is developing a collective understanding of the need for a way forward, which in turn takes a direction about what to do to follow-up the situation at Blueberry School as stated by Steven (44) right before the time available to complete the problem-solving work ran out.

Discussion and concluding remarks

The problem-solving work I have studied, based on the case narrative of Blueberry School, took place in groups of principals participating in a National Leadership Programme. Problem-solving work between individuals orchestrated around a case narrative in leadership programmes reflects a way of organising work that resembles what Van der Veer and Valsiner (1991) called 'experimental settings'. The research question aimed to give insight into and understand how groups of principals in such an experimental setting *do* problem-solving work together. Based on the close-up interaction analysis of problem-solving work done, I raised three aspects for discussion related to doing problem-solving work based on a case narrative: 1) how the coordination is performed, which means the ways in which the perspectives were given voice to become resources, 2) the timing of the problem-solving work, and 3) what characterises the actions and interactions in the group. References to the representations in the case are relevant for all the aspects to be discussed.

The analysis of this case-based problem-solving work reveals that the group of principals followed four sub-trajectories in their work process:

- To identify and frame the challenges of the Blueberry School; five main challenges.
- To examine and define the challenges of the Blueberry School; to determine what the problem is really about: questioning and analysing the challenges, categorising the challenges into three problem spaces.
- To identify follow-up activities for the Blueberry School; e.g., to compose a group to examine the psychosocial plan.
- Problem-solving–negotiating resolutions and direction: preliminary directions, direction statements, alternative statements and open-ended resolution and direction.

As such, the problem-solving trajectory as a whole can be seen as composed of four sub-trajectories. When identifying and framing the challenges, the group of principals focused on the challenges of the school, such as poor test results, bullying and low willingness to change. The group referred to and used the same types of representations retrieved from the case narrative throughout the entire problem-solving work. The sub-trajectory, 'examining and defining', started with the retrieved challenges which, during the trajectory, were gradually delimited into three problem spaces to be solved. The trajectory, 'follow-up activities', contained a collection of actions to be performed within the Blueberry School to solve the problems at hand. These three sub-trajectories were taken up and led to the open-ended resolution and direction in the fourth sub-trajectory: 'problem-solving–negotiation resolutions and direction'. Observing the perspectives given voice and how the participants drew on and used each other's perspectives and the representations when these three sub-trajectories intersected opened up the many layers of problem-solving work, which unfolded in the group of principals striving to handle the complexities of problem-solving work.

These sub-trajectories should be seen as interaction patterns that become constituted through sequences of actions by which these perspectives are given voice and used over time. This means that the sequences of action became aligned and combined, and 'looped' back and forth in time when the group of principals put forward perspectives that gave direction to their work. The looping back also implied that the perspectives became developed, depending on the questioning and interpretations of perspectives in use in the participant work on the object. The implication of this is that the perspectives change in function over the course of their actions and interactions; although their inherent feature may remain the same, their function changes.

As the sub-trajectories intersect, the individuals' perspectives interact and constitute the actions and interactions that make up the direction and resolution produced. More interesting, the analysis also shows how intersecting sub-trajectories elaborate how the group members also mobilised prior experiences that came to represent collective agency (Virkunnen, 2006). Since the sub-trajectories differ in timing, the interpretations of what is produced when they intersect are not given, but must be seen as contingent upon the context of problem-solving work and the object worked on (cf. Edwards, 2010; Engeström, 1999). The examining and defining sub-trajectory; to determine what the problem is really about, operates on a longer time-scale, as the challenges of Blueberry school and the object of their activity gain the groups attention throughout the entire problem-solving work. As such, it is evident that the case-based narrative supports both individual and collective agency and makes it possible for the participants to work on objects that are relevant and known to them (cf. Mumford et al., 2012)

As the participants in this experimental setting interacted, they mobilised perspectives or 'views from somewhere' (Holland & Reeves, 2001, p. 273). In their initiatives, socially situated, historically constituted practices came into play. The principals were engaged to act on the object; however, they seemed to strive with the object under construction and its pervasive tensions stemming from the diverse viewpoints. The viewpoints of those speaking from the position; what must be done at the Blueberry School and those speaking from the position; that the assignment must be done on behalf of the superintendent. It is evident that their engagement with the complex tension-laden object generated search actions (Engeström, 1999). However, these future-oriented actions were mainly directed towards finding solutions to the challenges at the Blueberry School rather than to the assignment given to them in the case narrative that the instructor/researcher read aloud before the problem-solving work started and again about 10 minutes before the time for their work ran out. This course of action corresponds with what Van der Veer and Valsiner (1991) pointed to: that experimental settings must be seen as a context of investigation wherein the instructors can introduce the participants for uniquely framed common objects to be solved and manipulate their structure in order to trigger, but not 'produce', the participants' framing and constructing of solutions to the object. The problem-solving work that emerged was often unstructured, characterised by unpredictable shifts in negotiating the *what* and *ways to solve* the problems of the school, as one of the participants expressed: 'we need to be more concrete, we beat around the bush in a way, we turn our attention towards many things here'. This was a challenge for the group's performance and exemplified a problem-solving practice constituting an interplay in which the participants' viewpoints only to some degree became explored, aligned, coordinated and converged into a collective interest over the common object, and which resulted in an outcome that did not meet their shared responsibility (cf. Engeström, 2011). As seen, the unfolding interactions and the intersection of individual and collective perspectives became resources that resulted in a narrower problem framing than the uniquely framed object for their work and an open-ended direction (cf. Vennebo, 2015).

Each perspective represents germs originating from and used in the unfolding trajectory of previous problem-solving. However, the analysis shows that the direction and resolutions for actual problems to be solved must be created in each particular case. The analysis also exemplifies how the interdependency or social order (division of labour) between the participants emerged and influenced the direction, in this experimental setting of a specific educational leadership practice, in the interplay of perspectives, the information activated from the case and the object worked on (cf. Edwards, 2010; Engeström, 1999). The direction is made by following the sequences of actions in which connections between the externalised perspectives are produced, and the 'loop' that works across the sub-trajectories and in the problem-solving trajectory as a whole. So, the direction is produced at the action level and at the level of the problem-solving trajectory. Moreover, the leader's actions exemplify how preliminary directions became produced as part of the work; by supporting and proposing perspectives, and through temporary confirmation of directions and recurring reminders about the object of their activity. However, from a more leadership point of view, no one was doing the coordination work needed to take care of their shared responsibility (cf. Engeström, 2011).

By applying CHAT to the analysis of doing problem-solving work in the group of principals based on a case narrative, it becomes evident that there is no uniform way of solving complex problems. The perspectives brought to bear on problems of practice to be solved function as potential resources, historically and culturally rooted, that create the direction for sequences of action; but in complex problem-solving, each participant gives voice to different perspectives that must be negotiated, developed and used in order to create temporary directions and resolutions. This means that the perspectives themselves are contingent upon the activities performed; in other words, the ways in which perspectives function as resources are conditioned by their modes and by the ways they are negotiated, manipulated, developed and used in the problem-solving trajectory. It is through the intersecting contributions from each group member that we gain knowledge about the doing of problem-solving and the directions and resolution produced. The use of CHAT and the 'perspective' concept in the study of problem-solving work clearly shows that each action performed can, in principle, be directed in one or another direction. Thus, I argue that in educational leadership practices, a guiding protocol that can inform and guide concrete problem-solving processes can be helpful to keep the direction of actions and interactions within acceptable frames.

Implications

My main finding is that case-based instruction, like that taking place in an experimental setting in the context of a leadership programme, with a group of principals working on problems of school practice, has the potential to work as an arena for problem-solving training among principals. The principals managed to activate and make representations of the case relevant in their work and to identify, frame and examine the challenges at hand. However, they strove to consecutively include these findings in their problem-solving trajectory, which resulted in an open-ended resolution and direction, meaning that the course of action was not kept in an acceptable frame. The implication of this finding is straightforward: case-based instruction for doing problem-solving work must also provide principals with strategies for working with complex problems of school practice. This is an approach that implies participation in problem-solving work through performing professional group discussion, which is seen as a crucial leadership practice. This type of practice cannot be reduced to individual training and performance, since professional group discussion is seen as a key to working out the complex problem at hand in this type of practice. One methodological implication of this is that research based on survey or interview data is not sufficient to understand the challenges of professional discussions in groups of principals related to problematic issues in school settings presented to them by a case narrative. We also need research that scrutinises the principals' actual actions and interactions during problem-solving work. This study has demonstrated how CHAT can be used as an approach to studying characteristic features of case-based problem-solving work by focusing on the continuous movement and interaction between individual and collective performance, tightly linked to dynamic representations in the case narrative and the object worked on. However further research is needed to be able to appreciate CHAT's potential to capture the complexity of problem-solving work in experimental settings.

References

Aas, M. (2016). Leaders as learners: Developing new leadership practices. *Professional Development, 43*(3), 439–453. doi:10.1080/19415257.2016.1194878

Aas, M., & Vavik, M. (2015). Group coaching: A new way of constructing leadership identity? *School Leadership & Management: Formerly School Organisation, 35*(3), 251–265. doi:10.1080/13632434.2014.962497

Avolio, B. J., Reichard, R. J., Hannah, S. T., Walumbwa, F. O., & Chan, A. (2009). A meta-analytic review of leadership impact research: Experimental and quasiexperimental studies. *The Leadership Quarterly*, 20(5), 764–784. doi:10.1016/j.leaqua.2009. 06. 006

Edwards, A. (2009). From the systemic to the relational: Relational agency and activity theory. In A. Sannino, H. Daniels, & K. D. Gutiérrez (Eds.), *Learning and Expanding with Activity Theory* (pp. 197–211). New York, NY: Cambridge University Press.

Edwards, A. (2010). *Being an Expert Professional Practitioner: The Relational Turn in Expertise*. New York, NY: Springer.

Engeström, Y. (1999) Innovative learning in work teams: Analyzing cycles of knowledge creation in practice. In Y. Engeström, R-L. Punamäki-Gitai & R. Miettinen (Eds.), *Perspectives on Activity Theory* (pp. 377–404). Cambridge: Cambridge University Press.

Engeström, Y. (2001). Expansive learning at work: Toward an activity theoretical reconceptualization. *Journal of Education and Work*, 14(1), 133–156.

Engeström, Y. (2008). *From Teams to Knots: Activity-theoretical Studies of Collaboration and Learning at Work*. Cambridge: Cambridge University Press.

Engeström, Y. (2011). Activity theory and learning at work. In M. Malloch, L. Cairns, K. Evans, & B. N. O'Connor (Eds.), *The SAGE Handbook of Workplace Learning* (pp. 86–104). London: SAGE.

Holland, D., & Reeves, J. R. (2001). Activity theory and the view from somewhere: Team perspectives on the intellectual work of programming. In B. A. Nardi (Ed.), *Context and Consciousness. Activity Theory and Human-Computer Interaction*, 3rd edn (pp. 257–282). Cambridge, MA: The MIT Press.

Hybertsen, I. D., Stensaker, B., Federici, R. A., Olsen, M. S., Solem, A., & Aamodt, P. O. (2014). *Evalueringen av den nasjonale rektorutdanningen*. Retrieved from www.udir.no/tall-og-forskning/finn-forskning/rapporter/Rektorutdanningen-oker-kvaliteten-i-opplaringen/

Jordan, B., & Henderson, A. (1995). Interaction analysis: Foundations and practice. *Journal of the Learning Sciences*, 4(1), 39–103. doi:10.1207/s15327809jls0401_2

Kolodner, J. L. (1997). Educational implications of analogy: A view from case-based reasoning. *American Psychologist*, 52(1), 57–66. doi:10.1037/0003-066X.52. 1. 57

Lumby, J., Crow, G. M., & Pashiardis, P. (2008). *International Handbook on the Preparation and Development of School Leaders*. New York: Routledge.

Miettinen, R. (2005). Object of activity and individual motivation. *Mind, Culture, and Activity*, 12(1), 52–69. doi:10.1207/s15327884mca1201_5

Mumford, M. D., Peterson, D., Robledo, I., & Hester, K. (2012). Cases in leadership education. Implications of human cognition. In S. Snook, N. Nohria, & R. Khurana (Eds.), *The Handbook for Teaching Leadership. Knowing, Doing, and Being* (pp. 21–33). Harvard: Sage Publication.

Taylor, D. L, Cordeiro, P., & Chrispeels, J. H. (2009). Pedagogy. In M. D. Young, G. M. Crow, J. Murphy, & R. T. Ogawa (Eds.), *Handbook of Research on the Education of School Leaders* (pp. 319–369). New York, NY: Routledge.

Timperley, H. (2011). *Realising the Power of Professional Learning*. Maidenhead, UK: Open University Press.

Tuomi-Gröhn, T., Engeström, Y., & Young, M. (2003) From transfer to boundary-crossing between school and work as a tool for developing vocational education: An introduction. In T. Toumi-Gröhn & Y. Engeström (Eds), *Between Work and School. New Perspectives on Transfer and Boundary-Crossing* (pp. 1–18). Amsterdam: Pergamon.

Young, M. D., Crow, G. M., Murphy, J., & Ogawa, R. T. (2009). *Handbook of Research on the Education of School Leaders*. New York: Routledge.

Van der Veer, R., & Valsiner, J. (1991). *Understanding Vygotsky: A Quest for Synthesis*. Oxford: Blackwell.
Vennebo, K. F. (2015). *School Leadership and Innovative Work Places and Spaces*. (Doctoral Thesis), University of Oslo, Unipub forl, Oslo.
Vennebo, K. F. & Ottesen, E. (2014). The emergence of innovative work in school development. *Journal of Educational Change, 16*(2), 197–216. doi:10.1007/s1033-014-9234-0
Virkunnen, J. (2006). Dilemmas in building shared transformative agency. *Activities*, 3(1), 44–66.

9 Cultural-historical activity theory framing and guiding professional learning in school-based development

Nina A. Vasseljen

Introduction

> School-based development means that the school, including school leaders and the entire staff, undergoes a workplace development process. The aim is to develop the school's collective knowledge, attitudes and skills when it comes to learning, teaching and collaboration. School-based competence development therefore deals with development that is school-based as well as the needs of both the teachers and the school as its starting point.
>
> (Directorate of Education and Training, 2012a)

Although many schools and municipalities in Norway are well on their way to building local competence development, authorities have found that the development of professional learning communities as a tool for school-based competence development has thus far been insufficient. For this reason, the 2017 national strategy for competence development (Ministry of Education and Research, 2017) pointed to decentralised competence development as one of the most important interventions. Local school-owners and leaders are given responsibility to identify local challenges and, accordingly, to develop school-based interventions. Teacher training should thus contribute relevant expertise based on the school's needs, and teachers, with the help and support of school leaders, should translate their experience and knowledge into a new and improved kind of teaching. This understanding of competence and collective analysis and development processes tends to result in the need for changes in routines, areas of professional responsibility and organisational structure within the school (Directorate of Education and Training, 2012b). Research has found that teachers, leaders and researchers experience school-based competence development as challenging (Dahl, 2016; Postholm, 2018). Collaboration among teachers in Norway has mainly been directed towards coordination and practical facilitation of day-to-day schooling, with minimal communication aimed at developing practices within the school (Junge, 2012; Kvam, 2018). Teachers experience relatively little collaboration related to developing what goes on in the classroom, and the entire collegium is rarely included in the process of development (Dahl, 2016). Teacher training needs to develop its role as a partner in school-based competence development (Dahl, 2016), and many school leaders lack good models for leading and directing development processes in their schools (Ministry of Education and Research, 2017; Postholm, 2018).

The study on which this chapter is based was a four-year project in which teachers and school leaders at a medium-sized Norwegian primary school applied Lesson Study (LS) as the method for school-based competence development. The project was guided by two researchers from teacher education – my colleague researcher, who focused on inclusive education and special needs, and myself, who focused on school development and leadership. Within LS, the teachers collaborated on improving the curriculum through collective planning, observing and evaluation of research lessons, and by focusing on pupils' learning processes and learning outcomes. Early in the project period, the following challenges were raised during meetings between school leaders and researchers: 'How can we stimulate powerful and knowledge-developing learning processes in the teacher teams?' and 'How can we expand the teams' learning processes to the organisational level?'

In this text, I use cultural-historical activity theory (CHAT) as the project's theoretical foundation and focus on how concepts and models from CHAT strengthened learning processes and leadership at all levels of developmental work. The text is framed by the research question: *How can CHAT frame and guide professional learning in school-based development?* This chapter starts with a presentation of the theoretical framework for the study and an overview of related research. Then, CHAT is presented in a separate section, before the study's context, and is followed by a presentation of the methodology and methods applied in the study. Next, the findings are presented and subsequently discussed. The chapter ends with a closing reflection.

Theoretical framework and related research

Both school-based competence development and professional learning community theory are based on the principle that teachers' profession competence is situated in their everyday experiences and is thus best developed when teachers, in collective processes, explore their own teaching practices. Professional learning communities are characterised by exploratory and developmental dialogues whereby teachers focus on the pupils' learning process. The role of the teacher is de-privatised, with the teachers becoming more autonomous and more pupil-centred in their work (Vescio, Ross, & Adams, 2008). Togsverd and Rothuizen (2012) described the role of today's teacher as being expanded from performance to exploration and encompassing the development of their own practice. Ertsas and Irgens (2017) used the term *professional theorising* to describe how teachers, by comparing their own experiences with research-based knowledge, can develop new understanding and knowledge. Professional theorising helps narrow the focus of the developmental work and also gives the analytical distance necessary for critical reflection and a meta-theoretical perspective (Ertsas & Irgens, 2017).

In high-performing schools, the professional group (in this study, teachers and school leaders) is collectively evolving (Hargreaves & Fullan, 2012). Collinson, Cook and Conley (2006) used the term *organisational learning* for systematic and recurring learning processes in which the school's collective and individual learning, as well as teaching and leadership, are enhanced. Professional learning communities evolve by questioning the values on which the organisation's practice is based, by developing new insight and knowledge, by communicating and sharing information, and by creating the capacity for the effective use of knowledge (Argyris & Schön, 1978).

In LS, which originated in Japan, groups of teachers seek to learn from their classrooms. A group of teachers choose a development or research focus for their own teaching and formulate goals for pupil learning and long-term development for a 'research lesson'. They plan in detail the research lesson, which one group member teaches while the others closely observe the pupils' learning. In this way, the group achieves a strong basis for analysing the pupils' learning outcomes, evaluating teaching and discussing their own learning after completing the research lesson. Finally, the teachers' groups meet to share and discuss their experiences (Dudley, 2013). The LS process of planning, acting, evaluation and sharing of experiences is often referred to as a LS cycle. And LS, as a teacher learning process, has been found to develop teacher collaboration, enhance teachers' professional and pedagogical knowledge, increase the quality of the teachers' planning and teaching, and strengthen the teachers' focus on the pupils' learning process and learning outcomes (Cajkler, Wood, Norton, & Pedder, 2014; Lewis, Perry, Friedkin, & Roth, 2012).

Even though learning discussions in professional communities have the potential to create development, this does not happen automatically (Horn & Little, 2010; Junge, 2012; Kvam, 2018; Timperley, 2008). Both Junge (2012) and Kvam (2018) found little evidence of challenges and problematisations in learning discussion. The conversations consisted mainly of descriptions of practice and exchanges of experiences related to alternative ways of applying existing knowledge, lacking analyses, research-based theory and professional terms that could have contributed to a new understanding. Standards for cooperation and communication, structured discussions and leadership are crucial to knowledge development (Horn & Little, 2010; Timperley, 2008).

Development from within or development based on the school's needs, as in school-based competence development, is characterised by the fact that teachers and school leaders in professional communities manage norms and standards, conduct active school development and contribute towards the development of a professional knowledge base (Dahl, 2016). This requires open-mindedness (Sellman, 2003) and professional uncertainty (Munthe, 2001), understood as questioning your work. Lillejord (2011) found, however, that Norwegian school and competence development is well anchored in the dissemination pedagogy, with 'implementations' and 'top-down' development achieved through courses. In such a culture, collective reflections, creation of meaning and collaborative learning will be experienced as demanding, unknown and subject to resistance.

Pondy (1978) used the terms *organisational surface structure* and *deep structure* to describe how easily recognised surface-level plans, strategies, visible leadership and organisation maps rest on a deep structure of basic conditions, such as values, norms, ethics and culture. Because the surface level is relatively concrete and easily dealt with, the significance of values and feelings may be at risk of being ignored, according to Irgens (2016). The deep level has a strong, but often hidden, influence on everyday life, and school development must maintain an interplay between the surface and deep levels: 'If quality development and improvement take place on the surface only, it may be just a form of surface treatment, a cosmetic change with limited durability, which leads to interventions and activities that may not result in a real change of local practice' (Irgens, 2016, p. 299, author's translation). School-based competence development requires deliberate leadership, supporting structures beyond introducing methods and the devotion of time to collaboration (Scribner, Cockrell, Cockrell, & Valentine, 1999): 'Leaders need to stand back and view the situation through a myriad of lenses' (Earl & Timperley, 2009, p. 6).

To understand, set a direction for and develop both the people and the organisation are central to several leadership theories (Leithwood, Harris & Hopkins, 2019). Within the theory of transformational leadership, the principal is described as a supporting and guiding role model who motivates teachers to shift their attention from their own interests to the common good of the community and the school. Professional development and intellectual stimulation among co-workers are emphasised, and school leaders communicate high expectations, delegate authority and give individual support and autonomy (Yukl, 2013). In distributed leadership theory, leadership practice takes place in the interaction between school leaders, followers and their situations, rather than as a function of one or more leaders' actions (Spillane, 2005, p. 146). Co-workers act as leaders due to the strength of their professionality and personality, without stripping formal leaders of their responsibilities and freedom of action (Spillane, Halverson, & Diamond, 2004). Interaction, coordinated leadership, regular meeting times, shared knowledge and the establishment of a collective practice through a variety of tools, structures and routines are all central to distributed leadership (Spillane, 2005).

Cultural-historical activity theory

In CHAT, we find models and concepts that envision the complexity of development processes, interaction within groups and interaction between groups in larger organisations (Engeström, 1987, 2001). Engeström's (1987, 2001) activity system allows us to visualise how activity and development take place in a social interaction between the individual and the environment, and how the many factors in the context mutually affect one other. There is a constant interrelation between the subject and the other factors, and the interaction between subject and object is mediated by these factors (Hirsh & Segolsson, 2017). CHAT describes both goal-directed action and objects for activities, where goal-directed actions move the practice towards the object of the activity (Wertsch, 1998). Leont´ev (1981) claimed that the object is 'the true motive' (p. 59), thus emphasising the importance of bringing together participants' efforts towards a common object by establishing a common understanding of the purpose of development work.

Tensions in and between the nodes in an activity system are potential triggers for developmental processes in the activity. Through expansive learning, contradictions can make participants transform the activity system by constructing a new object and concept for their collective activity and implementing this new object and concept in practice: They 'learn something that is not yet there' (Engeström & Sannino, 2010, p. 2). Expansive learning, which involves asking questions about basic assumptions and established practices and developing new understanding and new ways of acting (Engeström, 2001), can lead to qualitative transformations both at the level of individual actions and at the level of the collective activity and its broader context (Sannino, Engeström, & Lemos, 2016).

The term *boundary crossing* describes how professionals at work may need to enter territory about which they are unfamiliar and, to some extent, unqualified (Suchman, 1994), but also how participants can meet across ordinary group affiliation and 'face the challenge of negotiating and combining ingredients from different contexts to achieve hybrid solutions' (Engeström, Engeström, & Kärkkäinen, 1995, p. 319). In boundary zones, participants can show unified actions while, at same time, pursuing and making productive use of various perspectives. Diversity in perspective among group members does not need to be overcome by unity in order for collaboration to occur. Both unity and diversity are relevant for organisational development. The challenge is to determine which mechanisms work together to enable groups to maintain both unity and diversity (Akkerman, Admiraal, & Simons, 2012).

Within CHAT, we also find concepts and models related to development cooperation between practitioners and researchers. Developmental work research (DWR) (Engeström, 1987) is a formative intervention (Engeström & Sannino, 2010) methodology that promotes positive change in practices using a participatory, collaborative design. When practitioners face a problematic and contradictory object, the formative interventionist researchers' role is 'to provoke and sustain an extensive transformation process, led and owned by practitioners' (Engeström & Sannino, 2010, p. 15). A key outcome of formative interventions is agency among the participants, and an intervention that is not embedded and contextualised in the participants' meaningful life activity is unlikely to have durable formative influence in the long run (Engeström, 2011). Presentation of *mirror data* (Cole & Engeström, 2007), which the researcher collects and which reflects the practitioners' development process, and the researcher's introduction of theoretical and methodological resources can provide stimuli for development. Postholm and Moen's (2011) model for Research & Development (R&D model) visualises how DWR performs between teachers and researchers, including processes at various levels. They named Engeström's expansive learning cycle (1987; 2001), which represents the development process in formative interventions, as the primary level. At the secondary level, a meta-level, practice is reflected by using theories as an analysis tool. From a third level, which is a transparent researchers' platform, the researchers focus their research gaze telescopically (see Chapter 1 for a detailed description).

Context

In the DWR project, the LS was used as a method for developing the teams into professional learning communities to promote school-based competence development based on the needs of teachers and schools. This was the object of the project, and the desired outcome was that the pupils should learn more and flourish. The school's seven teacher teams, each led by one of the teachers (the lead teacher), completed nine LS cycles during the project period. Each cycle lasted five weeks, with four hours for planning the research lesson, one hour for teaching and observation, two hours for evaluation and two hours for the sharing of experiences between colleagues. Between the teachers' LS cycles, the researchers first met with the school leaders (principal and two middle leaders) and then with the school's development group, consisting of school leaders and lead teachers, in order to collaborate on further development of the project. The school leaders organised and managed the teachers' LS work and led the sharing of experience at the end of each LS cycle.

I, researching school development and leadership, continuously collected data through anonymous, structured reflection logs from teachers and school leaders and through audio recordings of the teams' LS conversations and the leadership's meetings between the LS cycles. In meetings with the school leadership and development group, I presented my ongoing analyses, compared the participants' experiences and the analyses with current theory, and suggested possible tools for further development of teacher collaboration and leadership. School leaders and lead teachers considered my input and discussed what they would emphasise in the leadership of the upcoming LS cycle. In order to strengthen the autonomy of both teachers and the school, from the beginning of the project, I did not participate in the teaching staff's LS work. Apart from this, I have participated on occasion and by invitation.

Methodology and methods

Ethnography and data collection

To develop an understanding of the work processes and how the learning culture was developed in the school, I conducted an ethnographic study (Wolcott, 2008). In the study, the following sources constituted the data material: project participant logs, audio recordings from teachers' LS work, audio recordings from meetings between researchers, school leaders and lead teachers, and my notes from process analysis and meeting preparations. I first made content logs (Jordan & Henderson, 1995) of the audio recordings in order to provide an overview of the data corpus. Next, I transcribed, verbatim, sequences containing leadership, exploratory talk or pedagogical choice, questioning and reasoning.

Data analysis

I conducted a three-part analysis process based on notes and transcripts. In the first phase, I searched for settings in which CHAT was used. In the second phase, these settings were separated according to which concepts and models were used, how they were used and by whom. Based on this sorting, I developed a two-part description of the situation: first, what was going on; and second, how CHAT was used to illuminate and drive the process further. To ensure the quality of the study, these descriptions were presented to the school leaders for a member check (Lincoln & Guba,

1985). Based on these descriptions, in the third phase, I conducted an analysis using open coding, as described by Strauss and Corbin (1998) in the constant comparative analysis method, and I narrowed the focus on the descriptions of the situations with the question: 'What did the use of CHAT contribute?' The categories developed during this process, which give an idea of how CHAT contributed, are as follows: 'Learning and development processes', 'Leadership', 'Structure' and 'Learning culture'. I present the findings in a two-part description of the situations: first, what was happening; and then, how CHAT was used.

The situations and the use of CHAT

Situation 1

The teaching teams' work in the first and second LS cycles showed few traces of pedagogical and didactic analyses and justifications. Large parts of the conversations moved directly from situation descriptions to solution proposals, and the teachers' professional competence largely remained tacit knowledge. In my analyses, I thought I would find very little learning and little activity associated with professional learning communities. However, the teachers' logs demonstrated that they had learned. They wrote:

> I've learned some tricks I can use on Smartboard. I have learned a lot about how my colleagues think about the order and organisation of a teaching session. I have learned several methods that I can use. Planning reminds me of all the important things that we need to think about before a teaching session.

This focused my attention on our use of the concept of learning. Did we define the term differently? Was the teachers' focus on development through sharing and application, whereas I sought analyses, hypotheses and professionally justified assessments?

The use of CHAT

Leont'ev's (1981) statement, 'The object is the true motive' (p. 59), led me to the questions: Do we who participate in the project have different understandings of what school development is? And, further, does this lead to our attention and actions being directed at different learning and development processes? Historical analysis with Engeström's (1987, 2001) activity system as an analytical tool demonstrated how LS created tensions in the subject-artefact-object triangle in most teams and led me to reflect on what happens when one of the three nodes in a balanced triangle change. Whereas LS (artefact) was intended as a tool for establishing school development through professional learning communities (object), it seemed that the teams did not understand it that way, but instead adapted it to their incorporated learning and collaboration culture, characterised by the sharing of experience and coordination. This appears in the teachers' logs: 'We were efficient and did a lot of planning. We had great progress, and we were able to plan the entire session in detail. I think we have the same opinion of the time it takes'. The analysis helped me develop issues for collective reflection in meetings with school leaders and lead teachers: What happens when we use development tools that challenge established learning views, development culture and interaction practices in a well-established development and collaboration culture? Does LS as a method of development represent a more radical and demanding change in the teachers' understanding of learning and cooperation than we had anticipated? What is needed for LS to become a tool that lifts team collaboration from experience sharing and practical adaptation to a professional learning community that can contribute to school-based development? Could it be that teachers lack competency in collective analytical and exploratory learning processes? The upper triangle of the activity system showed how the interaction between subject, object and artefact is of decisive importance for the 'power' in the LS work and made both school leaders and researchers aware that the method and allocated time were not sufficient for development.

Situation 2

Variation in the teams' work processes in the second and third LS cycle focused my attention on the teams as subjects in the LS work. In some audio recordings, I found many examples of exploratory conversation, educational and didactic analysis, and justified choices; in other recordings, I found only additions to analysis and reflection. Several lead teachers wrote in the log that they found it difficult to lead the team to exploratory conversations:

> I tried to ask questions. It was difficult, and it is something in which we all need training. Sometimes, I got the feeling that someone was offended because I asked questions about their choices and suggestions. It was difficult to keep structure in the conversation and challenging to push my colleagues to hold a deeper conversation. It is clear that we are not so accustomed to justifying our opinions and views in planning sessions, and that we feel a little threatened if anyone questions our opinions.

In audio recordings, I could hear how exploratory and analytical questions from the lead teacher led to hesitation in several of the teams, and how the conversations quickly turned back to practical clarifications, unjustified choices and constant shifting of topics that left much unresolved. Both lead teachers and the other teachers had written in start-up logs that they felt positive with respect to LS as a new and 'research-based' development method, but the lead teachers' logs showed that transferring knowledge about professional learning communities into practical action was a demanding process in most teams.

The use of CHAT

Suchman's (1994) description of boundary crossing as entering territory in which one might feel unqualified, in conjunction with the findings of lead teachers' logs, strengthened my understanding of LS as a demanding development method. The school leaders and researchers had, in the design of the project, considered the school's seven teacher teams to be good arenas for collective learning processes. Were we now in a situation where teachers and lead teachers experienced that LS, which should lead to a new form of both co-operation and leadership, instead jeopardised the support, security and 'feelings' of the teams? In formative intervention research (Engeström & Sannino, 2010), the researcher's role is 'to provoke and sustain an extensive transformation process, led and owned by practitioners' (p. 15). This definition led to the question: How can school leaders and researchers stimulate lead teachers and teams in demanding learning and developing transformation processes, without compromising their autonomy? How is challenge balanced with support? The questions were first discussed with the school leaders and then in the development group. Lead teachers elaborated on their experiences, which largely revealed challenges. I highlighted concrete examples of exploratory talk, or the beginning of such talk from all the teams' LS work. Based on theory, I justified why these were examples of good practice, and I showed how, based on these examples, I had drafted a template that could help the teams to structure the conversations and to ask analytical questions, especially in the LS cycle planning phase. Could this template be something to develop further?

Situation 3

As the final phase of each LS cycle, the school's seven teacher teams shared experiences from the completed cycle. In the first three LS cycles, the teams' experiences were presented orally and via posters, followed by space for questions and comments from colleagues. After the third LS cycle, both school leaders and teachers expressed a need to develop the sharing of experiences.

The use of CHAT

Analysis of the activity system uncovered tensions between the reflective and exploratory learning that now emerged in the teams' LS work, and the traditional presentation form used in sharing experiences in the entire collegium. Connected to the theory of boundary crossing (Akkerman et al., 2012), these tensions stimulated the school leaders to reflect on the LS cycle's experience sharing as an arena for organisational learning. Discussion of the question, 'How do we lift the learning processes in the teams' LS work to an organisational-level learning process?', led to the reorganisation of experience sharing in the fourth LS cycle, where groups of three teachers from different teams discussed issues developed from members' teamwork. The groups concluded the discussions by considering whether any of the issues were of significance for all teams at the school and, if so, ought to be considered at the organisational level, in processes led by the school leadership. This led to the theme 'Pupil collaboration' becoming the focus of collective research in the next LS cycle. Meetings between colleagues grew from being solely an arena for sharing experiences to also an arena for creating a collective focus for development. The new organisation provided valuable knowledge sharing and colleague guidance across teams.

Situation 4

Halfway through the project period, audio recordings and logs showed that both the content and form of collaboration in the teaching teams' LS work was in development. Several teachers wrote that they benefitted greatly from planning lessons together with colleagues, from school leaders or researchers participating in the teams' LS work, and from the implementation of the template. They wrote:

> It was instructive to hear how the others reflected on the teaching and pupil challenges. The researcher challenged us and made many constructive suggestions. We think we would have been stuck without the support we were given. It's good to have someone from outside who can give some input and direction along the way and perhaps ask questions differently. Had the research not been present, we would not have benefitted from the different perspectives she shared. The template was a good tool throughout the process; it gave us an overview and helped us to become more critical and reflect in a more structured way about what we are going to do. The template was very useful, and it challenged our thinking. Without the template, the academic and pedagogical analysis would probably have had only a minor role.

The template mentioned by the teachers was intended to strengthen the teams' structuring and ownership of their own learning processes. It was built around five phases: pre-analysis, brainstorming about learning activities, design of research lesson, acting out the research lesson and post-analysis. In the audio recordings from the pre-analysis and brainstorming phases, I could tell that some teachers were sceptical of pupils using active learning processes, but they were nonetheless willing to try. In the subsequent evaluation phase, I heard the same teachers express enjoyment with the pupils' involvement in and mastery of discovering learning activities; but they also expressed surprise that it had not turned into 'chaos'. One teacher wrote in the log: 'LS helps us see things from a broader perspective'. Others wrote: 'I want to work more systematically with collaborative learning from here on out' ... 'I want more focus on overall subject goals'.

The use of CHAT

During the analysis process, I reflected several times on the question, 'What is the basis for the teachers' choice of method and understanding of the roles of both pupil and teacher?' I now found that the node 'rules' was central for both discovering tensions and promoting development in the LS work. The teachers' grasp of curriculum and their safeguarding of long-term and overall goals presented in the curriculum were strengthened, and their understanding of the pupils' role and the role of teachers was moving towards active forms of pupil work and increased pupil participation. In the meeting with the development group, I was able to present mirror data (Cole & Engeström, 2007) with examples from logs and audio recordings that showed how the teams had steadily worked their way further into the content that constituted the node, 'rules'. Both attitudes towards and views on learning were the subject of collective reflection, and I could hear that the LS work elicited professional openness and uncertainty (Munthe, 2001; Sellman, 2003) among an increasing number of teachers. At the same time, statements like 'I don't think I would ever dare to carry out such teaching on my own' showed that transferring collective experience and understanding from LS to one's own teaching could be challenging. The question, 'What support do teachers need in order to transfer the experiences and knowledge from LS to their own teaching practices?', became a key issue in the next meeting of school leadership and researchers.

Situation 5

Time pressure as an ongoing experience led to some teachers questioning the benefits of the LS work between the eighth and ninth LS cycle: 'Is it worth using so many hours of collaboration for one good lesson?' The principal responded immediately that he experienced benefits from the LS work, both in teaching beyond the research lesson and in other collaboration contexts. Nonetheless, the teachers' question was an important signal: How to motivate school development when the development that takes place is overshadowed by everyday challenges? The situation inspired the principal and me, the researcher, to prepare a retrospective entrance to the ninth and final LS cycle: What development has taken place during the project period, and are the experiences and potential learning from the LS work transferable to other situations?

The use of CHAT

With the activity system as the conversation and evaluation framework, the teacher teams discussed 'What happened to development within the different nodes in the activity system during the project period?' This led to meta-communication about individual and collective learning, learning processes in teams and at the organisational level. They also reflected on LS, the template used by the teams, experience sharing and the activity system as a tool for development. During the analysis process, participants became aware of how the development work had not only increased teaching competence and strengthened school-based development (object) but had also expanded collaboration competence in the teams (subject), given increased professional awareness and curriculum knowledge (rules), strengthened the meeting time of colleagues as an arena for knowledge sharing and collective learning processes (community), led to new tools being developed and used for teacher learning and planning (artefacts), and evolved language, tools and arenas for development. Researchers and leaders became aware of the importance of highlighting and appreciating all the desired developments, or growth towards positive developments, during the project.

Discussion

The research question that served as the starting point for the study was, 'How can CHAT frame and guide leadership and professional learning in school-based development?' In the presentation of the findings related to the research question, the developed categories – 'Learning and development processes', 'Leadership', 'Structure' and 'Learning culture' – provide the structure for the discussion.

Learning and development processes

The DWR project (Engeström & Engeström, 1986) and LS embrace learning and development processes at many levels, and the study showed that models and concepts from CHAT have contributed to strengthening these processes. Formative intervention research (Engeström & Sannino, 2010) helped direct attention towards the subject of the learning or development activity – 'who owns the process' and 'who acts as the guide' – who is responsible for stimulating, provoking and maintaining the process of development. The study showed that an understanding of the pupils as the focus of teaching, with the teacher as a supporter and guide, as well as an understanding of the teachers as the subject of school-based competence development (with the school leadership and myself, the researcher, as supporters) provides a positive and necessary basis for development from within and 'agency among the participants' (Engeström & Sannino, 2010, p. 15).

The template, which is described in Situation 4, built on examples of good practice from the teams' LS work and was developed in interactions between me and the teacher teams through the last seven LS cycles. The template was intended to strengthen the teams' structuring and leadership of their own learning process in the LS cycles and was built around the five phases of pre-analysis, brainstorming about learning activities, design of research lesson, acting out the research lesson and post-analysis. The study showed that the template's pre-analysis phase strengthened the teams' processes of analysis and reflection by triggering the participants' knowledge, comparing it with theory and stimulating analytical processes. The brainstorming phase invited innovation and creativity in the development of learning activities. In the planning of the research lesson phase, the pupils' learning process was designed prior to the teacher's activity. It is clear from the study that this strengthened both the pupils' perspective in the teachers' planning and the pupils' activity in teaching. The focus for the observation made when teachers were acting out the planned lesson was based on hypotheses developed during pre-analysis, and the post-analysis strengthened the teachers' analysis and understanding of the interactions between different factors in teaching. The 'agency among the participants' (Engeström & Sannino, 2010, p. 15), the expansive learning cycle (Engeström, 1987, 2001) stimuli in the form of theory and tools, the activity system (Engeström, 1987, 2001) and the concept of expansive learning (Engeström & Sannino, 2010) (see Chapters 1 and 2 for a description of concepts and models in CHAT) were important concepts in the development of the template. The study showed that the template *supported* the teams' structuring of the conversations but *challenged* the content of the conversations. In this way, it strengthened the LS work and guided the teams into what is described as professional learning communities (Vescio et al., 2008).

The theory of boundary crossing strengthened the leadership's understanding that both unity and diversity are relevant for organisational development and help strengthen experience sharing and the teacher's meeting time as a boundary zone in which participants both find unified development areas and make productive use of various perspectives (Akkerman et al., 2012, p. 229). Learning processes were lifted from the team level to the organisational level and provided the basis for organisational development. The use of conversation tools that safeguarded both unity and diversity between the teams made it such that everyone received feedback about their own LS work and gave feedback in return. Common challenges were taken care of through analysis and development processes at the organisational level. The study showed that this strengthened the participants' outcome from sharing experiences, promoted learning processes in and across teams, and developed both teams and the organisation as professional learning communities (Vescio et al., 2008).

The activity system (Engeström, 1987, 2001) was a strong tool in the development of analytical competence, first at the level of research, and then among leaders and teachers. The system initially strengthened my development of mirror data (Cole & Engeström, 2007) by expanding the focus of analysis from the mediating triangle, which showed the acting subject using artefacts to act on the object, to also include the context. The experiences from the analysis work led me to initiate the process of collective analysis by modelling analytical questions and exploratory conversations aimed at both the development process and contextual conditions. This was done in meetings with the school leaders and the development group. The activity system was later used as a unit of analysis for the evaluation of the project in the whole collegium. The study showed that the activity system gave concepts to and developed our expertise in uncovering tensions in the organisation and finding measures that supported the development work. Findings in the project's final phase showed that tensions within nodes, so-called primary contradictions (Engeström & Sannino, 2010), have driven the learning processes and participants' reflections from a surface level to a deep level (Irgens, 2016). The concepts and models within CHAT have also strengthened the participants' language, meta-communication and awareness of their own learning process.

Leadership

The study showed that 'agency among the participants' (Engeström & Sannino, 2010, p. 15), 'to provoke and sustain an extensive transformation process' (Engeström & Sannino, 2010, p. 15) and mirror data, theory and tools as stimuli guided the leaders' and researchers' understanding and practice of leadership in the direction of both transformational leadership (Yukl, 2013) and distributed leadership (Spillane, 2005). School leaders, lead teachers and researchers facilitated, modelled, supported and stimulated learning and development processes, in and between different groups in the organisation, all of which strengthened the teachers' voices and autonomy in the project. The study showed that the teacher teams' use of the template correspondingly served to strengthen the pupils' voices and perspectives in the LS cycles.

The activity system as an analysis unit and the historical analysis contributed to continuous formative assessment in the project: Where are we going? How are we going? Where to next? (Hattie & Timperley, 2007). The activity system demonstrated the importance of a shared understanding of the object and served as a tool for uncovering tensions in the activity and recognising needs and opportunities for stimuli and support. With each team as a subject in the activity system and as the focus for the analysis, the development group adapted support and challenges to correspond to the teams' zone of proximal development (Vygotsky, 1978). In this way, theorising, tools for process development and participation in the teams' LS work grew as tools for the leadership. Additionally, the description of boundary crossing as territory in which they might be unfamiliar (Suchman, 1994) became a reminder to researchers and school leaders to balance challenge and support and, further, to appreciate and highlight all examples of the beginnings of growth towards desired practice.

The school leadership's continuous development of learning processes vis-à-vis colleagues' sharing of experience, which can be described as the teachers' boundary zone (Akkerman et al., 2012), strengthened project development at the school level. Through the use and development of various process tools, the leadership facilitated learning processes across teams that resulted in common development areas for the teams and the collective establishment of knowledge within the chosen area at the entrance to a new LS cycle. The leadership's use of theory as a stimulus for development contributed to professional theorising (Ertsas & Irgens, 2017) whereby implicit knowledge was made explicit, analytical distance and critical reflection were triggered, and common terminology was developed. The teams' sharing of experience and collective start-up of a new LS cycle emerged as a central arena for the exercise of educational leadership at the organisational level and an important arena for discovering and continuing the growth process towards expansive learning.

The study showed that through transparent analytical processes and the collective use of development tools, the leadership has promoted participants' development expertise. The template for the LS work, a corresponding structure in leadership meetings and the participation of school leaders and researchers in the teams' LS work all contributed to promoting learning and development processes and competence building within the organisation. This kind of organising and accomplishment made room for leading processes in line with distributed leadership (Spillane et al., 2004), where both formal and informal leaders could drive the process. This might strengthen future development projects and make the school more robust with a rotation of participating teachers and leaders.

Structure

The study revealed that CHAT stimulated the establishment of structures that framed and guided the DWR project. In the teacher teams' LS work, the template contributed to a sharp focus on development, critical reflection and increased creativity in the choice of methods. In the assembled collegium and in the development group and school leadership, similar analytical and exploratory structures contributed to the development of professional learning communities (Vescio et al., 2008). The structures provided a predictability that enabled the meeting leaders and participants to focus their attention on the content of the meetings.

With the expansive learning cycle (Engeström, 1987, 2001), Postholm and Moen's (2011) R&D model (see Chapter 1) and formative intervention research (Engeström & Sannino, 2010) as the starting point, I developed the model, 'Co-learning and co-leadership in school-based development', presented in Figure 9.1 below.

The model was developed as a tool for common understanding, leadership, planning, analysis and evaluation in DWR. It shows the structure of the DWR project, the anchoring in teachers' practice, the interaction between the different learning arenas and the holistic learning process in school-based competence development. As in Postholm and Moen's (2011) R&D model, the teaching teams' development of their own teaching is the primary learning and development arena. Experiences and knowledge from the teacher teams' LS cycles were brought to further analysis and knowledge building at the teacher community, the development group, the school leadership and the researchers' arenas. These processes provided co-leadership in form of stimuli and support back to the primary development arena, as visualized in the figure.

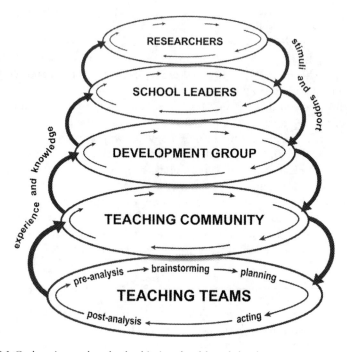

Figure 9.1 Co-learning and co-leadership in school-based development

Learning culture

The study demonstrated that models and concepts from CHAT became significant tools in the process of enhancing teachers' collective learning processes and in developing the professional role from being solely executive to becoming executive, exploratory and evolving (Togsverd & Rothuizen, 2012). Both the teaching teams' LS work and the collective processes at the school level show that the teachers' collaborative skills are developing towards those of professional learning communities (Vescio et al., 2008). The study revealed 'a climate where it is possible to challenge and prevail rather than merely conforming' (Hirsh & Segolsson, 2017), and where leadership is practiced as stimuli and support in processes 'owned by practitioners' (Engeström & Sannino, 2010, p. 15). The study also demonstrated that there are established processes of development that give the teacher teams room for professional autonomy, strengthen the school's collective focus on development and maintain the necessary shifting between surface and depth levels (Irgens, 2016) in the development work. The development processes have allowed for a more nuanced collective understanding of the concepts of learning and development, and the study showed that the participants' understanding of their own roles is developing in the direction of open-mindedness (Sellman, 2003) and professional uncertainty (Munthe, 2001), thereby stimulating professional development. More teachers are challenging their own teaching, as evidenced by their exploring and learning, and they are no longer 'rushing' to the practicalities in their LS work. They also exhibit an expanded perspective, contributing to development in teams other than their own as well as at the level of the school.

The activity system's presentation of development as a social interaction between the individual and the environment, where the many nodes constituting the context mutually affect one other, has made the participants aware that development cannot be understood as limited to goals and actions. The processes of analysis and development are not limited to the teaching, but also include the teams and the school as activity systems. The study demonstrated that the project's participants, through collective processes and professional theorising, have developed their professional language and have acquired the concepts of more nuanced descriptions and meta-communication.

Concluding reflection

Development strategies adopted from one culture to another, as LS, always pose the danger of adopting only the surface structure, not the deep structures, of the strategy (Stigler & Hiebert, 2016). The study revealed that while LS and the object of development based on perceived needs created uncertainty and a lack of operational competence in most teams at the start of the project, evaluations at the end of the project showed that the school has worked from the surface level to the deep level in terms of both LS structures and the activity system nodes. Such a development supports Stigler and Hiebert's (2016) contention that LS often requires a redesign of the context in which it is used.

CHAT and the theory of expansive learning emerged as a solid theoretical resource in the project and provided direction and a framework for both leadership and professional learning. Where LS as a method is aimed at developing teachers' planning, acting and evaluation of teaching, CHAT, in addition to strengthening the teams' LS work, has contributed to the processes of analysis and development throughout the school's operations. The study showed that CHAT has contributed to increased quality in the analysis and reflection processes at and across all the arenas in the school. This is visualised in the model, 'Co-learning and co-leadership in school-based development', which highlights the interaction between all arenas at school and a holistic school-based learning and development culture in the organisation.

References

Akkerman, S., Admiraal, W., & Simons, R. J. (2012). Unity and diversity in a collaborative research project. *Culture & Psychology*, *18*(2), 227–252. doi:10.1177/1354067X11434835

Argyris, C., & Schön, D. A. (1978). *Organizational Learning: A Theory of Action Perspective*. Reading, MA: Addison-Wesley.

Cajkler, W., Wood, P., Norton, J., & Pedder, D. (2014). Lesson study as a vehicle for collaborative teacher learning in a secondary school. *Professional Development in Education*, *40*(4), 511–529. doi:10.1080/19415257.2013.866975

Cole, M., & Engeström, Y. (2007). Cultural-historical approaches to designing for development. In J. Valsiner & A. Rosa (Eds.), *The Cambridge Handbook of Sociocultural Psychology* (pp. 484–507). New York: Cambridge University Press.

Collinson, V., Cook, T. F., & Conley, S. (2006). Organizational learning in schools and school systems: Improving learning, teaching, and leading. *Theory into Practice*, *45*(2), 107–116. doi:10.1207/s15430421tip4502_2

Dahl, T. (2016). *Om lærerrollen: Et kunnskapsgrunnlag* [About the teacher role: A knowledge base] Bergen: Fagbokforlaget

Directorate of Education and Training (2012a). *Rammeverk for skolebasert kompetanseutvikling på ungdomstrinnet 2013–2017* [A framework for school-based development in lower secondary school 2013–2017]. Retrieved from www.udir.no/kvalitet-og-kompetanse/nasjonale-satsinger/ungdomstrinn-i-utvikling/Rammeverk-skolebasert-komputv-utrinnet2012-2017/Skolebasert-komputv/

Directorate of Education and Training (2012b). *Rammeverk for skolebasert kompetanseutvikling på ungdomstrinnet 2012–2017. Vedlegg 6 Teoretisk bakgrunnsdokument for arbeid med organisasjonslæring* [A framework for school-based development in lower secondary school 2013–2017. Attachment 6 Theoretical background document for organizational development]. Retrieved from www.udir.no/globalassets/upload/ungdomstrinnet/rammeverk/ungdomstrinnet_bakgrunnsdokument_organisasjonslaring_vedlegg_6.pdf

Dudley, P. (2013). Teacher learning in Lesson Study: What interaction-level discourse analysis revealed about how teachers utilised imagination, tacit knowledge of teaching and fresh evidence of pupils learning, to develop practice knowledge and so enhance their pupils' learning. *Teaching and Teacher Education*, 34, 107–121. doi:10.1016/j.tate.2013. 04. 006

Earl, L., & Timperley, H. (2009). *Professional Learning Conversations: Challenges in Using Evidence for Improvement* (Vol. 1, Professional learning and development in schools and higher education). Dordrecht: Springer Netherlands. doi:10.1007/978-1-4020-6917-8

Engeström, Y. (1987). *Learning by Expanding*. Helsinki: Orienta-Konsultit Oy.

Engeström, Y. (2001). Expansive learning at work: Toward an activity theoretical reconceptualization. *Journal of Education and Work*, 14(1), 133–156. doi:10.1080/13639080020028747

Engeström, Y. (2011). From design experiments to formative interventions. *Theory & Psychology*, 21(5), 598–628. doi:10.1177/0959354311419252

Engeström, Y., & Engeström, R. (1986). Developmental work research. The approach and the application in cleaning work. *Nordisk Pedagogik*, 6, 2–15.

Engeström, Y., & Sannino, A. (2010). Studies of expansive learning: Foundations, findings and future challenges. *Educational Research Review*, 5(1), 1–24. doi:10.1016/j.edurev.2009.12.002

Engeström, Y., Engeström, R., & Kärkkäinen, M. (1995). Polycontextuality and boundary crossing in expert cognition: Learning and problem solving in complex work activities. *Learning and Instruction*, 5(4), 319–335. doi:10.1016/0959-4752(95)00021-6

Ertsas, Turid I., & Irgens, E. J. (2017). Professional theorizing. *Teachers and Teaching: Theory and Practice*, 23(3), 332–351. doi:10.1080/13540602.2016.1205013

Hargreaves, A., & Fullan, M. (2012). *Professional Capital: Transforming Teaching in Every School*. London: Routledge.

Hattie, J., & Timperley, H. (2007). The power of feedback. *Review of Educational Research*, 77(1), 81–112. doi:10.3102/003465430298487

Hirsh, Å., & Segolsson, M. (2017). Enabling teacher-driven school-development and collaborative learning: An activity theory-based study of leadership as an overarching practice. *Educational Management Administration & Amp; Leadership, Educational Management Administration & Leadership*. doi:10.1177/1741143217739363

Horn, I. S., & Little, J. W. (2010). Attending to problems of practice: Routines and resources for professional learning in teachers' workplace interactions. *American Educational Research Journal*, 47(1), 181. doi:10.3102/0002831209345158

Irgens, E. (2016). *Skolen: Organisasjon og ledelse, kunnskap og læring* [The school: Organisation and leadership, knowledge and learning]. Bergen: Fagbokforlaget

Jordan, B., & Henderson, A. (1995). Interaction analysis: Foundations and practice. *The Journal of the Learning Sciences*, 4(1), 39–103. doi:10.1207/s15327809jls0401_2

Junge, J. (2012). Kjennetegn ved læreres kollegasamtaler, og betydningen av disse for læringspotensialet i samtalene [Characteristics of teachers' dialogues, and the importance of the learning potential in these conversations]. *Norsk Pedagogisk Tidsskrift* [Norwegian Pedagogical Journal], 374–386.

Kvam, E. (2018). Untapped learning potential? A study of teachers' conversations with colleagues in primary schools in Norway. *Cambridge Journal of Education*, 48(6), 697–714. doi:10.1080/0305764X.2017.1418833

Leithwood, K., Harris, A., & Hopkins, D. (2019). Seven strong claims about successful school leadership revisited. *School Leadership & Management*, 1–18. doi:10.1080/13632434.2019.1596077

Leont'ev, A. (1981). The problem of activity in psychology. In J. Wertsch (Ed.), *The Concept of Activity in Soviet Psychology* (pp. 37–71). Armonk, NY: M.E. Sharpe.

Lewis, C., Perry, R., Friedkin, S., & Roth, J. (2012). Improving teaching does improve teachers: Evidence from Lesson Study. *Journal of Teacher Education*, 63(5), 368–375. doi:10.1177/0022487112446633

Lillejord, S. (2011) Kunsten å være rektor [Being a principal]. In E. Ottesen & J. Møller (Eds.), *Rektor som leder og sjef: Om styring, ledelse og kunnskapsutvikling i skolen* [Principal as leader and manager: About governance, leadership and knowledge development in school] (pp. 284–301). Oslo: Universitetsforlaget.

Lincoln, Y. S., & Guba, E. G. (1985). *Naturalistic Inquiry*. Beverly Hills, CA: Sage.
Ministry of Education and Research (2017). *Lærelyst – tidlig innsats og kvalitet i skolen* [Motivated to learn - early help and quality in school]. Oslo: Ministry of Education and Research.
Munthe, E. (2001). Professional uncertainty/certainty: How (un)certain are teachers, what are they (un)certain about, and how is (un)certainty related to age, experience, gender, qualifications and school type? *European Journal of Teacher Education*, 24(3), 355–368.
Pondy, L. R. (1978). Leadership is a language game. In M. McCall & M. Lombardo (Eds.), *Leadership: Where else can we go?* (pp. 87–99). Durham, NC: Duke University Press.
Postholm, M., & Moen, T. (2011). Communities of development: A new model for R&D work. *Journal of Educational Change*, 12(4), 385–401. doi:10.1007/s10833-010-9150-x
Postholm, M. B. (2018). Case A. In M. B. Postholm, A. Normann, T. Dahl, E. Dehlin, G. Engvik & E. J. Irgens (Eds.) *Skole- og utdanningssektoren i utvikling* [The school and the educational sector developing] (pp. 99–162). Bergen: Fagbokforlaget.
Sannino, A., Engeström, Y., & Lemos, M. (2016). Formative interventions for expansive learning and transformative agency. *Journal of the Learning Sciences*, 25(4), 599–633. doi:10.1080/10508406.2016.1204547
Scribner, J. P., Cockrell, K. S., Cockrell, D. H., & Valentine, J. W. (1999). Creating professional communities in schools through organizational learning: An evaluation of a school improvement process. *Educational Administration Quarterly*, 35(1), 130–160.
Sellman, D. (2003). Open-mindedness: A virtue for professional practice. *Nursing Philosophy*, 4(1), 17–24. doi:10.1046/j.1466-769X.2003.00113.x
Spillane, J. (2005). Distributed leadership. *The Educational Forum*, 69(2), 143–150. doi:10.1080/00131720508984678
Spillane, J. P., Halverson, R., & Diamond, J. B. (2004). Towards a theory of leadership practice: A distributed perspective. *Journal of Curriculum Studies*, 36(1), 3–34. doi:10.1080/0022027032000106726
Stigler, J., & Hiebert, W. (2016). Lesson study, improvement, and the importing of cultural routines. *ZDM*, 48(4), 581–587. doi:10.1007/s11858-016-0787-7
Strauss, A., & Corbin, J. (1998). *Basics of qualitative research: Techniques and procedures for developing grounded theory*. Thousand Oaks, CA: Sage Publications, Inc.
Suchman, L. (1994). Working relations of technology production and use. *Computer Supported Cooperative Work*, 2, 21–39. doi:10.1007/BF00749282
Timperley, H. (2008). *Teacher professional learning and development*. The Educational Practices Series - 18 Ed. Jere Brophy. Brussels: International Academy of Education & International Bureau of Education.
Togsverd, L., & Rothuizen, J. (2012). Argumenter for en utviklingsbasert førskolelærerutdanning [Arguments for a development-based pre-school education]. *Første Steg: Tidsskrift for Førskolelærere* [First step: Journal for pre-school teachers], 1, 50–55.
Vescio, V., Ross, D., & Adams, A. (2008). A review of research on the impact of professional learning communities on teaching practice and student learning. *Teaching and Teacher Education*, 24(1), 80–91. doi:10.1016/j.tate.2007. 01. 004
Vygotsky, L. S. (1978). *Mind in Society: The Development of Higher Psychological Processes*. Cambridge: Harvard University Press.
Wertsch, J. (1998). *Mind as Action*. Oxford: Oxford University Press.
Wolcott, H. (2008). *Ethnography – A Way of Seeing*, 2nd edn. Lanham: AltaMira Press.
Yukl, G. (2013). *Leadership in Organizations*, 8th edn. Essex: Pearson.

Index

achieving high educational quality 1–11
achieving teacher agency 91–107
action learning 20
action research 12–13
action triangle 15
activity system as research tool 17–20
adopting deep structures of strategy 141–2
aesthetic principles of arts pedagogy 54
AfL *see* Assessment for Learning programme
Akkerman, S. F. 5, 30, 48, 63, 97
Alexander, R. 75, 87
analysing data 45, 131–2
analysis as narrative 48–54; boundary objects as inspiration 54; toddler arts festival 48–53
anti-bullying 116, 118
applying theory 45–8; boundary objects as artefacts 47; interdisciplinary multimodality 47–8
arranging a toddler arts festival 48–53; blue space 51; evaluating the event 53; 'history' of participants 49–50; iPad space 51–2; playing with light 50–51; stocking space 52–3
artefacts 47; *see also* boundary objects
arts education 42–57; *see also* boundary objects
arts as legitimate subject 42–3
Askew, M. 75
assessment knowledge base development 100–101
Assessment for Learning programme 91–6; implementations 92–3
assessment literacy 91–3
autonomy 21, 91–2, 127–9, 131, 134, 138–9

Bakker, A. 5, 30, 48, 63, 97
bases for development 16–17
bicycle use 38
Bjørkås, Ø. 75
Black, P. 95
BLOOM app 51–2
blue space 51
Blueberry School 109–110
body language 120
boundary crossing 22, 27, 30, 37, 48, 59, 63, 68, 97, 130–39
boundary objects 42–57, 97; crossing boundaries 97; discussion 55; findings/analysis 48–54; introduction 42–3; theoretical framework 43–5; theory 45–8
Bowker, G. C. 97
brainstorming 135, 137
Brannick, T. 7
bridging road safety gap 26–41; *see also* road safety culture
Briseid, L. G. 61
Brown, J. T. L. 98
Brown, M. 75
Bulien, T. 75
bullying 110, 115–16

cascade model of school development 93
case study methodology 32–4
change in focus as bus passenger 38
CHAT perspective on problem-solving 110–112
CHAT as school research guide 14–17; origin/content of activity system 15–17
CHAT Situation 1 132–3; use of CHAT 132–3
CHAT Situation 2 133–4; use of CHAT 133–4

Index

CHAT Situation 3 134–5; use of CHAT 134–5
CHAT Situation 4 135–6; use of CHAT 135–6
CHAT Situation 5 136–7; use of CHAT 136–7
children's potential 75
co-construction of new knowledge 22
co-learning 140–42
Cobb, P. 86
coding 45
Coghlan, D. 8
cognitivism 45
coherence 60
Cole, M. 1, 43, 46–7
collaborating schools 13, 67
collaborative learning 15–17, 102–3
collaborative research 12–25; activity system/expansive learning cycle 17–20; CHAT as guide for researching schools 14–17; exemplar study 13–14; introduction 12–13; premises/possibilities for research 21–2
collective agency 4, 12, 18–19, 21, 120–23
collective collaboration 21–2
collective responsibility 27
Collinson, V. 127
commitment 98–100
communicating like a mathematician 73–90; *see also* working like a mathematician
competence development 96, 126–9, 137–8
concept of boundary objects 42–57; *see also* boundary objects
confidence 21
conflicts 16–17
Conley, S. 127
consensus through argumentation 87
constant comparative analysis 64, 132
content of activity system 15–17
context of Norwegian DWR project 94–5
Cook, T. F. 127
Corbin, J. 14, 132
Council for Road Safety 29
crossing boundaries *see* boundary crossing
Crossouard, B. 95
cultural artefacts 27–8, 30, 34, 36, 39
cultural differences 35–6, 39; interactions between pedestrians and drivers 35–6
culture of road safety within activity system 27–9; lifelong learning 29

Dahl, H. 75
daring to sing 49
data collection 43–4, 131

data use 102–3
data-driven changes 91–107
Dawes, L. 74–5
deep structure 128–9, 138–9
developing assessment knowledge base 100–101
developing knowledge of assessment literacy 94–5
developing practice 101
development of assessment literacy 91–3
development processes 137–8
development work research 5–9, 12–14, 16, 20–22, 27–33, 39, 91–107; bridging road safety gap 26–41; development of assessment literacy 91–3; DWP project 29–32
Dewey, J. 60
dialogic teaching 73–90; *see also* working like a mathematician
disrespect 36
diversity 130
division of labour 15–16, 28, 63–4, 118
drivers' rights 35–6
DWR *see* development work research

early childhood education and care 42–4, 48, 50, 53–5
ECEC *see* early childhood education and care
ECTS credits 95, 97, 99–100
educational assessment 91–107
educational tools for deeper understanding 39
Edwards, A. 61
elaboration of multimodal teaching 55
empirical data gathering 64
Engeström, R. 5
Engeström, Y. 4–5, 7–8, 14, 17, 27, 96, 129–30, 132
ensuring quality 45
envisioning complexity of development processes 129–30
Ertsas, T. I. 127
establishment of structures 139–40
ethics 27, 45, 78
ethnography 131
evaluating 'Playing with Light' event 53
examining challenges 115–16
examining operations 78–86
expansive learning cycle 6–9, 17–20, 30–31, 94–101, 129–31, 140; findings 98–101
expansive transformations 7, 29–32; planning/trying out solutions in real context 31–2

experimental settings 110, 120, 123
experimentation 120–23
exploring materials 49
externalisation 2–3, 7, 111

findings from expansive learning cycle 98–101; developing assessment knowledge base 100–101; informing/developing practice 101; participation in community activities 100; role of commitment 98–101
focus group interviews 44, 97–8
focus on systematic learning 12–13
follow-up activities 118–20
formative intervention methodology 96, 137–8, 140
fostering PD 108–9
frame for triad meetings 62–4
framing challenges 113–15, 120
framing PD using CHAT 126–44; *see also* school-based development
Frisch, N. S. 47
Fullan, M. 21

genetic law of cultural development 2
go-betweens 46, 48
Grimen, H. 60–61
Guba, E. G. 78
Gudmundsdottir, S. 43
guiding PD using CHAT 126–44; *see also* school-based development

Hannula, M. 43
Hargreaves, A. 21
Haug, P. 61
Hennessy, S. 76
Hiebert, W. 141
high-risk road groups 26–7
Hohr, J. 47
how CHAT can frame PD 137–41; leadership 138–9; learning culture 141; learning/development processes 137–8; structure 139–40
Howe, C. 75–6, 87
humility 21

identifying activity 78–85; modelling explorative work 79–81; monitoring pupils' work 81–3; orchestrating for agreement 83–5
illustrative case on dialogic teaching 73–90
implementing AfL 92–3
importance of school leadership 98–100
'Improving School Leadership' 109

independence 30
influence of lifelong learning 29
informing practice 101
initiation-response feedback 74–6
inspiration 49, 54; aesthetic principles 54; room as stage 54; techniques 54; *see also* boundary objects
instructor group problem-solving 113–20; examining challenges 115–16; follow-up activities 118–20; further examining challenges 116–18; revealing/framing challenges 113–15
integration 38
interactions between pedestrians and drivers 35–6
interdisciplinary multimodality 47–8
internalisation 2–3, 7, 111
International Journal of Education and the Arts 42
iPad space 51–2
IRE/F *see* initiation-response feedback
Irgens, E. J. 127–9
Issit, J. 75

job satisfaction 22, 116
Johnston, D. 75
Journal of Aesthetic Education 42
Junge, J. 128

Kärkkäinen, M. 5
Kazemi, E. 87
Kennedy, A. 21, 93
Klemp, T. 75
Korthagen, F. 58, 60, 62–3, 68
Kozulin, A. 45
Kress, G. 47
Kvam, E. 128
Kvernbekk, T. 61
Kyriacou, C. 75

lack of awareness of road risks 34–5
Lærerløftet strategy 12
'Language Use and Development in the Mathematics Classroom' *see* LaUDiM project
LaUDiM project 74, 77
leadership 138–9
learning culture 141
learning processes 137–8
learning/developing as professionals 67–9
Lee, Y.-J. 96
Leont'ev, A. 1–4, 9, 13, 76–8, 85–8, 129, 132; levels of analysis 85–8
Lesson Study 126–44

Index

Letnes, M. A. 47
levels of analysis 85–8
lifelong learning 29, 35, 39; and road safety 29
light installations 50–51
Light, P. 75
Lillejord, S. 128
limitations to actions 16
Lincoln, Y. S. 78
Littleton, P. 75
Loughran, R. 68
LS *see* Lesson Study
Luria, A. 1

mathematical literacy 73, 86
mathematics as social activity 73–4
maturation 37
mediated activity 45–6
mediation by tools 2, 46
mentoring student teachers 58–72; CHAT as frame for triad meetings 62–4; context 59–60; discussion 67–9; findings 64–7; introduction 58–69; literature review 60–62; research method 64
Mercer, N. 74–6, 87
Merriam, S. B. 43
Miettinen, R. 17
mirror data 6, 14, 18–19, 64, 130, 136, 138
modelling explorative work 79–81
modes of expression 47–8
Moen, T. 130, 140
monitoring pupils' work 81–3
multi-mediation 47
multi-voicedness 28–9, 111
multimodality 47–8, 50–52
Munthe, E. 61

'National Bicycling Strategy' 38
National School Leadership Programme 108–110
National Transport Plan 38; *see also* Vision Zero
Newnham, D. S. 13
Nilssen, V. 75
Nord University 29, 32

observation practice 61
open-mindedness 141
orchestrating for agreement 83–5
organisational learning 127
organisational surface structure 128–9, 138–9

origin of activity system 15–17; tensions as basis for development 16–17
ownership of activity system 16–17, 29
owning the project 16, 21, 134

participants in focus group interviews 44
participating in National School Leadership Programme 120–23; implications 123
participation in community activities 100
PD *see* professional development
Pimm, D. 86
pinpointing actions 78–85
planning road safety in real-life situations 31–2
'Playing with Light' event 44, 48–54
policy enactment 92
Pondy, L. R. 128
positivism 45
possibilities of research 21–2
Postholm, M. B. 33, 96, 130, 140
practice as element of teacher education 58–9
practice of leadership 138–9
premises of research 21–2
principals' participation in school leadership programme 108–125; *see also* problem-solving work
problem-solving training 123
problem-solving work 108–125; Blueberry School 109–110; CHAT perspective on problem-solving 110–112; discussion 120–23; in groups of principals 113–20; introduction 108–9; methodology 112–13; National School Leadership Programme 109
professional development 92, 94–5, 102–3, 108–9, 129
professional learning community theory 127–9
professional theorising 127
promoting school-based competence development 130–31
Pryor, J. 95
psychosocial environment 116, 118, 120
pupil collaboration 134–5

qualitative approach 32–4
qualitative observation study 112–13

Ragin, C. C. 43
re-examining challenges 116–18
real-life situations in road safety 31–2
realising data-driven changes 91–107
reciprocity 45

reducing serious accidents 27–8
reflection 14, 18–21
reflective equipment 29, 31, 34, 36–7
refugee youth and road safety 26–41; *see also* road safety culture
research into teacher education 59–60
responsibility 27
revealing challenges 113–15
Rhodes, V. 75
riding bicycles 38
risks of being a road user 34–5
road fatalities *see* traffic fatalities
road safety culture 26–41; development work research project 29–32; findings/discussion 34–9; introduction 26–7; methodology/methods 32–4; reflections 39; within activity system 27–9
Road Safety Day 32, 37–8
Robinson, V. 21
role of commitment 98–100
room as stage for arts pedagogy 54
Roth, W.-M. 96
Rothuizen, J. 127
Russell, J. 68

safety helmets 29
Sannino, A. 5, 7
school leadership 98–100
school-based development 126–44; context 130–31; cultural-historical activity theory 129–30; discussion 137–41; introduction 126–7; methodology 131–2; reflections 141–2; situations and use of CHAT 132–6; theoretical framework 127–9
schools collaborating in research 12–25; *see also* collaborative research
schools' openness to communication 66–7
schools unprepared for communication 65
seat belts 32, 34, 36–7, 39
Selander, S. 47
self-awareness 102–3
self-expression 46
self-regulation 36
sharing of experience 139–40
signalisation 46–8
situated social practice 95–7; boundary crossing/boundary objects 97; teacher agency 96–7
situations of CHAT 132–6
Skagen, K. 69
Skorpen, L. B. 75
socio-cultural theory 1, 14, 76–7
socio-historical contexts 112

Solstad, A. G. 58, 61–2
sources of data 44
specialisation 102
Staarman, J. K. 74–5
stagnation 7–8
Star, S. L. 97
Stigler, J. 141
Stipek, D. 87
stocking space 52–3
strategies for fostering PD 108–9
Strauss, A. 14, 132
studying processes 43
Suchman, L. 133–4
suggesting future directions 116–18
Suoranta, J. 43
systematic learning 12–13

teacher agency 91–107; discussion 102–3; findings 98–101; introduction 91–3; methodology 97–8; Norwegian context 93–5; theoretical framework 95–7
teacher education literature review 60–62
teachers' learning 21
teaching practice 13–14, 58–72; systematics of 13–14
technical tools for arts education 54
tensions 16–17, 28–9, 111–12, 129–30
theoretical framework of boundary object research 43–5; analyses and ensuring quality 45; data collection 43–4; focus group interview 44; methodology 43; other data sources 44
theory of activity 1
theory of boundary crossing 97, 133–5
thinking aloud 113–15
Thompson, C. M. 47
Timperley, H. 16, 20–21, 109
toddler arts festival participants 49–50
Togsverd, L. 127
traffic fatalities 26–7, 34
transformative agency 7, 93, 98, 103
transforming teacher agency 102
triadic mentoring of student teachers 58–72; *see also* mentoring student teachers
triangulation 45
trying out road safety in real-life situations 31–2
types of interaction 64–7; collaborating schools 67; schools not expecting communication 65; schools open to communication 66–7

understanding of road traffic concepts 34–9; creating deeper understanding 39; cultural differences related to traffic 35–6; lack of awareness 34–5; unfamiliarity with cultural artefacts 36–8
understanding school learning culture 131–2; data analysis 131–2; ethnography 131
unfamiliarity with road safety cultural artefacts 36–8; change on focus as bus passenger 38; use of bicycles 38; use of reflective equipment 36–7; use of seat belts 37
universal models 1–2
use of CHAT 132–6; Situation 1 132–3; Situation 2 133–4; Situation 3 134–5; Situation 4 135–6; Situation 5 136–7
use of reflective equipment 36–7
using data to inform 101
using formative interventions to achieve data-driven changes 91–107
using your body 49–50

Vadén, T. 43
Valsiner, J. 120, 122
Van der Veer, R. 120, 122
van Oers, B. 75, 86
Virkkunen, J. 13, 96
Virkkunen, L. S. 7
Vision Zero 26–7, 34
Vrikki, M. 76

vulnerability of refugees on roads 27, 34, 39; *see also* road safety culture
Vygotsky, L. S. 1–4, 14–17, 30, 45–8, 76–7

Wegerif, R. 75
well-being 110
Werner, S. 61
Wheatly, L. 76
WHO *see* World Health Organization
Wiliam, D. 95
William, D. 75
Wilson, B. 47
Wilson, M. 47
Wilson, S. M. 43
Wood, T. 75
working like a mathematician 73–90; discussion 85–8; findings 78–85; introduction 73–4; method 77–8; previous research 74–6; theoretical framework 76–7
workplace development process 126–7
World Health Organization 26

Xu, Y. 98

Yackel, E. 86

zone of proximal development 14–15, 17–18, 30, 37, 139
ZPD *see* zone of proximal development